CRITICAL FAILURES

CRITICAL FAILURES

MODERN JAPAN AND THE POSSIBILITY OF READING OTHERWISE

MIYABI GOTO

CORNELL EAST ASIA SERIES
AN IMPRINT OF
CORNELL UNIVERSITY PRESS
Ithaca and London

Number 226 in the Cornell East Asia Series

Copyright © 2026 by Miyabi Goto

All rights reserved. Except for brief quotations in a review, this book, or parts thereof, must not be reproduced in any form without permission in writing from the publisher. For information, address Cornell University Press, Sage House, 512 East State Street, Ithaca, New York 14850. Visit our website at cornellpress.cornell.edu.

First published 2026 by Cornell University Press

Librarians: A CIP catalog record for this book is available from the Library of Congress.

ISBN 9781501785665 (hardcover)
ISBN 9781501785672 (paperback)
ISBN 9781501785696 (epub)
ISBN 9781501785689 (pdf)

GPSR EU contact: Sam Thornton, Mare Nostrum Group B.V., Mauritskade 21D, 1091 GC, Amsterdam, NL, gpsr@mare-nostrum.co.uk.

For Eric

Contents

List of Illustrations ix
Note on Transliteration xi

Introduction: That Which Is
Casually Called Criticism   1

Part I: Discourses of Critical Reading

1. The Age of *Hihyō*   33
2. Critical Reading, Creative Production   62

Part II: Practices of Critical Reading

3. On Dividing: The "Literature and Nature" Debate   81
4. Knowing the Dancer from the Dance: The "Dancing Girl" Debate   112
5. Against Interpretation: The Submerged-Ideal Debate   132
6. The Community of No Referent: The Interrelation-with-Life Debate   158

Conclusion: Failing Well   179

Acknowledgments 193
Notes 197
Bibliography 225
Index 237

Illustrations

0.1. "Jitchi yūeki hakurankai no zu," in *Gōtō: Dai Nihon kokumin sen'yō jitchi yūeki taizen*, ed. Tamura Mie (Yūekidō, 1886), n.p.   5

1.1. An excerpt from Nishi Amane, *Hyakugaku renkan*, in *Nishi Amane zenshū*, vol. 1, ed. Ōkubo Toshiaki (Nihon Hyōronsha, 1945), 18   40

1.2. An entry of "Criticism," *Tetsugaku jii*, ed., Inoue Tetsujirō, Ariga Nagao, Kōdera Shinsaku, and Wadagaki Kenzō (Tokyo Daigaku Sangakubu, 1881), 21   43

1.3. "Shakoku," *Kokumin no tomo* 9 (October 1887): n.p.   53

Note on Transliteration

In most cases, I write Japanese personal names with family names first, given names second. Names of writers whose works are written in English are identified as they appear in publications. I follow the Japanese conventional practice and refer to canonical writers by their most known pen names (e.g., Sohō instead of Tokutomi, Ōgai instead of Mori). Writers who primarily used their real names are mentioned by their family names (e.g., Iwamoto for Iwamoto Yoshiharu). Japanese terms not established as loan words in English are italicized following the modified Hepburn style of romanization with macrons indicating long vowels. All translations of the Japanese texts are mine unless otherwise specified.

CRITICAL FAILURES

Introduction
That Which Is Casually Called Criticism

If we were to read and criticize a text, how would we do it? For those who profess literature in an academic setting, the question is a familiar one. Indeed, the act of reading involves a variety of paths. When we read a text, we often begin by identifying something unique and outstanding in the text so that interpretation can ensue. Some of us might further investigate the historical context within which the piece came into existence. We might ask who wrote the piece, in response to what event, or to address whom. Some might inquire into thematic features in order to illuminate what the text is about. It might also occur to us that looking at the technical production aspect of the text could be a good way to discern the material conditions that enabled the arrival of the piece. Various steps could be taken to make sense of the text—indeed, making (possibly better) sense of the text is what many of us hope to accomplish. We aspire to embark on our sensemaking adventures by assuming we have to be critical readers. A critical disposition constitutes an essential component in our reading practice, and it has been a topic of heated discussions among academic readers for many decades.

If methodologies of critical reading have long been contested among scholars of literature, over a hundred years ago young Japanese intellectuals too were grappling with the same question: what it means to read in a critical way. This book studies the discourses and practices of critical reading called *hihyō* that emerged during Japan's Meiji period (1868–1912). I pay special attention to discrepancies between what was posited as critical reading and what was executed in the name of critical reading in late nineteenth-century Japan, considering those discrepancies as failures that in fact pointed to generative possibilities of what critical reading could be. Many Meiji intellectuals struggled to bring their vision of critical reading to realization and experimented with methods of being critical in their reading practices. They mobilized intellectual conventions available to them and reinvented critical reading, its language, rhetoric, and style. While they did not successfully put into effect what they said about critical reading, their attempted practices at once gave rise to unexpected forms of criticism and engendered innovative approaches of engaging with and discussing what they read. The case of fin de siècle Japanese criticism thus shows us multiple examples of creative interventions in critical reading practice. Recollecting Japan's pursuit of critical reading and what came out of it introduces fresh insights into the practice that we now casually call criticism. It helps us move beyond the familiar, prescribed models of critical reading and invigorate our understanding of how we connect with what we read. In short, Meiji Japan's criticism helps us read otherwise.

Critical reading, as both concept and practice, became important to an unparalleled degree in Japan toward the end of the nineteenth century, along with the time's rapidly changing global dynamics. The nineteenth century witnessed colonial expansionism on the global scale, with East Asia one region in which the power hierarchy was pronounced. The situation did not leave Japan untouched, as China had been divided and semi-colonized by multiple colonial forces just across the shores. When the political regime transitioned from the Tokugawa shogunate (the Edo period, 1603–1868) to the Meiji monarchy in the late 1860s, the new Meiji state immediately and proactively had to take steps to avoid the fate of being colonized. Japan began to import an extraordinary number of books and technologies from Euro-Anglo-American colonial powers so that the country could equip itself with anything necessary, both material and ideological, to maintain its independence. Against a backdrop of Japan's inevitable participation in the global nineteenth century, which concurred with the socioeconomic changes on the domestic front, Japanese intellectuals began to clamor for the necessity of rigorous critical reading practice.

Consider the following image, an illustration of an exposition entitled "Jitchi yūeki hakurankai no zu" (An illustration of a practical and

THAT WHICH IS CASUALLY CALLED CRITICISM 3

useful exposition), included in the general reference book *Gōtō: Dai Nihon kokumin sen'yō jitchi yūeki taizen* (A collection of practical and useful matters for the people of great Japan) published in 1886.[1] This reference book focuses on the basic knowledge of people's daily needs, including new legal regulations, customs, and technologies recently introduced. With its many explanatory illustrations, the book presumably intends to help general readers understand things unfamiliar but useful to them. On the left side of the illustration, we see a banner reading, "selling books that are useful in the contemporary world." In the small space underneath the banner, books are stacked up high; there are piles and piles of them. If we look closely, we find different types of books, some bound in Japanese style with strings on their back, and some bound with hardcovers. Some are written in Japanese (or possibly in Chinese or some variant Sinography), while some others show European languages. The image thus shows a jumble of information, written in multiple languages and presented in various forms. And this information, drawn from multiple corpora of knowledge and in mutual negotiation or competition, circulated on the market.

Note the availability of those books to the general public at the exposition. The attendees' access to those books—especially ones written in Roman alphabets—reflects the information-import trade prompted by the global colonial tensions. Furthermore, the abundance of books, not just the ones with Roman alphabets but also the Sino-Japanese books, testifies to one major result that this trade brought about: a sudden surge in publications. With colonial pressure intensifying, Japan actively brought from abroad not only new knowledge in book form but also new equipment to facilitate the production and circulation of books. The number of newly published titles doubled between 1881 (5,973 titles) and 1888 (12,718 titles), and tripled in 1890 (18,720).[2] This sudden increase of published items was enabled by the growth of the print industry, which involved not only the introduction of new print technologies such as metallic movable type and steam presses, but also the building of more stable infrastructure such as trains and other rapid distribution systems.[3] The 1880s thus witnessed a material abundance of publications to be circulated, purchased, and consumed. In the face of this abundance, literate but not-so-wealthy readers needed guides, that is to say, reliable advice on how to most efficiently spend their money, time, and effort on reading. The practice of reading information analytically for assessment and judgment became necessary, then, because it could enable readers to make wise investment decisions.

For some Japanese youths, a particular skill set of reading came to assume vital importance, because they believed that their survival as Meiji elites hinged upon it. For them, reading enabled the youths to take a position within the changing social order under the new Meiji regime. In the illustration, we see a woman speaking to the bookseller and a man closely examining an item. Both figures appear to be parents, accompanied by small children. And while it is perhaps generally important for parents to think about their children's education, including their reading, in late nineteenth-century Japan the matter was particularly urgent for the former samurai class. Many samurai youth would have inherited their class privileges automatically had the social hierarchy of the Tokugawa period—samurai, farmers, artisans, and merchants—persisted, but with the collapse of the shogunate their privileges crumbled. Young generations of former samurai, many achieving adulthood toward the end of the nineteenth century, had to work to readjust and reinscribe themselves in an emerging, still unstable social environment. One way to accomplish this was to mobilize their cultural assets, in particular the high literacy of the privileged class: They could read books that contained newer information and thereby seek to reconfigure their elite social standing. Their high literacy, compared with the masses, assisted the effort to retain their status as refined, well-educated individuals who could bring benefit to society. In a growing sea of information, the literate youth could assert that they knew how to read and discern what would be worthy of readers' attention.

These intertwined sociohistorical and material factors facilitated a general consensus of critical reading's importance in late nineteenth-century Japan. Printed materials pervaded people's everyday lives; as literature scholar Kōno Kensuke notes, the "printed letters" (*insatsu moji*) served a defining role in Japan at a time when the country began to represent itself anew in language through such systems as taxation, education, conscription, and currency.[4] It is not a coincidence that in this illustration, the abundance of books in multiple languages is staged in an exposition; in this period, such events were typically held on the national scale and functioned to inculcate the very idea of "nation" in the minds of attendees. By gathering people and products in one place, expositions exhibited the reach of the national imaginary. The valorization of critical reading practice, in other words, went hand in hand with the building processes of the Japanese nation under the Meiji regime.

FIGURE 0.1. "Jitchi yūeki hakurankai no zu," included in Gōtō: *Dai Nihon kokumin sen'yō jitchi yūeki taizen*. Scanned from my own copy.

In the following pages, I will investigate an early history of critical reading in modern Japan by observing the struggles of young Japanese intellectuals, and the unexpectedly fertile forms of critical reading that they brought about when they attempted to institute the practice. While my discussion concentrates on late nineteenth-century Japan, my hope is that this book offers a refreshing point of reference to those who strive to imagine alternative ways of reading that the disciplinary training in literary studies in North America would not typically provide.

The Scope of *Hihyō*, a Japanese Mode of Critical Reading

The Japanese term that designated critical reading in the late nineteenth century, and still does, is *hihyō* (批評). This unambiguously Sinographic compound word became standardized as a translation of "criticism" and "*Kritik*" during the 1870s and 1880s, as I demonstrate in chapter 1. As if to reference the novelty of the translational kinship drawn between the Japanese term *hihyō* and those of Anglo-European origins in fin de siècle Japan, Meiji writer Tsubouchi Shōyō (1859-1935) mobilized a unique wording in his 1887 account, titled "Hihyō no hyōjun" (The criteria of *hihyō*). Shōyō begins his writing by stating:

> Literary culture in our country made an astonishing level of progress in the past couple of years. No, it is in fact an astonishing level of change. A great number of new books, ones that are different from conventional books in the nature of writing, the type of discussion, designs, and formats. Above all, *that sharp Western-style hihyō* came to be practiced here and there, and even journals that specialize in *hihyō* began to appear all over. In other words, while Oriental literature withered at long last, Western literature greatly came to prevail, together renewing the appearance of the literary world [emphasis added].[5]

Out of many examples of "change," Shōyō draws particular attention to the practice of *hihyō*: not any kind of *hihyō*, but specifically "*that sharp Western-style*" one. According to Shōyō, the sudden increase of this type of *hihyō* is a vital factor that recently transformed the literary landscape. His word choice shows that *hihyō* prevailing in the late 1880s was considered an essentially "Western" approach of reading, one that had only recently taken root in Japan and was distinct from existing reading methods. In Shōyō's writing, we observe a hint of the lingual and conceptual negotiation—the Japanese understanding of a Western practice expressed in the Chinese compound—at work surrounding critical reading in fin de siècle Japan. To underline the significance of this tension inscribed in the term, which I argue in this book ultimately leads to its generative failures, I use the Japanese term *hihyō* throughout.

It is necessary to remember that even though *hihyō* as a new, "Western" approach of critical reading gained traction and turned into a dominant style of intellectual reading practice in the late nineteenth century, this does not mean that it established a uniform definition at the time.[6] The nonuniformity of *hihyō*'s meanings can be observed even today; it does not take long for us to realize that the term encompasses a wide array of "critical" traits that various practices of reading bring forward. The breadth of its contemporary usages reflects the convoluted history of how *hihyō* evolved in the Japanese intellectual landscape.

One of the most common registers of the term *hihyō* denotes "reviews" of a given material, be it a piece of literary work or an art object, and this form of *hihyō* typically appears in journalism. Many periodicals such as daily newspapers and magazines have a column for this type of critical reading. Another usage indicates "scholarship," one in the study of literature—creative linguistic production such as poetry and prose fiction—in particular. Scholarly journals, monographs, and edited volumes that are published by university or specialized academic presses often serve as venues for this research-oriented reading activity. Additionally, there are many overlaps between *hihyō* and "contemporary thought" (*gendai shisō*) and "[critical] theory" ([*hihyō*] *riron*) in the academic setting, especially surrounding the field of literature. Furthermore, *hihyō* sometimes points to prose writing that is speculative and often philosophical, but not necessarily evaluating and passing a judgment on a given material or topic. This type of *hihyō* becomes akin to "reflective essay." We can remember the famous aphorism that Kobayashi Hideo (1902-83), one of the representative practitioners of *hihyō* in the twentieth century, presented in his 1929 debut essay, "Samazamanaru ishō" (Multiple designs): "Is not *hihyō* ultimately about speaking of one's own skeptical dream, about narrating dreams of the self with skepticism?"[7] As if to mirror this statement, many of Kobayashi's writings are self-explorative, disclosing what is streaming through his internal realm. As the fact that Kobayashi is typically referred to as a literary critic (*bungei hihyōka*) shows, reflective undertakings of this sort have been considered *hihyō* and belongings of the literary field in a large part of the twentieth century.[8] Related to this register, *hihyō* also refers to a broader, "humanistic institution." To be more precise, the *hihyō* in this sense points to a commitment to fostering new forms of sensibility and receptiveness and to cultivating self (and often other entities as well) by way of reading. Going beyond the confinements of the academy into the public sphere, this type of reading practice becomes synonymous with the spirit of liberal arts experiences or the orientation toward general culturedness at times, and dilettantism at others.[9]

It is certainly not that the different meanings of *hihyō* in the current usage are independent of one another; all of them are premised on the act of reading, and thus oftentimes they are entwined. Nonetheless, those differences are noteworthy, as they show traces of linguistic and conceptual negotiation through which *hihyō* came into being and developed since the late nineteenth century. Note, for instance, references to "literature" or *bungaku* that underlie many of the meanings of *hihyō*. While those references indicate that modern Japanese *hihyō* revolved around the literary sphere, it is important to remember that the meaning of literature itself went through transformations.[10] This means that the relationship between *hihyō* and literature and, by implication, its contours that evolved along with what was considered literary cannot be considered fixed. Such an aspect of *hihyō*'s history testifies to its amorphousness, showing that from the very beginning, its meaning was unstable.

This instability is essential for us to understand *hihyō* and its proceedings. Throughout this book, we will observe that a diverse range of its "critical" registers in contemporary usage was already present, sometimes obviously, some other times latently, in the discourses and practices of *hihyō* that emerged in the late nineteenth century. The "critical" quality of *hihyō* has never been monolithic, accounting for why Meiji intellectuals had to struggle extensively to establish *hihyō*. Precisely for that reason, their attempted practices of critical reading began to assume experimental, innovative forms. This book attempts to restore the unstable state of *hihyō*, considering that its instability was what enabled unique proceedings of Meiji Japan's critical reading.

The Confusion of Being "Critical"

Hihyō gathered momentum in the specific historical context of fin de siècle Japan because many intellectual figures considered *hihyō* to be an essential practice that would cultivate Japanese minds and pave the way for a new, strong nation capable of rivaling colonial forces. Then-leading intellectual figure Tokutomi Sohō (1863–1957) captured the zeitgeist when in 1888 he declared, in tones of urgency and excitement, "Japan at the present moment is facing the age of *hihyō*."[11] A serious problem ensued, however. While young intellectuals recognized the importance of *hihyō*, they were unsure how to proceed because *hihyō*, which was posited in strong association with the "Western" model of critical reading such as "criticism" and "*Kritik*," had yet to be formulated in Japan. Contemporary readers of Japanese texts might consider the translation between *hihyō* and criticism or *Kritik* obvious; to young Meiji elites, however, the connection was not self-evident. As noted previously, Shōyō stated that "Western-style *hihyō*" had only recently surfaced in Japan, changing the landscape of publications. That Shōyō needed to qualify his use of the term *hihyō* as "Western-style" indicates a distance between a Western-style of critical reading and its non-Western counterpart, namely, a practice that his readers would generally understand as critical reading. The strong attention to *hihyō* in the late nineteenth century thus came with a considerable degree of confusion, a collective uncertainty about what a new style of critical reading might entail, and how the "critical" component of the reading practice in Anglo-European genealogies might differ from one extant in Japanese traditions.

Meiji intellectuals found themselves baffled. Indeed, there was a diverse range of practices in Japan, ones that focused on qualitative evaluation and can now fall under the umbrella of critical reading, that had been performed long before the arrival of the Meiji period.[12] In the realm of poetry, for instance, discourses on poetic composition (*karon*) had demonstrated Japanese intellectuals' attempts to stipulate the criteria of aesthetic judgment since the Heian period (794–1185). Editorial notes on collected poems, too, often exhibit reflection on how to evaluate poetry, as shown in Ki no Tsurayuki's preface to *Kokin wakashū* (Collection of poems from ancient and modern times) compiled in the early tenth century. As to prose writing, efforts to articulate how to read at times took the form of fiction. One of the most famous examples is the "Fireflies" chapter of Murasaki Shikibu's *The Tale of Genji* (circa early eleventh century), in which Genji lectures on the pros and cons of reading fiction to Tamakazura. *Mumyōzōshi* (The nameless book), presumably written by Fujiwara no Shunzei no Musume in the early thirteenth century, also presents an assessment of existing literary works and proposes interpretations of them in the guise of female characters' group discussions. Furthermore, exegeses were a common practice, especially on widely known works, as with Motoori Norinaga's Genji Monogatari *tama no ogushi* (The jeweled comb of *The Tale of Genji*, 1799).

Among varied traditions of critical reading that predate the Meiji period, of particular relevance here is that of classical Chinese learning because of its foundational position in early Meiji's intellectual sphere. Classical Chinese studies had long existed as a corpus of knowledge, a distinct system of intellectualism that constituted the Sinosphere—the language cosmopolis facilitated by the Chinese writing system in broader Asian regions for more than a millennium.[13] The youth of the Meiji period, especially those who belonged to the samurai class in the former shogunate era, were typically trained in classical Chinese studies. In such studies, dividing lines between disciplines do not manifest in the way that disciplines are systematized in the Anglo-European academy, as reading classical Chinese texts often involved studying philology, ethics, legal studies, and recitation performance all at once. The body of classical Chinese texts grew by incorporating elaborate commentaries and annotations, and learning those appendages was also an essential part of critical reading practice in classical Chinese studies. Born and raised in the late nineteenth century, Meiji elites inherited the genealogies of knowledge in classical Chinese studies and internalized the idea of what critical reading meant in their own terms throughout their childhood education. They knew how to read and be critical about what they read in the ways that had been inculcated in them.

If there were rich genealogies of critical reading practice in Japan, what Meiji elites had experienced as critical reading in their traditions of literacy training was not necessarily commensurable with a "Western-style" of critical reading that had been nurtured in a different order of knowledge. Contemporary scholar Emmanuel Lozerand further complicates the incommensurability between these modes of critical reading, in the course of tracking the genealogies of reflective discourses about literary production in Japan:

> [T]he majority of reflections on Japanese literature prior to this period [the late 1880s] were written in the context of existing writing practices, in particular poetic, which required writers, whether amateur or professional, to assimilate a body of references and continue in the tradition of canonical texts. Fundamentally, these ancient "literary critiques" paid little heed to newly published books—an expression which in any case is meaningless when referring to past centuries—and were not aimed at pure readers. Whether directly or indirectly, their objective was always to help or encourage people to write.[14]

If the emphasis of the traditional "literary critiques" produced in Japan was more on "writing" and on teaching how to compose better poetic works, as Lozerand describes, what the youth of Meiji Japan encountered as a "sharp, Western-style" *hihyō* did not appear comparable with those traditions. The qualitative difference between readerly traditions became salient when Japan proactively began to introduce Euro-Anglo-American forms of intellectualism on a significantly larger scale in the nineteenth century. There is a famous anecdote that exemplifies a distance between the two manifestations of critical reading: Shōyō "wrongly" made a moral, not an analytical, argument, when he attended an English literature course at the University of Tokyo and was given an assignment to "criticize" the character of Gertrude from Shakespeare's play *Hamlet*.[15] Shōyō's "mistake"—apparently he received a failing grade in that assignment—testifies to the type of confusion felt by him and his contemporaries about what it takes to read something in a "critical" way.

Meiji intellectuals registered *hihyō*'s importance, and many of them, including Shōyō, thought that it had to be practiced rigorously to bring benefit to Japan. Yet this *hihyō* had to be different from what they had done when they read Japanese poetry, prose, or classical Chinese texts. The critical reading practice conceived in late nineteenth-century Japan had to be a recently introduced "Western-style *hihyō*," that is, something unprecedented in the country. *Hihyō* was required to be new, and as such its ways and workings were yet to be conventionalized.[16] With the question of how to differentiate *hihyō*'s methodologies from existing approaches of reading yet to be explored, its contours remained amorphous. It reached an impasse as soon as it became a major concern for Meiji Japan, when the people who were about to practice it were unable to discern how to move forward.

Under these circumstances, Meiji intellectuals were compelled to reinvent critical reading in the name of *hihyō* based upon what they understood by digesting information freshly acquired from Anglo-European genealogies of reading. They attempted to delve into the question of what it means to read in a newly critical manner, asking among themselves what exactly was expected in *hihyō*. As a result, discourses about critical reading began to proliferate toward the end of the nineteenth century in Japan. The emergence of those reflective discourses marks the first instance in the history of Japanese reading practice where the nature of critical reading itself became a common, broadly shared subject of discussion. This means that the novelty of late nineteenth-century *hihyō* lies not only in a call for a new mode of reading but also in the elaborate unfolding of metadiscourses, in other words, discourses that discuss the practice, what it should be, and how it should be done.

Throughout those metadiscourses, Meiji intellectuals made conscious, collective efforts to institute a new critical reading practice. Yet because of the imperative for newness, they struggled to put in concrete terms the technicalities of the practice. As I demonstrate in part 1 of this book, the discourses surrounding *hihyō* at that time could only propose abstract, extremely high ideals—*hihyō* as "fair," "all-encompassing," "objective" assessment of "every" existing publication—without fleshing out the practical details of what needs to be done to accomplish those ideals. In the end, they did not achieve their stated ends in beginning to assess given objects in the name of *hihyō*. Far from being "fair," "all-encompassing," or "objective," their critical reading practices were oftentimes partial, personal, and manipulative. What they produced as *hihyō*, therefore, did not meet the high but vague criteria.

Recasting Failures

The Japanese criticism practiced in the late nineteenth century failed. More important, it failed in a strikingly generative way by producing unprecedented rhetoric and forms of critical reading. My use of the term "failure" exclusively denotes the discrepancy between what was posited and what was executed as *hihyō*, that is, the disconnect between the lofty, vague ideals and the actual incarnation of *hihyō*. To be more precise: Meiji intellectuals' attempts to exercise critical reading did not become realized in a compelling form, not because they were incompetent to evaluate their objects with precision, nor because their thoughts were naive, outmoded, and incompatible with the Anglo-European models of critical reading that they pursued, but because the ideals initially posited for the practice were unrealistic. Indeed, the failures that I discuss in this book do not point to futility, loss, rejection, or defeat. On the contrary, I attempt to displace failure from a negative, often emotion-ridden judgment by bearing witness to productive, if inadvertent, results invoked by the failing.

I make this motion to decouple failure from negativity, as I recast failure as a site of creative possibilities. Take a moment to reflect on failure and its potentially generative workings. As art critic Lisa le Feuvre asserts, "Failure, by definition, takes us beyond assumptions and what we think we know."[17] Failure forces us to notice what is generally considered successful and, by implication, the arbitrariness of the boundaries of success. Here in the twenty-first century, in which existing sociocultural norms of gender, class, and ability have to be scrutinized, Jack Halberstam argues, the "static models of success and failure" no longer hold valid and need to be dismantled.[18] Halberstam writes, "Under certain circumstances failing, losing, forgetting, unmaking, undoing, unbecoming, not knowing may in fact offer more creative, more cooperative, more surprising ways of being in the world."[19] Failure, in short, creates room for alternative forms of engagement, allowing us to realize there are other paths to explore the thing that we failed.

Meiji Japan's *hihyō* embodies such a manifestation of generative failure. Fin de siècle Japan invested in the idea of establishing critical reading while not quite knowing what it entailed on a practical, empirical level. Resultantly, *hihyō* as practiced in late nineteenth-century Japan did not achieve what it promised, be it fairness or impartiality. Yet as I show in part 2 of this book, in their struggles, Japanese practitioners composed strange and fascinating types of critical reading. In one case, *hihyō* stylistically staged its claim and demonstrated a clever interplay between form and content, while completely refusing to engage with what it was supposed to read and evaluate on the semantic level (chapter 3). At other times, *hihyō* disguised itself as a fiction, thus ceasing to maintain an appearance of objective judgment, while widening the reach of critical language into the creative realm (chapter 4). Another case of *hihyō* generated an unexpectedly anarchic, carnivalesque effect in its use of language by resuscitating literary conventions that were considered unfitting as critical language at the time (chapter 5). *Hihyō* also gave rise to a long-lasting readerly community by failing to articulate what it needed to articulate the most (chapter 6). As these examples show, Meiji Japan's *hihyō* ended up bringing about surprisingly creative, even graceful outcomes exactly when it failed to fulfill its ideals. These cases demonstrate *hihyō*'s failures actually amplified its horizon and enriched how it did what it did. And because Meiji Japan's *hihyō* unfolded in ways that broke with expectations, it counterintuitively illuminates what critical reading could be. I emphasize the poiesis of failures, the moments that flashed through the ruins of words accumulated in the late nineteenth-century Japanese *hihyō*, to glimpse alternative visions of criticism.

It is important to underline the accidental nature of Meiji *hihyō*'s failures, as I intend to dissociate *hihyō*'s failures from telos.[20] The failures of late nineteenth-century *hihyō* were the spontaneous outcome of Meiji intellectuals' struggles, and came into existence as the practitioners groped in the unknown for new modes of critical reading. The disjuncture between what was said and done as *hihyō* was uncalculated, unregistered, and unclaimed. None of these Meiji intellectuals intentionally ignored the ongoing discussions about critical reading. None consciously tried to defy the normative ideals of critical reading speculated upon in their time, nor willingly or deliberately pursued failures. The practitioners were aware neither that their *hihyō* did not correspond to the high, abstract standards set for the practice, nor that their failures gave rise to those felicitous moments that I describe in this book. What I posit as generative failures is thus not a driving force fully recognized or solicited by those who failed. Meiji intellectuals had to struggle because *hihyō* itself was not self-evident to them. In other words, they did not know what they were initiating. This very fact is crucial to my argument because I situate their "not knowing" as a source of their creative strength. I categorically separate what took place in the name of *hihyō* in late nineteenth-century Japan from what I read in it in my here and now. It is I, as a belated reader of fin de siècle Japanese criticism, who designate the discrepancies between theory and practice of *hihyō* as failures and stumble upon the wealth of its failures.

Hihyō crafted language, grammar, and style of its own, even though its originality was not recognized as such in the immediate context. Discrepancies between theory and practice, a kind that I feature in this book, have often been too flatly narrativized in scholarship as manifestations of intellectual immaturity in Japan amid the modernization. As opposed to such an approach, the emphasis of this book is on encountering those failures and reclaiming their generative outcomes—even if they did not fulfill what was promised. The failures came into being as a result of Meiji practitioners' wrestling with the question as to what it is to read in a newly critical way. This means that *hihyō*'s failing moments were inhabited by various directions into which critical reading could develop. When tracing the ways in which *hihyō* unfolded in late nineteenth-century Japan, I withhold as much as I can from simply reducing *hihyō*'s failures to historical events. I insist on leaving the discrepancies unfastened, on lingering in the unknownness of what it takes to be critical. In so doing, I aim to extend the failures' reach beyond the context of late nineteenth-century Japan.

This is where I underline the connection between the fin de siècle Japanese intellectual sphere and literary studies in the twenty-first century. What comes after the deliberation over *hihyō*'s failures is not a predictable narrative of modernization theory, which typically thematizes the distorted, idiosyncratic formation of the modern Japanese psyche, but rather twenty-first-century literature scholars' surprise encounter with the varied manifestations of critical reading. At first glance, late nineteenth-century Japan may not seem to offer illumination or guidance when we ponder questions of critical reading practice. Temporal and geographic remoteness aside, the peripherality of Japan is legibly pronounced in the ways in which disciplines are organized in North American academic institutions—consider for example the limited availability of Japan studies programs in the United States. And yet, I suggest that instead of dismissing Meiji Japan's *hihyō* as a dated, local, poorly executed example of critical reading, we begin thinking in terms of likeness. More than two decades into the twenty-first century, our work as critical readers has become less relevant or less self-evident. Regardless of what each of our job descriptions says, we are confronted with questions of how we relate to our objects of study, with what sort of energy, and to what effect in society beyond the confines of academia. The pressure is urgent as we face the chronic endangerment of our positions. In the same way that those of us in literary studies in the current century are pushed from multiple directions to reconfigure how to engage critically with what we read, so too the emerging generation of Japanese youth who came of age in the final two decades of the nineteenth century struggled to discern what being critical might encompass. Both parties made a commitment to ceaseless, ardent search for possibilities of reading well, if not better.[21] It is this commitment to envision shapes of critical reading that brings together academics in the twenty-first century and Japanese intellectuals from the fin de siècle.

Moreover, the Japanese case is informative to us because what materialized as critical reading in late nineteenth-century Japan shakes our assumptions about criticism: When we read the discourses and practices of critical reading from late nineteenth-century Japan, we perceive that what took place in Japan over a hundred years ago are not quite similar to the conventions of critical reading known to us. The case of fin de siècle Japan thus defies our norms of reading texts in a critical fashion, our familiar criteria of judgment. Precisely because Meiji's *hihyō* arrived at something unintelligible to us when it attempted to become critical, it invites us into a realm of the unknown, a realm in which we cannot determine the effectiveness of our common understanding of critical reading. While I do not intend to present *hihyō* as a new reading method that contemporary literary studies must adopt, the varied ways in which

Meiji Japan's *hihyō* failed to meet its promises offer productive points of reference for us as we seek to reimagine our reading practices and, by extension, our relationships with the texts we read.

Reading *Hihyō*'s Failures in the Postcritical Age

Failing can be generative "under certain circumstances," says Halberstam.[22] This point matters to contemporary scholars of literary studies because the current scene of knowledge production is one of those "circumstances" that would benefit from learning about how to fail—and how not to inherit precedent.

To begin, consider the current state of literary studies. Literary studies in the Anglophone world, contemporary scholar Joseph North maintains, has been, and still is, operating in the "historicist/contextualist" paradigm in the past few decades, in which "works of literature are chiefly of interest as diagnostic instruments for determining the state of the cultures in which they were written or read."[23] If the study of literature only adheres to and reinforces cultural specificities, North warns us, scholars of literature end up instrumentalizing what they read and reducing it to a mere "occasion for writing cultural history."[24] North's point was identified by Japanese intellectual Karatani Kōjin already in the late 1990s. Referencing the trends of cultural studies and postcolonialism prevalent in Japanese and American academia at the time (Karatani was affiliated with Columbia University at the time), Karatani berated contemporary scholars for "regressing into empiricism and positivism, while pretending to be theoretical by using established theories in a somewhat clever way."[25] Karatani's frustration was directed at those who were satisfied by offering cultural and historical facts of the "base" (*kabukōzō*) without advancing into a theoretical, "superstructural" (*jōbukōzō*) level of knowledge, while still considering their own works as the cutting edge of scholarship.[26] If we exclusively value cultural and historical elements only to claim their singularities, one of the likely consequences would be, according to English scholar John Guillory, the eruption of "surrogational politics" in the discipline of literary studies, in which "the curriculum becomes the site of a proxy war," and texts would end up serving surrogacy agencies for "context," or the truth value of cultural history.[27] If the pursuit of details itself became an end of academic work, and if those details were used predominantly to highlight cultural idiosyncrasies, such attitudes would ultimately proceed to define and essentialize borders, instead of crossing them. Inadvertent or not, when the existing paradigm of knowledge imposes such limitations on our work, it is worth considering not inheriting, or failing to stay in, it.

To delve further into the discipline of literature, think what sort of scholarship has been expected and counted as adequate work of critical reading. Since the last century, scholars largely came to favor a particular mode of critical reading, that is, a skeptical kind that reads for revelation of a text's secrets. Such a style of critical reading widely affected the ways in which the success of academic work was measured, defining the thresholds of what can, and should not, be done in scholarship. When the codes for success have been predetermined, delimiting what we do, perhaps we can take a moment to think about not meeting, or failing to reinforce, those codes. As Halberstam maintains, failing in this context illuminates the limits of "certain forms of knowing and certain ways of inhabiting structures of knowing," and thereby generates room for not-reproducing certain configurations of knowledge.[28] If we fail in that way, we may dislocate the shackles of preset modes of reading and, by implication, knowing. Then we may be able to open ourselves up to alternative ways of being critical, engaging with texts, and producing knowledge.

In fact, attempts to address currents of critical reading and problematize the fossilization of methodologies have already begun. A brief overview of the self-reflective discussions around critical reading will help to contextualize the trajectories of contemporary discourses.[29] As early as the 1960s, Susan Sontag challenged critics' "fancy that there really is such a thing as the content of a work of art" and their "perennial, never consummated project of *interpretation*" of it.[30] Sontag's view makes a stark contrast to Frederic Jameson's call in the early 1980s to "always historicize."[31] The "ordinary reader" would simply think that "the text means just what it says," claims Jameson, and therefore, critics need to exercise "'strong' rewriting" of the text so as to disclose the "mechanism of mystification or repression" that is masked on the surface and bring to the fore a "latent meaning behind a manifest one."[32] The Jamesonian disposition of reading constitutes a thick pillar of the school of hermeneutics of suspicion, representative figures of which include Karl Marx, Friedrich Nietzsche, and Sigmund Freud. As Paul Ricoeur puts it, the suspicion-driven interpretations central to this school make painstaking efforts to reveal meanings camouflaged or erased. This is because to suspicious minds, consciousness is primarily "false," and therefore, the "fundamental category of consciousness is the relation hidden-shown."[33] What Ricoeur calls "suspicion" prompts the proneness to read "symptoms" in the text. In their 2009 essay, Stephen Best and Sharon Marcus identify the dominant reading methodology among scholars of literature as "symptomatic reading," which takes "meaning to be hidden, repressed, deep and in need of detection and disclosure by an interpreter."[34] Bruno Latour in the early 2000s draws attention to the reductive, hence easily reproducible, nature of suspicious or symptomatic reading methods, asserting that those methods would likely reach the same conclusion for any text under scrutiny. If any critical inquiry ultimately says "[t]here is no sure ground anywhere," wonders Latour, "[a]re we not like those mechanical toys that endlessly make the same gesture when everything else has changed around them?"[35] And if we are turning into reading machines that repeat the same motion in the name of criticism, "[w]hat has become of the critical spirit?"[36] Latour's rhetorical questions display his frustration that critique in our time ceased to be critical.

Eve Sedgwick reasonably identifies the reading style normalized through the school of hermeneutics of suspicion as a strong theory. Quoting psychologist Silvan Tomkins, Sedgwick glosses a strong theory in the following way:

> Any theory of wide generality is capable of accounting for a wide spectrum of phenomena which appear to be very remote, one from the other, and from a common source. This is a commonly accepted criterion by which the explanatory power of any scientific theory can be evaluated. To the extent to which the theory can account for "near" phenomena, it is a weak theory, little better than a description of the phenomena which it purports to explain.[37]

Sedgwick characterizes the suspicion-driven, strong theory–based reading as paranoia, reframing it as a drive that seeks to expose causal relationships, often buried, between historical happenings and cultural products. Paranoid reading, in other words, strives to extract a coherent narrative out of contingencies. To the paranoid, nothing comes as a surprise: The goal is to reconfirm presumed narratives so that paranoia can be soothed. Ideology critique epitomizes paranoid reading. The revelations that ideology critique brings to the fore may at first appear horrific. As Jameson made clear, that is precisely why the "political interpretation" of texts needs to be prioritized.[38] And yet if ideologies seep into every corner of our lives, what ideology critique pursues is in a sense always anticipated and already narrativized. According to Sedgwick, it is the anticipatory, indisputable nature of paranoid reading that becomes its methodological limitations. The very likely, if not alarming, result of the proliferation of paranoid reading, backed by strong theories of suspicious minds, is the tautological, inevitable confirmation of the same presumptions and, by extension, the preempting of the conception of other attitudes for reading.

When interpreting cultural products, we may feel an urge to unveil the secret agendas hidden under the surface, expose their complicity with state violence, divulge the politics of the apolitical, and also, mention the heroic moments of resistance buried in some of them. For several decades, those who study literature and write about cultural products encountered or reproduced, whether knowingly or unwittingly, variations of those arguments. But although such scholarly narratives sound familiar, and we can safely confirm that they offer critical readings of texts, at issue here is their very familiarity: Even when we already know what will come from our reading, we still follow the impulse and repeat the same patterns of inquiry to say "gotcha." This is certainly not to negate those methodologies entirely: there is value in reading "behind," "beneath," and "beyond" texts. Yet if readerly behavior becomes akin to an "automated reflex-action," as Latour warns us, our claim to the position of "critical" readers may no longer hold valid.[39]

Specifically, when it comes to the Meiji period, the subjects under investigation tend to be explained, all too easily and predictably, through narratives of modernization. The overwhelming pressures of modernization and its multilayered, long-lasting effects existed indeed, but modernization alone should not be a default finishing line that conveniently wraps up scholarly deliberations on the era. The processes through which *hihyō* unfolded in the late 1880s into the 1890s were far from straightforward. The ways in which Meiji intellectuals theorized critical reading and put their theories into practice were so wildly varied that they refuse to be narrativized in a generally applicable, if not reductive and repeatable, strong theory, no matter how prevalent the intensity of modernization appeared in the context of late nineteenth-century Japan. Imagine a speculative scenario in which I said at the end of this book, "the discourses and practices surrounding critical reading in late nineteenth-century Japan were messy because the country was experiencing transformative forces of modernization at the time." This statement itself might be valid, supported by a strong theory of modernization. Yet such a narrative is prewritten before I write it; as such, restating it as conclusion does not broaden our understanding of *hihyō*—or of anything. While I too operate in what North calls the "historicist/contextualist" paradigm to a fair extent, I intend to treat Meiji Japan's *hihyō* more than yet another "occasion for writing cultural history."[40] I aim to examine details without directing them toward a single convergence point or common denominator of Japan's modernization or explaining them away as cultural idiosyncrasies. I am compelled to explore what other vocabularies and visions I can assemble and compose, not just as a Japanologist but also as a literature scholar, based on my reading experiences of Meiji *hihyō*.

To that end, think how we can fail to reproduce certain patterns of critical reading, and how else we can read. We can draw on many alternative models that have been proposed against the predominance of suspicious, symptomatic, or paranoid reading practices, often fortified by strong theories. Sontag, for instance, did not simply reject hermeneutical practices. Instead of excavating and eventually vandalizing the text in the name of hermeneutics, she advocated an "erotics of art" that would allow critical reading to "show *how it is what it is*, even *that it is what it is*, rather than to show *what it means*."[41] The entire fall 2009 issue of the literary journal *Representations*, to which the aforementioned essay by Best and Marcus serves as an introductory note, is dedicated to various conjectures about surface reading. Surface reading asks how we can become attentive to surfaces, not the depth, of texts that "have been rendered invisible by symptomatic reading."[42] Franco Moretti's call to distant reading can be added to the list of alternative reading models. Distant reading shows no interest in interpretation of texts—be it reading "more" of them or reading them "more closely"—and instead approaches text as components, trends, and collectable data.[43] Michelle Boulous Walker proposes slow reading as a way of resisting "institutional reading," that is, the "largely professional reading undertaken in the university that occurs within a culture of speed and haste—of publish or perish."[44] Slow reading, Boulous Walker argues, directs us away from a professional skill set of reading that prioritizes time efficiency for sheer informational gain and, in so doing, helps us recuperate the "love of wisdom (the instituting moment)," which has long been overshadowed by the "forensic desire to know (the instituted moment)."[45]

Scanning the contemporary discussions over reading methods, Rita Felski delineates the limits of the dominant postures of criticism while entertaining possibilities of productively undoing them. Now broadly grasped as postcritical reading, the body of Felski's scholarship presents revitalizing ideas: We can generate something constructive out of our reading experiences, instead of ripping apart everything we read;

we can engage with what we read without disregarding or suppressing such affective responses as attachment, enchantment, and shock, which are often intertwined with ethical and political implications[46]; and we can "articulate a positive vision for humanistic thought" and "recognize the potential of literature and art to create new imaginaries," when the disciplines of humanities need to defend, more than ever, their value.[47]

Failing to be critical in a prescribed way points to a path to bringing constructive energy into our reading practices in the postcritical age. As an afterword to the brief sketch of postcritical reading, I wish to clarify two points. First, the postness of postcritical reading does not equate to the discarding of those intellectual genealogies that we inherited, often with deep reverence.[48] Whatever objects we study, we certainly question, doubt, and sometimes become obsessive and skeptical in our inquiries. The emphasis here is not on doing away with those dispositions but on "creat[ing] new imaginaries" for the texts we encounter. Second, postcritique does not aim at prescribing a new model of critical reading that might replace suspicion, paranoia, or skepticism. One reason why the call for postcritique was met with a backlash is that a proponent of postcritical reading does not describe an alternative way of reading in concrete terms.[49] Yet when the imperative of postcritique is to envision possibilities of forming a personal, affective, hence always singular, relationship with what we read and, by extension, with the world in which our reading experience takes place, what we need is not another fixed model of reading but room that allows us to acknowledge the bounds of our reading experience.[50] Studying Meiji Japan's discourses and practices of critical reading creates such room, helping us see how fixed our reading practice might have been. What emerged as *hihyō* in late nineteenth-century Japan failed to be true to its ideals, and its failures draw a map of paths that are not quite intelligible to us. I read for those meandering paths, ones that are muddling but still reveal varied outcomes of attempts at critical reading, and I seek to execute my reading in a critical, yet not necessarily censorious way. In short, I read Meiji Japan's *hihyō* in order to think through how we can read in the postcritical age and demonstrate our passion and competence as critical readers, without reflexively replicating what we have internalized as normative reading methodologies.

As I deliberate over this question, I am reminded of what Sedgwick (via Tomkins) explored as a weak theory: "little better than a description of the phenomena," a weak theory does not aim at reaching an all-encompassing, causal, comprehensive explanation because it operates on the time- and space-specific scale. It is indifferent to creating a narrative of the whole. It does not utilize parts for the comprehension of something larger. It alerts us that we may be paranoid if the conclusion that we are about to offer appears familiar. Most important, a weak theory persists in attending to the irreducibility of details and the messiness of reality. If a strong theory, in being strong enough to encompass many cases across time and space, cannot adequately account for the confusion, inscrutability, and generativity that surrounded fin de siècle Japanese criticism, perhaps the ways in which *hihyō* evolved in Meiji Japan could be understood only in an opposite manner, that is, through a weak theory. Proceeding with the details allows me to assemble, rather than dismantle, my objects of study with "care and caution."[51]

My analyses thus rely on close reading of the details, and I treat the details not as evidence of Japan's specificity but as trajectories of attempted critical reading. Throughout this book, I elaborate on various rhetorical moves and strategies manifested in Meiji practitioners' writings, and examine multiple instances of misreading. If we put on hold the drive for suspicious, symptomatic, or paranoid reading—a drive inculcated in the mentality of many contemporary scholars of literature—then perhaps we may be able to begin experiencing at first hand the strange, rich, kaleidoscopic directions in which late nineteenth-century Japanese criticism unfolded in search of new criticality. We can then envision differently our relationship to *hihyō* and flex our perspectives on what critical reading could be without being entirely consumed by a narrative of modern nation-building verified by a strong theory. I suggest that we read fin de siècle Japanese criticism as one of the possible footholds from which we reorient ourselves toward texts that we read, evaluate, and write about. This book hopes to serve as an open invitation to imagining otherwise how we read.

Overview

Meiji Japan's *hihyō* was invoked as a powerful intellectual device in the late nineteenth century. Yet it has not enjoyed strong scholarly attention in the field of Japanese literature in North America. Well-studied figures such as Shōyō and Mori Ōgai (1862–1922), who have been consistently positioned as key players in the development of modern Japanese literature by many scholars, produced a fair amount of writings concerning *hihyō*. Unlike their prose fiction, however, their *hihyō* writings have often been marginalized in scholarship. This deprioritization of Meiji *hihyō* may reveal, in part, the narrow temporal scope of the discourses and practices of *hihyō* at that time. That is to say, what was discussed about, and exercised as, *hihyō* in the late nineteenth century was "in play" only for a limited period in their immediate context, and not beyond. Those discourses and practices flashed into the new media space established for *hihyō*, and their information value was quickly eclipsed by other print materials. As such, it may now appear that Meiji *hihyō* no longer communicates anything enlightening to contemporary readers. However, its existence delimited and still defines the bounds of success, in other words, the range of successfully valorized scholarly objects (such as prose fiction) produced in and since the Meiji period, if only from the periphery. This book conjures the unattended discourses and practices of *hihyō* for their very peripherality, and I intend to do so, not to disturb the center-periphery dynamics, but to stay with the periphery.

In the following chapters, my attention is directed at what enabled the construction of *hihyō*, what was discussed about *hihyō*, and what materialized as *hihyō*. It is important to remember that in the process of *hihyō*'s construction, a diverse range of reading methods that had been practiced before the Meiji period were retroactively subsumed under a category of *hihyō*. That being the case, I am less concerned with etymological recuperation of *hihyō* or the prehistory of Japanese critical reading, but more with the negotiation of *hihyō* as an object of discussion, as well as a mode of reading practice experienced from the late nineteenth century onward. Instead of hypostatizing Meiji *hihyō* as a foundation of inquiry, I seek rather to remain cognizant of the uncertainty inscribed in it.

To clarify how I approach *hihyō* while being attentive to its amorphousness, I note media historian Ōsawa Satoshi's dexterous tracking of the processes through which discourses called *hihyō* came to be systematized in the early twentieth-century print media environment. The mass production and popularization of print materials from the late 1920s into the middle of the 1930s prompted the formation of a particular media environment that prepared the proliferation of *hihyō*: Examining such factors as specific patterns of writing, forms of publication, and infrastructure that supported the previous two, Ōsawa argues that it was the "media environment" that "produced *hihyō*."[52] In the beginning of his study, Ōsawa poses a provocative question, asking if there was ever an activity that deserved the moniker *hihyō* in Japan.[53] The point of Ōsawa's question lies in its unanswerability: It is a rhetorical question in which the answer can be either yes or no. However, as long as the question is formulated this way, the answer, be it a yes or no, ultimately boils down to positivism and search for origin. When origin is at stake, an infinite movement of identifying links, whether obvious, arbitrary, or missing, ensues, typically by presuming a fixed locus of meaning somewhere that awaits us. Yet the quest for something decisive and essential may become easily mired in tautology and obsession because an origin of meaning, singular and intact, may exist nowhere. A question that entails an origin search, therefore, imposes a not-so-constructive restriction upon itself and cannot be sustained. Fully aware of this limitation, Ōsawa swiftly changes the course of his inquiry from "what *hihyō* was and now is" to "how it existed and still does." I introduce this shift in perspective, from "what" to "how," as I delve into late nineteenth-century *hihyō*. Taking the question, "how" Meiji Japan's *hihyō* came into existence, as my point of departure, I hope that this book will become an extension of what Ōsawa's project initiated, moving back in time from the early twentieth century that Ōsawa analyzes to the late nineteenth century, thereby broadening the temporal scope of "how *hihyō* existed" in Japan.

Part 1 consists of two chapters and elaborates on the emergence of *hihyō* as an intellectual reading practice in late nineteenth-century Japan. *Hihyō* was actively constructed in this period, yet the establishing processes came with confusion. The two chapters in part 1 detail the Japanese experiences of instituting critical reading practice and lay the groundwork for part 2, in which I investigate the varied forms that critical reading took at the time.

Chapter 1 contends that the institutionalization of *hihyō* in Meiji Japan was facilitated by the creation of material space through which it could be written into existence, and that the production of that material space preceded Meiji intellectuals' general consensus as to how to practice critical reading. After reviewing the ways in which leading intellectuals of the time conceptualized *hihyō*, I track a media history of its establishment, that is, how it began to take a material shape in print media. Toward the end of the 1880s, a media space exclusively dedicated to *hihyō* began to appear in major journals, the examples of which include *Shuppan geppyō* (Monthly reviews of publications, 1887–91) and *Kokumin no tomo* (The nation's friend, 1887–98). The individuation of the space of *hihyō* was quickly popularized by the early 1890s. The physical space on paper (how it exists), not the content (what it is), thus designated *hihyō* and delimited its boundaries. *Hihyō*, in other words, first and foremost cultivated a primary habitat on paper, where it could begin to prosper. The spatialization of *hihyō* in material form was itself the message, as what was contained in it could immediately turn into a manifestation of critical reading, regardless of its content and quality.

Chapter 2 further investigates the emerging stage of *hihyō* by looking into representative discourses that surfaced in 1880s print media, with special attention to two points: the relationship that *hihyō* began to form vis-à-vis literature, and the unrealistic ideals that Meiji intellectuals imposed upon *hihyō*. Soon after *hihyō*'s importance to Meiji Japan was recognized by young intellectuals, it began to forge an exclusive connection to literary production. Subsequently, a media space specifically used for the critical reading of literary work began to appear. After showing the building of the *hihyō*-literature connection in print media, I examine one of the earliest attempts to theorize *hihyō* in Meiji Japan, namely, an essay titled "Hihyōron" (A theory of *hihyō*) proposed in 1888 by leading intellectual Ōnishi Hajime (1864–1900). "Hihyōron" is unique not simply because it intends to formulate *hihyō*'s stand in relation to creative work such as literature but also because it posits one of the oft-mobilized, high ideals of *hihyō* at the time, that is, *hihyō*'s privileged distance from what it reads. As if to reflect a contemporary discourse that posited the division of (intellectual) labor as a necessity for the efficient progress of the Japanese nation, Ōnishi's theory emphasizes divisions between critics and creators, critical language and creative language. In so doing, "Hihyōron" insists that *hihyō* needs to maintain its exceptional status as an impartial, detached judge. Importantly, however, the essay also contradicts itself by asserting that in order for *hihyō* to succeed, it is required to merge with the creative work that it assesses and temporarily undo the dividing line. Ōnishi's writing does not resolve the self-contradiction, as he leaves the exact mechanism of distance and nondistance unexplained. "Hihyōron," in other words, fails to explain itself as a theory of *hihyō*. I will recast this failure in Ōnishi's account as a distinct moment inhabited by possibilities of *hihyō* creating itself. The *hihyō* conceptualized in his theory has to be open for transfigurations specifically into things creative. As such, Ōnishi's vision enlarges the scope of what *hihyō*, at once a critical and creative reading practice, can become.

"Hihyōron" also serves as a gateway to four chapters in part 2 of this book, each undertaking a case study of *hihyō*'s failures and unraveling the unexpected, innovative ways in which late nineteenth-century Japanese criticism unfolded. The cases are debates—the "Literature and Nature" debate, the "Dancing Girl" debate, the submerged-ideal debate, and the interrelation-with-life debate—that occurred in the media space of *hihyō*.

These cases are selected for scrutinization for their form (debate), timing (around 1890), and topic (literature). The form of debates—specifically public exchanges of ideas, the missives bartered in print—effectively brings to light the stakes of practicing *hihyō* in the open, intellectual space of fin de siècle Japan. The timing of these debates—all four of them taking place soon after *hihyō* began to be spatialized in print media toward the end of the 1880s into the early 1890s—shows that the years surrounding "Hihyōron" hosted a moment at which the inaugural, conscious efforts to conceptualize *hihyō* concurred with the collective ventures into actually practicing it. In addition, each instance of *hihyō*, assuming a form of a debate, addresses in varying ways the question of how to do critical reading in relation to literary writing and, in so doing, shows the ways in which the boundaries of *hihyō* and literature were negotiated. Meiji intellectuals often read each other's published work, be it a reflective essay, opinion piece, or literary composition, and publicly commented on it in print. Their *hihyō* sometimes prompted further responses and turned into heated debates. Debate participants thus exercised critical reading at different stages as they continued to read and respond to refutations from other discussants. Interestingly, those debates proceeded as if to fill in the lacuna of "Hihyōron" by demonstrating *hihyō*'s creative turn. Based on a logic of division of labor, Meiji intellectuals strove to distinguish a language used for *hihyō* from other linguistic functions such as literary ones. Yet the *hihyō* practiced throughout those debates often ended up mobilizing literary conventions, thereby undermining the premises of *hihyō*. I contend that the failure of critical language in those debates actually made radically creative gestures in inventing *hihyō*.

Chapter 3 features the 1889 "Literature and Nature" debate and investigates a manifestation of *hihyō*'s failure, that is, how *hihyō* may address a topic at hand if it ignores what it criticizes. In the debate, Ōgai and Iwamoto Yoshiharu (1863-1942) disputed the divisibility of "literature" from "nature." While they read and criticized each other and exchanged missives in print media, their interaction soon collapsed because Ōgai disregarded his opponent's words and logic. Despite Iwamoto's effort at clarification, Ōgai continued to misread Iwamoto and imposed the meaning of "science" upon Iwamoto's "nature." In this almost violent semantic suppression, the fundamental promise of *hihyō*, first and foremost as a reading practice, fell through; as a result, no sensible interaction ensued. And yet, the broken correspondence between Ōgai and Iwamoto in fact performed the very thing they were debating:

it divided "literature" from other disciplines. Ōgai's *hihyō* did not attend to his opponent's discourse, but his distinctively "scientific" method of building an argument, resembling the theory of scientific observation and experiment proposed in Émile Zola's "The Experimental Novel" (1880), approximates in form his claim about the division that had to be made between literature and science. Ōgai's responses in the debate thus show a performative way that late nineteenth-century Japanese criticism addressed a subject matter while failing to carry out its task of (semantic) reading. As such, this case study offers a reference point from which to develop new potential shapes that critical reading might take.

The "Literature and Nature" debate is my first case study because it has the broadest scope, demonstrating that the idea of division of intellectual labor manifested not only in the literary realm but also in adjoining political and societal spheres. With its thematization of disciplinary differences between science and literature, the debate underwrites the contemporary desire to individuate something out of a larger mass for further specialization. The chapter thus indicates that the institutionalization of *hihyō* was not an isolated phenomenon but an example of modern knowledge systematization.

The next two chapters contemplate how Meiji practitioners' collective urge to register a critical language independent of other forms of linguistic use emerged, and how this urge was betrayed by their own practice. Both chapters feature *hihyō* failing in dividing critical language from creative language: first from fiction, and next from playful writing, respectively. Chapter 4 focuses on a dispute prompted by the publication of Ōgai's novella "The Dancing Girl" ("Maihime") in 1890, and conjectures about *hihyō*'s failure to sustain independence from fiction. Soon after the appearance of "The Dancing Girl," leading intellectual Ishibashi Ningetsu (1865-1926) problematized the inconsistency in character depiction manifested in the story, inviting vehement responses from the author. Oddly, the exchange of *hihyō* between Ningetsu and Ōgai maintained a façade of fiction, as both writers assumed fictional personae in their writings. Furthermore, as the debate unfolded, it ended up providing alternative endings of "The Dancing Girl." The discourses on critical reading generally emphasized the objective distance that *hihyō* ought to maintain from what it criticizes and, by extension, fiction. And yet such categorical distinction completely collapsed in this debate. That blurring of the boundaries, however, counterilluminates the arbitrariness of what we consider the language appropriate for critical practice. As such, the debate carves out room to conjure freer ways to exercise critical reading.

Chapter 5 analyzes the submerged-ideal debate between Ōgai and Shōyō in the early 1890s, and examines *hihyō* parodying itself and thereby failing to maintain the appearance of seriousness. When Shōyō as a Shakespearean scholar published his lecture notes on *Macbeth*, remarking that his methodology of reading was one of noninterpretation, Ōgai challenged the noninterpretative method as irresponsible, misrepresented Shōyō's claims, and never squarely responded to clarifications. The exchange unsurprisingly did not bridge the rift between the two, and yet the debate took a surprise turn when Shōyō changed the style of his writing into parody. Playful writing known as *gibun*, full of wordplays and allegories, was suppressed as an "outmoded" literary convention in the scene of writing in late nineteenth-century Japan, especially in the discourses surrounding *hihyō*. Shōyō's writings clearly did not meet expectations for a new, sober style of critical language. The accidental resurgence of the "unfit" literary device, however, dislocated the tension of the dispute and brought Ōgai's pen to a halt. The Shōyō-Ōgai exchange shows one model of unfastening the binds of critical language—what it should say and how it should be expressed—deeply inculcated in the minds of twenty-first-century scholars of literature. The debate is also noteworthy because it was one of the earliest instances in Japan in which the stakes of interpretation as a critical reading method—"read for interpretation or not," which is a very familiar question to us—were publicly contested.

The next and final chapter of the book takes a different approach to *hihyō*'s failure and examines its long-lasting effects, that is, what emotive responses its failure could possibly stir among readers. Chapter 6 takes up the 1893 interrelation-with-life debate, in which Kitamura Tōkoku (1868-94) and Yamaji Aizan (1865-1917) battled over the purpose of literature, and investigates the paradox of Tōkoku's *hihyō*. Tōkoku took issue with Aizan, who claimed the instrumental quality of writing practice, and instead advocated the purity—or absolute independence—of literature in the world. During the debate, however, Tōkoku left unexplained the most important part of his idea, that is, what constitutes the purity of literature. Without providing sufficient indications of what he needed to say, Tōkoku's account against Aizan digressed from the initial topic—the purpose of literature—and became monologic. His *hihyō*, in other words, failed to represent itself adequately in verbal form and was unable to engage with its opponent. Paradoxically, however, Tōkoku's writing has a major impact on the scene of writing in Japan: Although his central claim remained unarticulated, the notion of "pure literature" or *junbungaku* still persists in the twenty-first-century literary world. The privileged Akutagawa Prize (established in 1935), granted semiannually to writers of "pure literature," exemplifies the continuing effect of Tōkoku's rhetoric. I show that in spite of the failure of Tōkoku's *hihyō*, his recourse to specific grammatical structures, that is, the use of deictics, has allowed readers to interpret and appropriate "pure literature" at will and facilitated their commitment to the idea. Part 2 ends with the analysis of the Tōkoku–Aizan dispute because this case uniquely illuminates the position of readers. The inadvertent evocation of readerly participation prompted by the failure of Tōkoku's *hihyō* affords us an opportunity to reflect on our own relationships with readers, without whom our critical reading practice may not be validated.

The four case studies enrich our understanding of what took place as critical reading in late nineteenth-century Japan. *Hihyō* produced at the time engendered diverse forms of critical reading exactly when it failed to realize its ideals. These cases of *hihyō* do not conform to what twenty-first-century scholars typically consider criticism. Yet precisely because of the nonconformity to familiar hermeneutic models, fin de siècle *hihyō* shows examples of what intellectual flexibility, imagination, and creativity for critical reading might look like.

We cannot undo the failures of late nineteenth-century Japanese criticism when it did not meet its own high standards. In its failures, however, we can read moments that may unwind us from the familiar standards of how we do what we do in literary studies, of which critical reading is a constitutive part. This book strives, however weakly, to bring contemporary readers closer to failures of critical reading in the past of a foreign land and, in so doing, offers a moment away from the pressure of having to be critical in a certain way. To read Meiji Japan's *hihyō* is to be confronted by opportunities to reflect on how our critical practice might be prescribed, structured, and delimited. If we can engage intimately with what took place as critical reading in Japan over a hundred years ago, we can embrace those opportunities as felicitous possibilities that allow us to consider how we might perform readings otherwise.

PART I

*Discourses of
Critical Reading*

CHAPTER 1

The Age of *Hihyō*

> Our age is the genuine age of criticism, to which everything must submit.
>
> —Immanuel Kant

In 1888, Tokutomi Sohō, a young, vibrant journalist, gave a fervent speech on the importance of *hihyō* in contemporary Japan.[1]

Japan at the present moment is like a starving person and, therefore, the country needs to refrain from selecting what is appropriate for itself. The responsibility of selection thus goes to intellectuals of the time. Those who are starving do not discern a difference in any food. It is only natural that the Japanese, who had been in the dark cave like bats, suddenly saw the sun lights and felt deeply impressed. Precisely because of that, Japan should not forget about the way of selection. That is why Japan now needs *hihyō* the most, a kind of *hihyō* that is precise and rigorous. When we say *hihyō*, we might think of finding fault with things. But *hihyō* definitely does not mean that. The task of a *hihyō* practitioner is not to discover the truth but to make a judgment of truth and advertise it. Out of all the matters that exist in the world, a *hihyō* practitioner discerns the most appropriate one in his time and place, commends it to the public, and diffuses it to the world. Japan at the present moment is the age of *hihyō*. Especially when it comes to Euro-American civilizational matters that are unfamiliar to the Japanese, a *hihyō* practitioner must conduct *hihyō* of what is most suitable to us and make it relevant to our needs.²

Sohō delivered this speech as a founder of the Min'yūsha School (Society of people's friends, established in 1887), a school of thought and also a press that aimed to cultivate and invigorate discussions on a variety of sociopolitical, econocultural topics. The primary audience of his speech was the young, educated, male audience of Hongō Seinenkai (The youth association of Hongō, Tokyo). The speech was reproduced from the shorthand version and first published in two consecutive installments in intellectual journal *Rikugō zasshi* (The universe).³ The excerpt above is an abridged version reprinted in Sohō's own platform, *Kokumin no tomo* (The nation's friend, launched in 1877), run by the Min'yūsha School. The repetitive incarnation of the same claim in different venues demonstrates Sohō's investment in the idea: Contemporary Japan is at an important historical juncture, facing the age of *hihyō*.

As if to echo a tone of urgency looming in the utterance of Immanuel Kant, Sohō's discourse implies an underlying message: Without the intervention of critical reading, imminent misfortune will not pass, and something unpleasant will follow. While Kant's imperative stems from his grappling with the limits of human intellect in eighteenth-century Germany, what permeates Sohō's speech is a concern about how to navigate Japan's civilizational crisis amid the shifting global power dynamics of the nineteenth century. Commodore Matthew Perry's surprise visit in 1853 opened the country to the Euro-Anglo-American economic, colonial, and military powers, beginning with unequal treaties. These powers were already ubiquitous in East Asia, with China being ripped apart right across from Japanese shores. Against such a backdrop, Sohō argues that "[i]n order for our half-civilized country to stand equal to fully civilized Euro-American powers," it needs to "appropriate Euro-American civilization, which goes one step ahead of us." Yet "selection" is not easy, Sohō admits, as infinite matters might fall under the category of "Euro-American civilization." This is where Sohō sets *hihyō*'s mission: There is an immediate need for "precise and rigorous" *hihyō*, one that makes appropriate "selections" for present-day Japan. And for that purpose, according to Sohō, practitioners of *hihyō* must serve seriously by acquiring five distinct qualities: "disinterestedness" (*muyoku*), "fairness" (*kōhei*), "sincerity" (*seijitsu*), "learnedness" (*gakushiki*), and "intelligence" (*sōmei*).⁴ In his assessment of post-shogunate Japan as in the process of producing and resituating itself in the world, Sohō clearly relies on the logic of civilizational hierarchy, with Euro-Anglo-America ("civilized") at the top, Japan in the middle ("half-civilized"), and others at the bottom. Sohō's vision of the future unfolds by extending the same logic: If Japan successfully exercises *hihyō* and appropriates what it selects for the country, Japan will become the "one that has Western-like civilization and stands tall at the center of Oriental barbarians."[5]

Beyond the appearance of civilization hierarchy running through Sohō's account, I am particularly struck by the connection that he delineates between Japan's crisis and *hihyō*, that is to say, the importance he ascribes to "critical" reading practice for rectifying the "critical" situation of the country. As if to reverberate with Greek term *krino*—to distinguish and make a judgment—from which English term "criticism" originated, Sohō designates *hihyō* as a decisive agent that can and must save Japan from its predicament. I take note of this point in order to highlight that *hihyō* was conceived as a new mode of reading during one of the most transformative periods in Japan's history. Because of that context, *hihyō* had to be hyperaware of its task—to read in a critical way to resolve a crisis—from the inception in the late nineteenth century. Such a hyperawareness, which we can observe in prolific discussions about the nature of *hihyō* at the time, makes Meiji Japan's *hihyō* a distinct case in the history of critical reading in Japan and elsewhere.

Late nineteenth-century *hihyō* had to be cognizant of itself also because, despite the enormous scale of the critical reading project for the nation under construction, it was unsure of how to execute the assigned task. The mission to provide critical reading of Western civilization and guide half-civilized Japan out of its crisis was overwhelming. What made the situation more challenging was that, as discussed in the introduction, the commercial publishing industry was growing and diversifying at an ever-increasing speed while Japan negotiated with the worlds' shifting hegemony. The sight of a massive number of print materials, volumes that could never possibly be consumed in their entirety, furthered a sense of urgency in Meiji intellectuals' call for legitimate critical reading practice. The problem was that no one really knew what kind of shape such critical reading might take in the name of *hihyō*. It is reasonable that *hihyō* must embody "disinterestedness," "fairness," "sincerity," "learnedness," and "intelligence," as Sohō envisions. Nevertheless, beyond those abstract ideals, how to read critically—in an unprecedentedly "critical" way to select useful information and save the country at the present moment—was not obvious.

What ensued from these historical circumstances is particularly unique because *hihyō* proceeded into a drastic direction, finding its way to establish itself in form first in print media. While intellectuals were still in the middle of seeking defining ways and workings of *hihyō* upon which a majority could agree, many major periodicals targeting generations of young, educated readership individuated a section dedicated to *hihyō* in their issues in the late 1880s and turned into a stronghold of the practice. Said differently, precisely because of the uncertainty about how to exercise a new mode of critical reading, *hihyō* first materialized as a space specializing in the practice from which it could be deployed. Journals were particularly appropriate media to incorporate the space of *hihyō* for their medium specificity: Unlike daily papers that had to provide new information at a fast pace within a limited word count, weekly or monthly periodicals, generally working with a broader time and spatial frame, could publish longer, more thoroughly crafted pieces for selection, evaluation, and judgment.[6]

It was only natural that the spatialization of *hihyō* took place in print media and went hand in hand with the emerging process of what Jürgen Habermas posits as the public sphere in Meiji Japan: Critical reading practice carved out itself within a site for public, critical discussion.[7] Along with the rapid development of the publication industry in late nineteenth-century Japan, print media, especially periodicals designed by and for well-informed, male youths such as Sohō's *Kokumin no tomo*, served as primary forums for open contestation, exchange, and dissemination of ideas. As Kyu Hyun Kim describes, that Tokugawa society had already prepared the ground for civilian discursive fields by nurturing material, consumer culture and fostering national, political consciousness helped to bolster the construction of the public sphere in the new era.[8] As soon as these media began to function as platforms for the formation of public opinions, they created the space of *hihyō*, at once solidifying the base for critical reading practice and inviting more discussions about it. Indeed, these media spaces were "public" only insofar as privileged intellectuals were concerned.[9] Moreover, the degree to which print media were "public" was in constant negotiation with state control, as they were susceptible to law and censorship.[10] These constraints notwithstanding, rendering a tangible shape for critical reading practice in the public discursive sphere helped to establish its legitimacy. Through this form of spatialization, *hihyō* began to stand by itself as a valued intellectual practice, and as a result, whatever appeared in the space became *hihyō*, regardless of whether or not it convincingly executed the task of selection. The institutionalization of *hihyō* in Meiji Japan was thus facilitated by the creation of physical space on paper through which its circulation could be enabled.

As Sohō described, Japan in the 1880s was facing the "age of *hihyō*." The cultivation of a space exclusive to *hihyō* took place against the changing geopolitical landscape of Japan vis-à-vis the world in the late nineteenth century. Given the centrality that the practice of *hihyō* garnered in the public discourse during the twentieth century, the material emergence of *hihyō* at this historical juncture marks a pivotal moment of print media history in Japan. Yet differently from the Anglo–European model that Habermas draws, in which critical discursive practice was gradually and naturally institutionalized, the case of *hihyō* underwent a rather abrupt and forceful experience, showing the conscious, more explicit production of critical reading practice as part of the public sphere.[11] The spatialization of *hihyō*, the inversion that *hihyō* existed as a material space first before a general consensus about its mechanism, punctuates the strong sense of self-awareness that *hihyō* had to develop at the time. As such, Japan entered the "age of *hihyō*" in the 1880s not just because Meiji intellectuals recognized its necessity; more important, it was an appropriate caption because *hihyō* had to drive itself into production.

Hihyō Under Translingual Negotiations

While Japan found itself in the "age of *hihyō*," the contours of the practice were amorphous. The lack of clarity of *hihyō*'s workings manifested in, and also had much to do with, the fact that the term itself was wavering. The term "*hihyō*" as a translation of English "criticism" and German "*Kritik*" came to be used in the 1870s and widely recognized by contemporary intellectuals in the late 1880s. The trajectories that this term undertook involved Western languages, Chinese characters, and the Japanese lexicon. In that sense, it is fair to say that the term "*hihyō*" came into common usage as a result of what Lydia Liu calls "translingual practice," that is, the process of negotiation and confrontation between "China, Japan, and the West at the site of translation or wherever the languages happen to meet."[12] The early appearances of "*hihyō*" as a Japanese term were highly unstable, exhibiting the traces of translingual negotiation. The very instability of the term at this point anticipated the uncertainty that Meiji youth felt toward the practice of *hihyō*.

One of the earliest mobilizations of "criticism," the English term, in the Meiji period took place in *Hyakugaku renkan* (The circular relations of one hundred learnings), a book-length transcription of lectures given by elite intellectual Nishi Amane (1829–97) around 1870.[13] As a high-rank retainer serving for the Tokugawa clan during the Edo period, Nishi was trained in the Chinese classics, Dutch, and English and had the privilege of spending a few years at Leiden University in the 1860s to study Western philosophy and international law on a shogun's mission. After the Meiji Restoration, while working for the new Meiji government using his linguistic and educational expertise, Nishi also assumed a position of an enlightenment thinker and contributed to the introduction and diffusion of Anglo-European-based systems of knowledge in the Japanese context. The lectures Nishi gave, as well as the resulting compilation of *Hyakugaku renkan*, were conceived as his explanations of the taxonomy and organization of Anglo-European encyclopedic knowledge.[14] The iconic opening passage of *Hyakugaku renkan* shows Nishi's intent on introducing a foreign corpus of knowledge to his Japanese disciples: "The English term *encyclopedia* derives from an ancient Greek term, Ενκυκλιος παιδεια [sic]. It means to educate children by putting them in a circle. Therefore, now in my translation of *encyclopedia* I posit it as *hyakugaku renkan*, the circular relations of one hundred learnings."[15] As such, *Hyakugaku renkan* was an early, path-breaking component of Nishi's enlightenment project.

However, as a transcribed, written text, *Hyakugaku renkan* exhibits linguistic anarchy, for lack of a better term, because it mobilizes multiple languages and writing styles side by side. The text is dotted with English, French, and sometimes Greek words for the terms that are yet to be commonly accepted in Japanese in the late 1870s. The ubiquitous chaotic effect also manifests when the text describes "criticism" (in English) in the introductory chapter, as one of the five constitutive learnings under "belles lettres" (in French). I include an image of this section, as well as its partial transcription to highlight the messiness of the text:

に　　　　　　佛語
西洋文章のことを　Belles-lettres と云ふあり。英語 Humanities 或は Elegant Literature.
　　　　　　　　　好　文字　　　　　　　　　　人　道　　　高上ノ　文 章

THE AGE OF *HIHYŌ* 39

英國文章をヒマニッチと云ふ意は則ち Mental Civilization なる意にして、
字
心ノ　開　化

凡そ文字なるものは心を開くものなれば、

文字をヒマニッチ即ち人道と云ふに至れり。…

文章に五ツの學あり。　Rhetoric, Poetry, History, Philology, Criticism.
話スコノ術ト辭書ニ見ユレハ奇麗ニ文章ヲ書ク學ナリ
文章學　詩　歷史學　語原學　論辨學　義理上ニ原ツキテ
書ク文章ナリ

Belles-lettres を學ふものは、此の五學をなさゝるへからす[16]

To twenty-first-century readers, the passage looks like a jumble of languages, composed of a mixture of Japanese alphabets, Chinese characters, and several Anglo-European terms. In addition, the text shows a distinct style of typographic presentation. The Anglo-European words are often accompanied by explanatory paraphrases written in Japanese alphabets and/or Chinese characters and presented in a smaller font size, presumably to assist the reader's understanding. Unfortunately, though, such a presentation style intensifies the messiness of the text.

Below I give my closest rendering that approximates the semantics of the passage. I have used parentheses for Nishi's smaller raised font and quotation marks for Nishi's smaller lowered font:

Writing[17] can be referred to as Belles-lettres (French), meaning "great letters," in the West. The English word is Humanities or "the way of humans," or Elegant Literature or "lofty writing." In England, writing (letters) is humanities, which means Mental Civilization or "mental enlightenment." Because any letters of the alphabet would open human minds, letters came to be referred to as humanities, the way of humans. . . . There are five learnings in writing: Rhetoric (the dictionary says this is the art of speech, and therefore it is the learning of writing in a neat way) or the "learning of writing"; Poetry or "poetry"; History or the "learning of history"; Philology or the "learning of etymology"; and Criticism or the "learning of logical discussion and discernment, which points to writing produced based upon the sense of reason and obligation." Those who study Belles-lettres cannot do without these five learnings.

The obvious difficulty in reading this passage comes not because of the translation but because it moves laterally between languages and expressions. For example, the single term "criticism" is explained in two different paraphrases: "learning of logical discussion and discernment" and "writing produced based upon the sense of reason and obligation." In

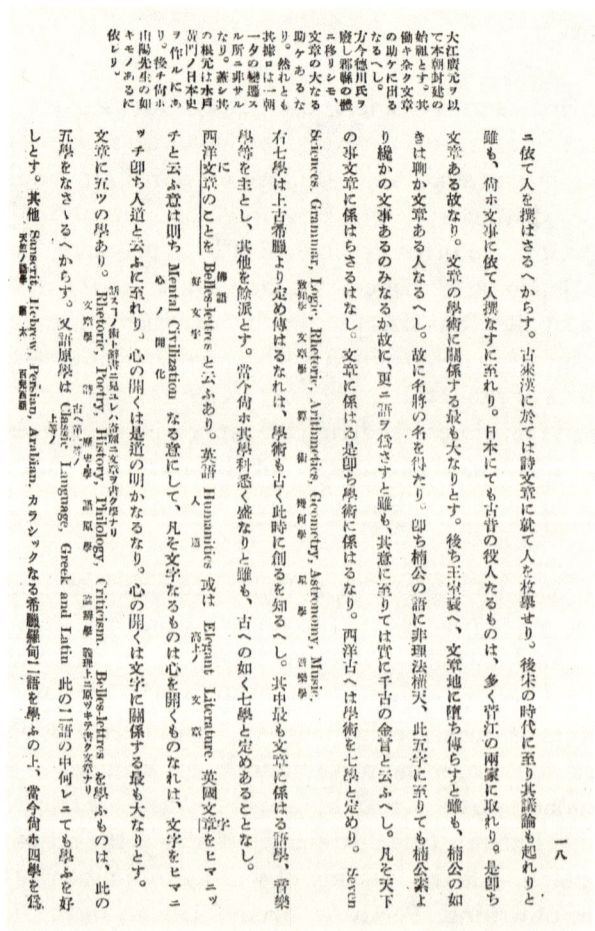

FIGURE 1.1. An excerpt from Nishi Amane's *Hyakugaku renkan* shows the chaotic linguistic juxtaposition in the text. Reprinted with permission by Nippon Hyōronsha.

THE AGE OF *HIHYŌ*

Nishi's account, "criticism" is painstakingly constructed out of a mixture of words. Yet the very attempt to elucidate what it is results in wordiness, which ironically undermines the comprehensibility of the explanation. Such an effect persists because, instead of clarifying the semantics of the term in a concise way, Nishi's text foregrounds the traces of how he attempted to transplant a foreign system of knowledge in Japan.

The chaos surrounding "criticism" in *Hyakugaku renkan* is furthered by the fact that Nishi revises his word usage. In the introductory section previously quoted, Nishi mobilizes *"ronben-gaku"* (論辨學, literally the "learning of logical discussion and discernment") as a Sinographic rendering of an English term "criticism." Later, he consciously negates this initial decision while also misremembering his original word choice. I quote a passage from the "Literature" section of *Hyakugaku renkan* to observe these fluctuations[18]:

Rhetoric の中に又一ツの學あり。之を Criticism といふ。總論中之を明辨術と譯せしは非なり。　　　　　　　　　　鑒裁術

　　　メキヽ　　　　　　　　　メキヽ
即ち看定といふことにして、文字を目刺し是非を辨別して文に書く所の學なり。

此文章は一種の別なるものにて、散文及ひ詩の如きものにあらす。

Essay 及ひ Review 等を書く所の學は皆此 Criticism なるものより出る所なり。
試體　　　題跋

The following is the semantic approximation of the passage:

> Within Rhetoric, there is another learning, called Criticism, meaning the "art of reflection and judgment." It was wrong of me to translate this term as the art of clear discernment in the introduction.[19] That is, making a judgment (as a connoisseur); it is a learning of judging letters (as a connoisseur), distinguishing its good and bad, and putting the judgment into words. This kind of writing is a distinctive one, and it is not like prose or poetry. The learning of such writings as Essay or "exploratory composition" and Review or "preface and postscript" is all coming from that which is called Criticism.[20]

In this excerpt, "criticism" is accompanied by Sinographic *"kansai-jutsu"* (鑒裁術, literally, the art of reflection and judgment), which according to Nishi is a more fitting translation of the English term. He also notes that his initial choice to represent English "criticism" was wrong. When he does so, however, he mistakenly negates *"meiben-jutsu"* (明辨術, the art of clear discernment), not *"ronben-gaku"* (論辨學, the learning of logical discussion and discernment, the writing produced based upon the sense of reason and obligation) as the word he initially chose. This difference could have been a simple misremembering on Nishi's part, or a transcriber's clerical mishandling. Regardless, the point is not that there is a discrepancy in Nishi's usages, but that *Hyakugaku renkan* presents at least three different Sinographic compound words of English "criticism"—"*ronben-gaku*," "*meiben-jutsu*," and *"kansai-jutsu"*—each of which is then further fleshed out with extra words.

Consciously or otherwise, such terminological wavering appears frequently in *Hyakugaku renkan*, and is indicative of lingual and conceptual negotiations experienced by early Meiji intellectuals like Nishi. There is no question that *Hyakugaku renkan* is a translingual text. This text embodies the translingual practice, however, not because it demonstrates intricate negotiations between the "host language" and the "guest language," as Liu suggests, but because it challenges such a schematic configuration of host vis-à-vis guest.[21] I understand the "trans-" part of translinguality specifically as that which cannot be reduced to any single linguistic origin, host or guest. Multiple manifestations of English "criticism" in Nishi's text defies the possibility of localizing language and renders which is a host, and which is a guest undecidable. What *Hyakugaku renkan* effectively shows us is that that which was called "criticism" and later turned into *"hihyō"* was inhabited by irreducible multiplicity and in-betweenness from the start.

The process of translingual production of critical reading involved multiple possibilities to transform English "criticism" into Japanese usage, be it "discussing" (*ron*, 論), "discerning" (*ben*, 辨), "clearing" (*mei*, 明), "reflecting" (*kan*, 鑒), or "judging" (*sai*, 裁). Clearly, the path for "criticism" was not singular in 1870s Japan. While the map of Anglo-European encyclopedic knowledge that Nishi strove to explain was pregnant with various routes toward "criticism," it did not quite settle the English term's final destination. For readers who demanded to reach the point in the fastest way, such as Meiji youths who found themselves in the age of crisis, Nishi's map was less illuminating. As we know, none of the terms that Nishi presented ended up taking root in Japan as a common translation of "criticism," as the Japanese language ultimately landed on *"hihyō"* over others.

What facilitated *"hihyō"* in becoming dominant was most likely *Tetsugaku jii* (A vocabulary collection of philosophy), an English-to-Sinograph dictionary compiled in 1881 by Inoue Tetsujirō and his peers at the University of Tokyo, Meiji Japan's first public university (established in 1877). Inoue, one of the earliest graduates of the University of Tokyo, earned his degree in philosophy, spent several years in Germany, and was

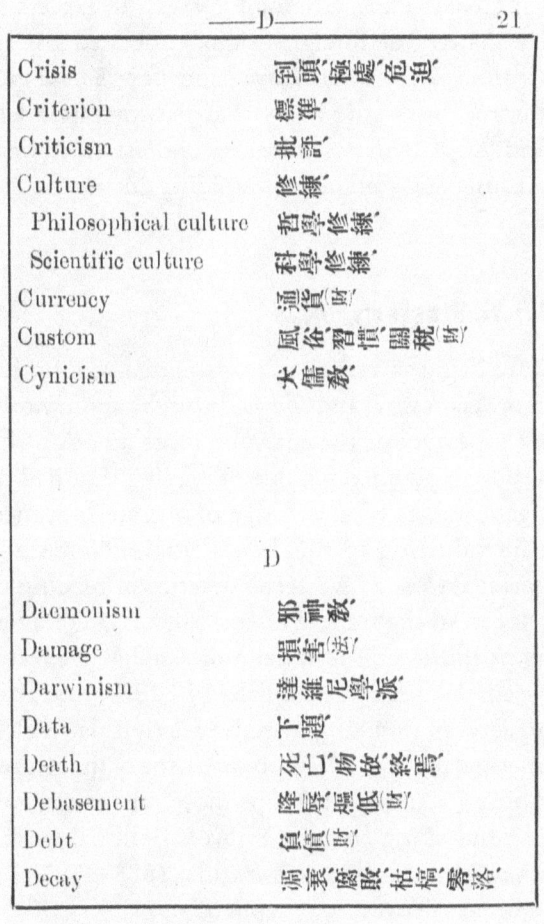

FIGURE 1.2. An entry of "criticism" in *Tetsugaku jii* shows that the term *"hihyō"* is unambiguously juxtaposed to "criticism," creating the appearance of an equation. The clarity of *Tetsugaku jii*'s presentation is evident in contrast to figure 1.1. Reprinted with permission by the National Institute for Japanese Language and Linguistics.

well-informed in genealogies of European thought. In compiling this dictionary, Inoue and his team accumulated a vast number of academic jargon terms, primarily of English origin (with German influence), and offered Chinese-based compound words as semantic equivalents.[22] The dictionary's first edition presents the equation of "criticism" and "*hihyō*," marking one of the earliest instances in which these two terms were visibly brought into mutual association.[23] Unlike Nishi's *Hyakugaku renkan* that displays terminological wavers, Inoue's *Tetsugaku jii* is simple and unambiguous. It seems that this clarity in presentation affected the ways in which Meiji readers, groping for words to express a wide range of unfamiliar matters of foreign origin, processed the information. We do not entirely know why "*hihyō*" and not "*kansai-jutsu*" came to signify "criticism," but we do know that the correspondence between "criticism" and "*hihyō*," or *hihyō*, as we now understand it, was established by way of translingual negotiations unfolding during the 1870s into the early 1880s.

Chinese *Hihyō*, Western *Hihyō*

Hihyō came into being as a result of translingual negotiations. And yet, the equation of "criticism" and "*hihyō*" brought about nothing of definite form or shape. Out of the equation arose a notion that *hihyō* was essentially a foreign practice, a mode of reading that had developed in the distinct genealogies of knowledge of a more "advanced" civilization. In the introduction to this book, I have referenced Tsubouchi Shōyō's remark: *hihyō* as a "Western" practice of reading that became prevalent in Japan in the middle of the 1880s.[24] Takata Sanae, one of the founding members of Tokyo Senmon Gakkō (predecessor organization of Waseda University, established in 1882) and editor of daily paper *Yomiuri shinbun* (Reading by selling daily), also a close friend of Shōyō, commented on the contemporary scene of literature in his 1886 writing, exhibiting a similar, perhaps more schematic, conception of *hihyō*.[25] Upon conducting *hihyō* on Shōyō's fictional work, *Tōsei shosei katagi* (The characters of modern students, 1885–86), Takata prefaces by positing a binary between two types of *hihyō*:

> Chinese *hihyō* focuses on praising, while Western *hihyō* specializes in stabbing. While Chinese writings consider the judge's evaluation invaluable, there are many Western writings that cannot

endure a *hihyō*-practitioner's stab and end up being eaten by a silverfish. When I think about it intently, Chinese praise-centrism not only turns into blandishments eventually but also achieves no real benefits of *hihyō*. A brief version of it is usually nothing more than flowery words to compliment the author. Even a detailed version does not illuminate the strength of the text that common readers cannot easily understand nor disclose the points that common readers often cannot see. It is merely a "commentary," namely, annotation. The essence of *hihyō* is in continuous, devoted hard work. . . . Now that I reflect on it, the reason why Western literature develops daily at a rapid speed and keeps up with the progress of the world is that *hihyō* practitioners of Western literature never fail to do their jobs. They raise what needs to be raised, suppress what needs to be suppressed, and they do so without mercy.[26]

Chinese *hihyō* and Western *hihyō* in Takata's writing are placed at polar opposites: The former brings about little benefits, while the latter makes a significant contribution to the world of literature, as it "stabs" and weeds out unfit writings. Takata paints this binary, only to negate the traditions of "commentary" and "annotation" that have been practiced in the Sinosphere, including Japan, as less desirable in contemporary Japan. Such a formulaic conception of different reading practices reflects the civilizational hierarchy Meiji intellectuals imposed upon themselves. The appropriateness of comparing these two aside, the gap between Chinese *hihyō* and Western *hihyō*, the former falling under the umbrella of "Oriental literature" in Takata's writing, was conceived not only as a spatial distance (the Orient [including Japan] versus the West); it was also a qualitative distance (backward versus advanced) premised upon a linear progression of human civilization. Takata's rhetoric insinuates that if Japan were to establish a critical reading practice in the name of *hihyō* for its further advancement in the global scene, it needed a "civilized" kind of critical reading that was utterly new and foreign to Japanese practitioners. The foreignness, as well as the hierarchy, inscribed in the term intensified a call for *hihyō* in Japan, but also produced uncertainty about the actual execution of the practice.

Hihyō had to recreate "Western *hihyō*," yet as a new mode of critical reading in Japan it had no preceding, immediately familiar model besides the one from the West. The uncertainty about the newness prompted a number of heated discussions that revolved around the nature of *hihyō* toward the end of the nineteenth century. Nevertheless, what each of them envisioned as *hihyō* was far from concrete. They could only produce discourses about ideal but abstract qualities of *hihyō* with no clear exposition, no practical details about how to achieve them. Take Takata's 1887 writing, "Hihyō no hitsuyō" (The necessity of *hihyō*), for example. Concerned about the deteriorating quality of published items, Takata emphasizes the need for *hihyō*: "It is truly astonishing that more books are produced today. There is no day that daily papers have no advertisements for books. Why do these bad books even sell? While bad books sell, good books can't be published. Even if good books are made, bad ones will drive them away . . . , [that is why] *hihyō* needs to flourish."[27] Yet Takata concludes his account only by saying that "those with an unreserved, fair, and insightful demeanor must appear everywhere and bad-mouth publications all their lives, to the best of their ability with their tongues and pens, . . . , for the purpose of improving literature."[28] No additional discussion about who has such a "demeanor" or how to "bad-mouth" is provided. Shōyō's call for the establishment of *hihyō*'s criteria came out in the same year, and yet similar to Takata's discourse, the gist of Shōyō's claim remained on an abstract level. Shōyō states: "I need to speak about the true character of *hihyō*, but of course it cannot be explained thoroughly here. The ultimate core of *hihyō* is, in short, to establish the just criteria. In other words, *hihyō* needs to be premised upon the truth, develop syllogistically, and make an analytic judgment."[29] The criteria for the critical reading practice must be installed because there are none as of now, which itself is a reasonable statement. Yet nowhere in this essay or in his writing career did Shōyō elaborate on the "truth" upon which *hihyō*'s "analytic judgment" could be based. Indeed, such an idea "cannot be explained thoroughly" not just in this essay but anywhere. Again, Sohō saw the task assigned to *hihyō* was enormous, a practice that makes objective selections—oxymoronic, indeed—out of a vast body of Western knowledge and makes them relevant to contemporary Japan.[30] Yet it is obvious that no practice could encompass such a wide scope. Sohō's gesture, as well as others, suggests that among the discourses that circulated as *hihyō* at the time, nothing was adequate to lift "half-civilized Japan" into "full civilization." Their writings were thus negatively prescriptive rather than positively descriptive: They deliberated on what was missing, yet did not articulate practical details on how to train practitioners, how to establish *hihyō*'s criteria, or how in actuality to proceed with critical reading. Without clarification on the concrete proceedings of *hihyō*, the arrival of an ideal, "Western-style" of *hihyō* in Japan was only deferred to the future.

Creating Space for *Hihyō*

To break the deadlock, fin de siècle Japanese intellectuals took a drastic measure: They established *hihyō* within print media, allocated physical space to it, contained certain discourses within the space, and designated them as *hihyō*. Put differently, the space was prepared in which *hihyō* could be written into practice, and whatever was enclosed in the space could become *hihyō*, regardless of its content or quality. That motion itself pointed to a radical, in a sense very creative, inversion. As major journals began to create a separate space, often in the form of columns, dedicated solely to the practice of *hihyō* toward the end of the 1880s, *hihyō* acquired stronger visibility. Moreover, enclosure of *hihyō* in a specialized media space also pushed open the scope of *hihyō*: No longer just a selector of what was valuable, it also entailed managing a massive influx of information and, by implication, creating information value itself. The development of *hihyō* was thus tightly linked to market mechanisms—supply (what *hihyō* can offer) and demand (what consumer-readers need)—of the printing trade.

Intellectual historian Kimura Naoe traces multiple instances at which the term *"hihyō"* surfaced in intellectual discourses, especially in print media, during the first two decades of the Meiji period. According to Kimura, the first periodical that established a special section for *hihyō* was *Tōyō gakugei zasshi* (Journal of Oriental arts and sciences, launched in October 1881).[31] This journal was initiated by the highest class of elites, such as aforementioned Inoue, affiliated with the University of Tokyo. As such, Kimura points out, *"hihyō"* was still an "academic jargon term" in the early 1880s, its usage limited to a handful of elite readers within a closed community.[32] The topics featured in *Tōyō gakugei zasshi* were diverse, ranging from scientific matters (Darwinism, chemistry, medicine, genetics, physics, geography) to arts and humanities (Confucianism, fine arts, Western philosophy). The journal created a section called "Ronpyō" (evaluation discussion) in its sixth issue in March 1882 and quickly updated the section title to "Hihyō" in the seventh issue that came out in the next month.[33] Notably, the first (and only) piece of *hihyō* appearing in the "Hihyō" section, written by Inoue, was on Tang philosopher Kan'yu (Han Yu, 768–824) and his Confucianist essay called "Gendō" (Original path). Importantly, Inoue's *hihyō* was composed in *kanbun*, a Sinographic writing style that had been adopted in Japan over a millennium ago and developed locally as a privileged writing form since then. Reading a classical Chinese text and writing about it in *kanbun* style requires a profound level of literacy and special disciplinary training, and the appearance of *kanbun* was not uncommon in *Tōyō gakugei zasshi* throughout. Given the prevalence of *kanbun* in this medium, Inoue's *hihyō* piece and its recourse to *kanbun* underwrites the selective nature of *Tōyō gakugei zasshi*, attesting to the high expectations that the journal had from its readership. It would be some years before the term *"hihyō"* left the small circle of the affiliates of the University of Tokyo and came to be recognized by a broader readership as a new mode of critical reading practice.

The case of *Chūō gakujutsu zasshi* (Central academic journal, established in 1885) is important because it demonstrates that *hihyō* was more diffused in the middle of the 1880s with the elitism attached to it fading. *Chūō gakujutsu zasshi* was launched and run by those who were affiliated with Tokyo Senmon Gakkō: Takata and Shōyō, who graduated from the public University of Tokyo but shifted their institutional affiliation to privately instituted Tokyo Senmon Gakkō as administrative instructors, were the journal's architects and frequent contributors. Given the fact that Tokyo Senmon Gakkō was founded in 1882 by Ōkuma Shigenobu (1838–1922), who had worked at the center of the Meiji government but was abruptly dismissed in 1881, a group of people surrounding this private school assumed a distinct position in the intellectual sphere that was not entirely bound by the University of Tokyo, the highest, most authoritative institution of knowledge production. Organized by the affiliates of Tokyo Senmon Gakkō, *Chūō gakujutsu zasshi* helped to disseminate new knowledge to a broader audience beyond the narrow circle of privileged elites at the University of Tokyo.

Chūō gakujutsu zasshi individuated *hihyō* into a new section in its twenty-first issue published in February 1886. According to their editorial announcement made in the twentieth issue of December 1885, the journal decided to separate a *hihyō* section after considering a series of *"hihyō* that readers have been offering since the inauguration of the journal."[34] What the journal calls readers' *"hihyō"* is summarized in five points: 1) reduce typographical errors, 2) use clearer and more plain phrases and sentences, 3) include lecture notes from academic institutions, 4) include a column for evaluations of books, and 5) reorganize pages for general readability.[35] Clearly, the journal established the "Hihyō" section in response to the fourth point. What the readers actually said when they requested a special column and who the readers were are not identified in this announcement. Nonetheless, this trajectory is noteworthy for two reasons. First, *Chūō gakujutsu zasshi* formed a reciprocal relationship with its readership. The journal paid attention to, accepted, and perhaps expected requests from readers, while readers saw this medium as a site of participation. Secondly, *Chūō gakujutsu zasshi* understood the readers' input as a "*hihyō*" directed at itself. This indicates that the journal identified itself as a receiver of *hihyō*, that is, as an object to be read and criticized. There was, in other words, a self-awareness on the journal's part that it was exposed to critical reading from anyone who had a chance to read it. The appearance of the "Hihyō" section in this particular medium, itself a reflection of a readerly *hihyō*, thus shows that the reach of *hihyō* expanded, as compared with the case of *Tōyō gakugei zasshi* and its limited circulation.[36] It is not a coincidence that the first piece of *hihyō* presented in the newly created "Hihyō" section in *Chūō gakujutsu zasshi* was Takata's "*Tōsei shosei katagi* no hihyō" (A *hihyō* of *Tōsei shosei katagi* [The characters of modern students]), in which Takata dissociates "Chinese *hihyō*" from "Western *hihyō*." When Takata contrasted the two genealogies of *hihyō* only to denounce "Chinese *hihyō*," his word functioned as condemnation for *Tōyō gakugei zasshi* and, by extension, the University of Tokyo and its elitism, exemplified by Inoue's Sinographic *hihyō*.[37]

Other journals followed suit and began to establish space for *hihyō*. Among them, *Shuppan geppyō* (Monthly reviews of publications, launched in August 1887) is particularly noteworthy for two reasons. First, as it described itself, *Shuppan geppyō* was Japan's "very first journal that specializes in the *hihyō* of publications."[38] The inauguration of this medium meant that *hihyō* served not merely as a part of a print medium but also as a standalone theme of an entire journal. Furthermore, unlike *Tōyō gakugei zasshi* (University of Tokyo) and *Chūō gakujutsu zasshi* (Tokyo Senmon Gakkō), *Shuppan geppyō* had no fixed institutional base. The journal's institutional independence indicates that *Shuppan geppyō* operated primarily on a commercial basis as opposed to an educational one, and that its expected readership was broader than the academic community. The journal's mission statement reflects its attention to the present state of the market, as well as its attempt to carve out a niche, as it describes emerging concern arising from the abundance of print:

When we look at the current state of book publications, the number of new publications is increasing day by day. In addition, a recent study says that there are as many as fourteen or fifteen new titles coming out a day on average. The increase in numbers probably indicates a symptom of progress. However, that alone is insufficient to assess the progress, unless we examine the cause of the increase and the quality of the increased matter.[39]

As noted in the introduction, the number of new publications grew rapidly in the 1880s.[40] Yet as *Shuppan geppyō* explains, the quantity does not ensure that the quality of those publications has been improving. *Shuppan geppyō*'s mission statement expresses its concern: "With the state of new publications described above, it must be said that the increase actually keeps our literary world in the dark."[41] Indeed, this growing volume might in fact "darken" the publication world, making it more difficult to grasp what is actually happening. "To save our literary world from the darkness," *Shuppan geppyō* aims to "illuminate the truth of new publications in the light of fair and rigorous *hihyō* and enable people in the world to judge the good and bad without difficulty."[42] The journal thus assigns itself the task of curating what to read out of numerous publications, "a mixture of good and bad," that continue ever more rapidly to appear.[43] The logic of selection is clearly at work: For consumers of limited resources, *Shuppan geppyō* actively presented itself as a selector of information—what piece is worthy of their money, time, and effort—to assist them in making wise investment decisions. A congratulatory message from Yatabe Ryōkichi upon *Shuppan geppyō*'s inauguration identifies the journal's primary function as "the yardstick for selecting new publications" for a general audience, namely, those who "wish to buy, read, and benefit from books"[44] In this way, the case of *Shuppan geppyō* shows *hihyō* beginning to appeal to a larger, less privileged audience, and justifying its value in reference to the growth of the print industry.

The inauguration of the *hihyō*-centric medium further pushed other journals into creating a space for *hihyō*. A month after the launch of *Shuppan geppyō*, *Kokumin no tomo* announced the creation of a "Hihyō" section.[45] Organized by Sohō and affiliates of the Min'yūsha School, many of them young, Christian, people's rights advocates, *Kokumin no tomo* rapidly grew into the most influential journal among young intellectuals-to-be in fin de siècle Japan. After its initial launch in February 1887, the journal printed 6,800 copies in August, 7,800 in September, 9,300 in early October, and a full 10,000 in the late-October tenth issue.[46] There is a correlation between the inauguration of this journal and its growth in the late 1880s and the virtual disintegration of the Freedom and People's Rights Movement enabled by severe state oppression in the early 1880s. Put differently, *Kokumin no tomo* arrived at a time when political activism, as well as opportunities for direct participation in the political sphere, ceased to be readily available for the coming generation of the educated male. To the youth generation who could not easily proceed in a political direction at the time, *Kokumin no tomo* timely showed an alternative path they could take: journalistic activism. This can be observed in its subtitle, *Seiji, shakai, keizai, oyobi bungaku no hyōron*, which can be approximately translated as "evaluative discussions of politics, society, economy, and literature." *Kokumin no tomo* was clear about its identity from the start: It offered *hyōron* or discourses evaluating these topics. As Emmanuel Lozerand puts it, *Kokumin no tomo* "aimed essentially to create the intellectual conditions conducive to the birth and development of a genuine public sphere."[47] Having no institutional affiliation, be it a political party or academic entity, *Kokumin no tomo* and, by extension, the Min'yūsha School helped young readers foster a vision of what evaluative discourses, apart from direct political action, might be able to accomplish. The reform of this trendsetting journal is an important barometer; given this journal's increasing readership and wide-reaching influence, its decision to accommodate *hihyō*'s spatial independence was itself a major statement, clarifying that *hihyō* was now a concern not just of established intellectuals but also of a younger and broader readership that was growing into the position of intellectuals.

Kokumin no tomo's prospect of spatial reorganization was announced in the eighth issue published in September 1887, and it took material shape in the next issue that came out in early October 1887. After the reform, the journal was divided into seven sections, with a new, independent "Hihyō" section, one of the seven:

- Kokumin no tomo: editorial articles, offering precise discussions on important political, social, economic, and literary problems.
- Special Contributions: useful articles by famous politicians and literati.
- Essays: interesting essays on literature and politics.
- Miscellaneous Record: a variety of important information concerning other news and statistics.
- Letters from Readers: prominent opinions shared by the readers.

- Hihyō: original *hihyō*—detailed and short pieces—of newly published books and of editorials featured in papers and journals.
- Current Topics: unique, summative but piercing, evaluations on domestic and international affairs.[48]

All seven sections are "evaluative discourses" of some sort, the topics ranging from urgent political issues to statistical data.

This structure suggests three points about the ways in which *Kokumin no tomo* delimited *hihyō*. First, when *hihyō* became an independent section, it was conceived as taking written, published discourses as its exclusive object. Of the seven, "Hihyō" is the only section to feature studies of written and published materials ("books," "papers," and "journals"). This does not mean that other sections exclude discussions of published items. "Kokumin no tomo," for instance, picks up anything the editorial team considers "important," and many contributors published their writings in "Special Contributions" and "Essays," touching on what was on their minds. Those sections naturally include topics of relevant publications. Yet the reorganized table of contents articulates that discussions in the "Hihyō" section revolve only around published items. This means that the object of *hihyō* is not all the phenomena of the world, but specifically and only words printed on paper. *Hihyō* here is thus compartmentalized and delineated as written, published discourses about written, published discourses.

Second, *hihyō* had to be "original," suggesting the existence of a "nonoriginal" kind of *hihyō* in circulation. According to literature scholar Komori Yōichi, *Kokumin no tomo*'s emphasis on the originality of *hihyō* was made specifically against a backdrop of the growth of the publishing world. Concomitant with the rapid increase in publication quantity, the industry was prioritizing quick mass production over quality, hence *Shuppan geppyō*'s lament for "a mixture of good and bad."[49] The claim to *hihyō*'s originality, Komori argues, marked *hihyō*'s independence from the ever-more-commercial publishing industry.[50] *Kokumin no tomo* promises that it will provide "original *hihyō*," as opposed to conventional flattery or clichéd advertisements, so that the quality of a publication is individually assessed. This declaration pointed to the necessity of a new quality-control system immune to the trend of mass-produced, low-quality publications.

Third and most important, *hihyō* is presented as information as valuable as other kinds included in the rest of the journal. *Kokumin no tomo*, though divided into seven sections, offers itself as a meeting ground, a

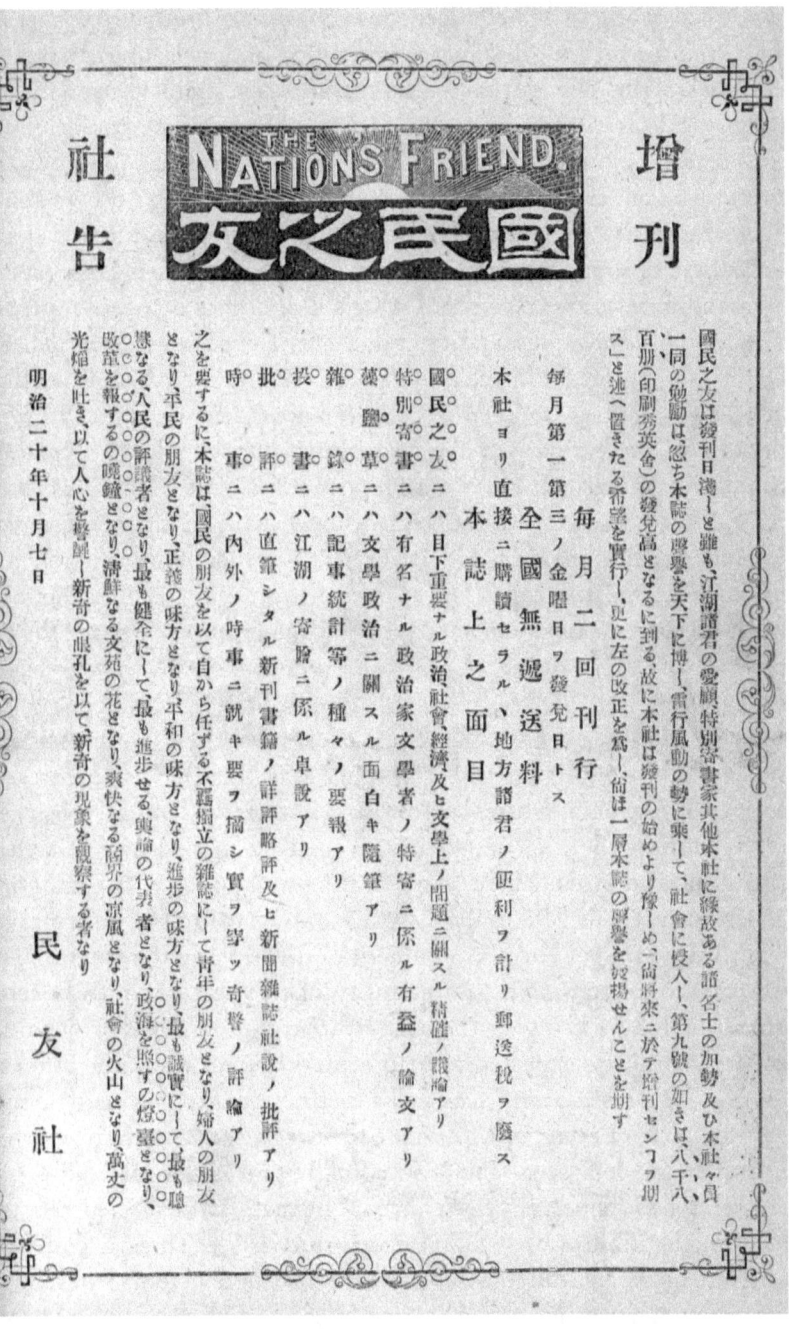

FIGURE 1.3. "*Shakoku*" (announcement) appears on the reverse side of the cover page of the ninth issue of *Kokumin no tomo*. Reprinted with permission by the National Institute for Japanese Language and Linguistics.

point where otherwise heterogeneous subjects are brought together for the single purpose of "discursive evaluation," and each subject has to be equally worthy. The journal makes this message legible by providing a list of sections in the announcement. The effect of the list, apparently innocuous, cannot be underestimated because it gives rise to new cognition of the information provided. To quote Walter Ong's classic study: "Lists range names of related items in the same physical, visual space. Print develops far more sophisticated use of space for visual organization and for effective retrieval."[51] Ong's idea of lists helps us approach *Kokumin no tomo*'s presentation of its own structure—in this journal, "Hihyō" is important in the same way as "Kokumin no tomo" (leading articles) and others are, and these sections are independent but "related" because all are "evaluative." The difference is purely topical: Discussions of politics primarily fall in "Kokumin no tomo"; those of books about politics most likely appear in "Hihyō." By visualizing the contiguity of sections in print, the list helps clarify the new order of information and, by implication, new cognition of information value. Delimiting *hihyō* in these ways, *Kokumin no tomo* justified the creation of space for the practice and, in so doing, solidified a ground upon which *hihyō* began to prosper.

The radicalness of spatialization of *hihyō* in these journals is not simply in the inversion that the space was created first before the arrival of a general consensus on *hihyō*'s workings, but also in their realization of the importance of information management that the space substantiated. These journals were well aware of the situation confronting them: The ability to sort a massive volume of information was turning into a crucial component of their appeal to readers. *Hihyō* was tasked to convert a vast quantity of publications into selected quality items. By bringing the heavy traffic of ubiquitous print under control, *hihyō* was expected to help readers discern the value of information. As a result, *hihyō* acquired a distinct quality as discourse that could attach, or even produce, value to other discourses in the market. For many readers, what the *hihyō* actually said about selected pieces mattered less than what was selected. The material space dedicated to *hihyō* made publications' commodity value visible. The space of *hihyō* sent an unambiguous message: Works featured here are worthy of attention, irrespective of the particular content of *hihyō*. In this newly emerging model of circulating discourses, saying something about publications was itself becoming a commodity, a saleable and buyable product that could stand alone. The space of *hihyō* in print media thus functioned as a self-promoting device by which *hihyō* as a specialized reading practice began to be sustained.

Hihyō on Hihyō

The ground was prepared. *Hihyō* was ready to grow. Yet this did not mean Meiji intellectuals were comfortable with what was practiced as *hihyō* in the space assigned to it. While Japanese intellectuals intended to set standards to practice it by introducing different ideas, those ideas were themselves contested ones. The "literary," for instance, could be "historiography."[52] The "beautiful" could point to "ethics."[53] The "natural" could mean "divinity" for some, "science" for others.[54] The definitions of these concepts varied to a great extent, depending on one's literacy and educational background. There was still no system of agreement in place about concrete workings of critical reading methodologies, and Meiji intellectuals were generally dissatisfied with the state of *hihyō*. Interestingly, dissatisfactions expressed against extant *hihyō* were themselves considered *hihyō*. This means that the search for *hihyō*'s limits itself circulated as *hihyō*, composing a highly self-referential, *hihyō*-on-*hihyō* structure, or what Lozerand calls its "metadiscourse spiral."[55] The early correspondence between *Shuppan geppyō* and *Kokumin no tomo* exemplifies this loop of *hihyō* on *hihyō*. If the late nineteenth century was the "age of *hihyō*," that was not simply because *hihyō*'s importance was recognized, but also because *hihyō* had to be highly conscious of itself and its (im)potency in its self-production.

The very first text that *Shuppan geppyō* chose as its object of *hihyō* was Sohō's 1886 work *Shōrai no Nihon* (The future of Japan), a piece that he wrote prior to establishing *Kokumin no tomo*, presenting his vision of the potential path for a new Japan. In the preface to this text, Sohō states, "I am writing this pamphlet solely because I wish to distribute it to my comrades and ask for their *hihyō*."[56] This remark indicates that *Shōrai no Nihon* predicted, or possibly attempted to induce, derivative, evaluative discourses surrounding itself as *hihyō*. *Shuppan geppyō*'s selection of this text was thus a response to the invitation from Sohō. This must have caught Sohō's attention, as *Kokumin no tomo* immediately registered the new publication of *Shuppan geppyō*: "*Shuppan geppyō* is a monthly journal that specializes in *hihyō* of books. I read their first issue. (Putting aside the right or wrong of their *hihyō* for the time being) I was pretty impressed by their ways of *hihyō*: their fairness, respectfulness, and the fact that they seem to understand the idea of literature to some degree."[57] This brief comment appeared in the "Miscellaneous Record" section of the eighth issue of *Kokumin no tomo*, before its own "Hihyō" section was established. Two months later when the new "Hihyō" section was in place, *Kokumin no tomo* revisited *Shuppan geppyō* and acknowledged the positive outcomes of the latter as the "bold, unreserved attacks against bad customs in the literary world."[58] Both journals thus reciprocated *hihyō* as they prepared the space for it, establishing a relationship as producers and receivers of *hihyō* mutually.

However, *Kokumin no tomo*'s favorable take on *Shuppan geppyō* did not last, and the former began to express negative assessments. In the "Letters from Readers" section of the twelfth issue, *Kokumin no tomo* included a note from an anonymous reader, titled "*Shuppan geppyō e no jogen o kou*" (Asking for advice to *Shuppan geppyō*):

> *Shuppan geppyō* already brought its third issue into the world. I have thoroughly examined each of them, but I have not yet seen a reputable evaluation that impressed me. *Shuppan geppyō* generally praises anything that is a little bit incomprehensible and finishes up short. Therefore, there is nothing distinctly different in their *hihyō* from daily newspapers' hackneyed *hihyō* written only for advertisement purposes, even though that was exactly what they condemned as unsatisfying. Then, when it comes to a matter that is intelligible to anyone, they exercise *hihyō* upon it by producing a lengthy entry, challenging it from every aspect, and in the end rejecting it by concluding that "this book does not deserve our *hihyō*." They are doing all this in the lengthy *hihyō*. The practitioners of *hihyō* at *Shuppan geppyō* usually remain anonymous, thereby assuming no responsibility for their *hihyō*.[59]

The writer of this letter places emphasis on what *Shuppan geppyō* is not doing right in *hihyō*. Clearly, he (*Kokumin no tomo*'s readership was predominantly male) is dissatisfied with *Shuppan geppyō*'s performance because contrary to what the journal declared in the mission statement, its *hihyō* does not "illuminate the truth of new publications."[60]

Beyond the sense of general disappointment with *Shuppan geppyō*, this letter is noteworthy because it is directed not toward *Shuppan geppyō* but toward *Kokumin no tomo*: "You, *Kokumin no tomo*, are *Shuppan geppyō*'s comrade in the world of literature. Why don't you make an exhortation to them occasionally? That is what I earnestly expect you to do."[61] The letter asks *Kokumin no tomo* to assess, call out, and intervene in *Shuppan geppyō*, so that the latter may reorient itself in its initial mission as a specialized *hihyō* practitioner. What the writer of the letter means by the term "exhortation" points to the active examination of *Shuppan geppyō* to help it improve its *hihyō*. In other words, the letter requests that *Kokumin no tomo* conduct more rigorous "evaluative discussion," or *hihyō*, upon *Shuppan geppyō*. Such a gesture has at least two implications. First, the relationship between these journals, that is to say, their mutual recognition as both producers and receivers of *hihyō*, was discernible to readers to the extent that they could imagine its expression in *hihyō*. Second, that *Kokumin no tomo* decided to print this letter shows the journal registering the problem of *Shuppan geppyō*, validating the letter writer's disappointment in the *hihyō*-centric medium, and perhaps even entertaining the possibility of following the exhortation. *Shuppan geppyō* needs to be a target of *hihyō*, and *Kokumin no tomo* is the one to execute it. The letter thus underwrites *Kokumin no tomo*'s self-recognition as a qualified executor of *hihyō* that could even take a *hihyō* specialist as its object.

Another manifestation of the *hihyō*-on-*hihyō* motion can be seen when the vector of *hihyō* was reversed, and *Shuppan geppyō* began to act as a media space to evaluate *Kokumin no tomo*. In the "Hihyō" section of the seventeenth issue of *Kokumin no tomo* (March 1888), a short piece of *hihyō* on Īda Ō's *Mohō tetsugaku* (Philosophy of imitation) appeared. The author of this *hihyō* harshly states, "there seems no deep philosophical principles in what Īda describes, . . . its structure clumsy, its judgment off the point, its wordings complicated with no clarity. Īda's work will make readers suffer when they attempt to get its gist."[62] To this piece of *hihyō*, the original author of the evaluated work, Īda, returned a refutation, but by turning to *Shuppan geppyō* to publish his piece.[63] Mentioning that his initial response to *Kokumin no tomo*'s *hihyō* was rejected for publication in *Kokumin no tomo*, Īda states: "What I am dubious about is what the *hihyō* practitioner [of *Kokumin no tomo*] meant by the 'depth' and what he had as his evaluation criteria. I have no clue what sort of criteria he used to determine the depth of my work."[64] Īda's complaint addresses the obscurity of the standards on which *Kokumin no tomo*'s *hihyō* practitioner relied when the critic concluded that there was "no deep philosophical principles in what Īda describes." In *Shuppan geppyō*, a journal exclusively publishing *hihyō*, Īda's remarks on *Kokumin no tomo* too were packaged as a *hihyō*. Just as the anonymous letter writer directed his problem with *Shuppan geppyō* at *Kokumin no tomo*, Īda chose *Shuppan geppyō* to express dissatisfaction with *Kokumin no tomo*'s handling of *hihyō*. *Shuppan geppyō* decided to publish Īda's comment, suggesting that this *hihyō* specialist journal considered Īda's piece—a condemnation of *Kokumin no tomo*'s disposition of *hihyō*—appropriate to the medium. While *Kokumin no tomo* was expected (or at least willing) to serve as a space to assess *Shuppan geppyō*, *Shuppan geppyō* also offered itself as a venue in which to check *Kokumin no tomo* for quality. The relationship between the journals, reciprocal producers and receivers of *hihyō*, was thus reinforced as they exchanged *hihyō* between each other.

The correspondence between these journals exemplifies *hihyō*'s "metadiscourse spiral." When they exchanged *hihyō*, one medium's *hihyō* of the other itself became an object of *hihyō*. Indeed, *hihyō* was posited as written, published discourses about written, published discourses. Instead of conducting *hihyō* upon selected primary materials, such as scholarly books and literary works that would help contemporary Japan move forward, their *hihyō* focused on what the other medium did wrong as *hihyō*. In this loop structure, saying "what you do as *hihyō* is not right" itself became the content of their *hihyō*. In this way, *hihyō* continued to search for its own limits, even as its importance was recognized and space created.

Vistas of *Hihyō*

There is nothing surprising about *hihyō*'s self-referentiality. When *hihyō* was recognized as a vital practice, it was proposed as an utterly different style of critical reading, unprecedented in Japan. There was no locally available model for critical reading in Japan to follow—or at least so thought young Japanese intellectuals at the time. In that sense, *hihyō* had to draw out of itself a model that could continue to replicate, and, as such, the discourses surrounding it had to assume a heightened sense of self-consciousness. Discussing what emerged as *hihyō* only to contradict it was an essential part of the process of delineating *hihyō*'s boundaries. The structure of self-reference was programmed in the institutionalization of *hihyō* from the outset.

Literature scholar Noguchi Takehiko remarks that the language of modern *hihyō*—rhetoric, style, vocabulary—was "violently produced" by rupturing itself from the rich genealogies of Edo literature.[65] I agree with Noguchi's observation, yet I suggest expanding his claim in the following: The "violence" was not only in the pressure of having to create new language or in the overwhelming task of selecting valuable information out of an innumerable mass, but also in the necessity of constant self-reflection that *hihyō* had to carry out. From the very beginning, Meiji Japan's *hihyō* was impelled to cast its gaze upon other discourses while simultaneously having to attend to itself. On the one hand, *hihyō* had to sort out information and organize a catalog of publications worthy of readers' investment; on the other, *hihyō* needed to rationalize itself as yet another form of information to be processed and evaluated. *Hihyō* constantly had to say at once, "You are not good enough as *hihyō*—and neither am I." The emergence of *hihyō* was thus "violent"—not only outwardly but also internally.

Yet when it comes to critical reading, such violence does not necessarily point to limitations because internecine strife may open room for something else, for alternative possibilities of reading, to flow in. A remark of Ishibashi Ningetsu, one of the young intellectuals who proclaimed the importance of *hihyō* in late nineteenth-century Japan, well captures this sentiment of productivity. Writing in *Kokumin no tomo*, Ningetsu assesses three of his contemporary writers and acknowledges their contributions to the literary world. One of the figures he singles out is Mori Ōgai, and he examines Ōgai's recent piece of *hihyō*, which itself is an evaluation of the current scene of literary production. About Ōgai's discourse that appeared in his *hihyō*-centered journal *Shigarami zōshi* (The weir), Ningetsu states:[66]

> [Ōgai] rigorously evaluates practitioners of *hihyō* on literature from last year without leaving anything out. I cannot affirm that his assessment nailed everything. Nonetheless, he meticulously examined contemporary *hihyō* practitioners with his aesthetic eyes, elucidating the beauty of their poetic tastes and remedying their evil practices, for which I cannot help but express my deepest gratitude.... If there were nobody to exercise *hihyō* upon *hihyō* practitioners, they would end up decaying in stagnation.[67]

Ningetsu conjectures that practitioners of *hihyō* need to be exposed to and examined by other practitioners. We can see in his own writing a movement into which *hihyō* practitioners are drawn: Ningetsu reading Ōgai, Ōgai reading others, and all of them practicing *hihyō* and directing it at each other. If we follow Ningetsu's logic, his *hihyō* is also subjected to someone else's. And if we consider that Ningetsu's writing performs its own claim by anticipating someone else's *hihyō* cast toward itself from the future, the implication is that *hihyō* cannot escape itself. Ningetsu's writing thus confirms two constitutive qualities of *hihyō*. First, it is at once a subject that reads and an object that is read. Second, and more important, as long as *hihyō* presents itself as *hihyō*, it must self-referentially include itself within the range of its object. Whatever it says about other *hihyō* therefore not only targets others but returns to itself reflexively. The idea that *hihyō* as a subject takes itself as an object may sound self-canceling, but it is also possible to see such duality of *hihyō* as inviting. This duality unfastens a hierarchical relationship that typically determines the relationship between the subject that reads and the object that is read. When the hierarchy between reading subject and read object no longer holds in *hihyō*, it gives rise to an infinite impulse for *hihyō* to carve out moments for reading and self-reading. From the unnerving, self-canceling quality of *hihyō*'s movement, inexhaustible possibilities for *hihyō* to produce and reproduce itself may arise.

Such a movement of reading and self-reading is not uncommon when being critical in reading is at stake. Thinking about the emergence of *hihyō* in fin de siècle Japan, I am reminded of a set of questions that Paul de Man asked in one of his seminal essays: "Is criticism indeed engaged in scrutinizing itself to the point of reflecting on its own origin? Is it asking whether it is necessary for the act of criticism to take place?"[68] Japanese practitioners of the Meiji period were all too aware of their *hihyō*'s impotence—or at least so they thought—and had to ask themselves whether they were being critical in the "correct" way. The question was indeed tautological, but if "such scrutiny defines, in effect, the act of criticism itself," as de Man says, what took place for and as *hihyō* in late nineteenth-century Japan was exactly the constitutive "act of criticism."[69] For those of us who read as academics and have to be self-reflective about our own reading practices after de Man, the loop structure that the discourses surrounding *hihyō* demonstrated appears familiar, even obvious. Needless to say, we are under increasing pressure to read differently to justify our raisons d'être as academic readers, and we constantly search for ways of validating and invalidating our own readings. We fear that our reading practices lapse into inertia, being labeled as useless. We wish to read better in an unprecedentedly critical way, and that attitude has become our default. I have tracked the emerging processes of critical reading called *hihyō* in this chapter to underline, not the idiosyncrasy, but the familiarity, of the Japanese case of handling critical reading. More specifically, through the examination of the uncertainty and self-referentiality imprinted in the discourses of *hihyō*, this chapter attempted to highlight the milieu, a surprisingly relatable one to us, that Meiji intellectuals reached in haste in their concerted efforts to institute critical reading of their own. If there is comparability between these two milieux, it is worth investigating what happened in the Japanese case and how Japanese practitioners struggled to bring a new mode of critical reading into existence. The remainder of my book will tell more detailed stories of their efforts and the varying manifestations of their failures in keeping up with their own efforts, in hopes that we can bear witness to the generativity inhabited in their failures.

CHAPTER 2

Critical Reading, Creative Production

Hihyō was posited as a new mode of critical reading that would pave the way for Japan to attain full civilization and, as such, it had to serve as a selector, organizer, and producer of valuable information. The task of *hihyō* was to engage with varied types of information, namely, published items that were increasing at a rapid pace along with the growth of the print business. Out of many categories of publications to be read critically, I single out one specific category, "literature," in the remainder of the book, and contemplate the relationship that *hihyō* formed vis-à-vis literature.

As soon as *hihyō*'s importance to Japan was recognized and its space created, a call for specialization within the practice began to emerge. That is to say, while it was conceived already as a distinct form of critical reading practice, there were movements to divide it further into more narrowly focused compartments, so that each could offer more precise, expert reading of its object. *Bungaku*, now often unreservedly translated as "literature" in English, was one category in which *hihyō* was expected to specialize. Yet like *hihyō*, *bungaku* was yet another amorphous concept that underwent processes of institutionalization in fin de siècle Japan: It was contested, to be eventually forged as a form of art, as a national, cultural property. Existing scholarship has unraveled the complicated, multilayered trajectories through which a particular style of writing gained traction among writers and became valorized as *bungaku* during the second to third decades of the Meiji period.[1] For present purposes, suffice it to say that while the term *bungaku* had pointed to a corpus of knowledge based on historical and ethical writings in the genealogies of Japanese and, by extension, Sinographic intellectual traditions, as in classical Chinese studies discussed previously, its nature and telos narrowed down into an aesthetic category in the late nineteenth century. In the same way that *hihyō*'s meanings vary, the contours of this *bungaku*, and from here on I use the English term "literature" for ease of reference, have never been stable, as they carry with them the traces of translingual negotiations.

The attention to literature and the breadth of meanings inscribed in it is crucial to our understanding of *hihyō* because arguably literature and *hihyō* have evolved hand in hand, while informing each other since the late nineteenth century. Precisely because the boundaries of both *hihyō* and literature were not cemented, they formed a reciprocal relationship: What was considered to be literary at a given historical juncture greatly affected what it was to be critical, and vice versa. We can still see their closeness. For instance, *hihyō* encompasses a wide variety of meanings—from "reviews" to "humanistic institution," as I described in the introduction—with each register directly or indirectly evoking things literary. Furthermore, since the late nineteenth century, *hihyō* almost always meant *bungei hihyō* (literary criticism) for many decades.[2] In addition to the fact that critical reading (as in the sense of commentaries and annotations) was an essential part of the literary training in the Sinosphere, that both *hihyō* and literature shared recourse to language as a primary medium of expression, as opposed to other nonlinguistic objects of *hihyō* (paintings, for example), fostered their affinity. Therefore, to reflect on the relationship between *hihyō* and literature is at once to think about the relationship between critical language and literary language, and how they align with, or distance from, one another. In fin de siècle Japan, *hihyō* was expected to be a strictly critical language, distinct from other applications of language, while also having to invent itself. In that context, the imaginary, fictional, and creative use of language often at work in literary writing served as a reference point for *hihyō* to fashion a language for its critical use, while simultaneously posing a challenge to the alleged independence of *hihyō*. When a critical language needed to devise itself in an unprecedented way, hence having to be creative, the possibility of separating a critical language from a creative one was put in jeopardy. Due to this convoluted relationship, I believe literature to be a useful site through which to interrogate *hihyō* and its use of language.[3]

Hihyō's Special Connection to Literature

The narrow register of literature—literature as creative, aesthetic writing practice—became prevalent during the middle of the 1880s, and periodicals specifically investing in those types of writing began to emerge. The inauguration of journal platforms, such as *Kagetsu shinshi* (New journal of flowers and moon, established in 1877), *Garakuta bunko* (Rubbish heap library, established in 1885), *Miyako no hana* (Flowers of the capital, established in 1888), and *Shinshōsetsu* (New novels, established in 1889), exhibit the growing interest in establishing media space exclusively for creative writing.[4] Along with the rise of these literature-focused mediums, other general-interest journals such as *Jogaku zasshi* (Women's magazine, launched in 1885) and *Kokumin no tomo* began to patronize literature in the sense of creative writing in their own spaces so as to entertain and attract readers. Toward the end of the 1880s, literature came to be more strongly associated with creative linguistic activity, and less with broadly humanistic writings as deployed in classical Chinese studies, to be categorized as an aesthetic form of expression.

What concurred with the redefining of the boundaries of literature, as well as the establishment of the media space for creative writing, was a discursive phenomenon that positioned *hihyō* as an advance guide to literature. We may remember Tokutomi Sohō's 1888 declaration of the "age of *hihyō*," the logic of which is that *hihyō* needs to lead half-civilized Japan to full civilization. The discourse on *hihyō*'s necessary precedence before literature was a variation of the "age of *hihyō*" rhetoric, demonstrating the same logic. One of the earliest manifestations of this rhetoric appeared in the early 1880s. In an editorial essay in daily newspaper *Meiji nippō* (Meiji daily) in 1883, an anonymous writer emphasized the task of *hihyō* in relation to literature thus:

> If *hihyō* was practiced vigorously, the consequences would be that the world of intellectuals would be spontaneously invigorated, and that people would naturally begin to pay attention to important matters to the extent that an urge to thoroughly understand their principles would arise. For that reason, in order to correct the errors of history, illuminate the dexterity of poetic writing, discover matters' principles, and to help knowledge make progress, *hihyō* should be the strongest device.[5]

The title of this entry, "Meiji nendai no bungaku o ronji awasete hihyō no hitsuyōnaru yuen o toku" (Discussing literature in the Meiji period and also explaining the reason why *hihyō* is needed), is self-explanatory: We can understand why we need *hihyō* if we look at the current state of literature (because it is not performing well). Thus as early as the beginning of the 1880s, *hihyō* was positioned as a precursor to what it reads, including "poetic writing." Beyond this instance, Tsubouchi Shōyō asserted in 1887 that "if sharp learnings of *hihyō* are actively exercised and bring about the benefits of selection, it won't be too long until we see the truly marvelous progress of literary fortunes."[6] Takata Sanae said the same thing in reverse in 1886: "Oriental literature shows symptoms of stagnancy and regression, as it is withering and inert. This is because *hihyō* practitioners insufficiently carry out their responsibilities: They neglect their mission and only voice a series of flattery to no avail."[7] By the time the 1880s came to an end, the idea of *hihyō* as a guide to literature—literature specifically as creative writing—was prevalent in the scene of writing.

Out of many instances that invested in the idea of *hihyō* as a precursor to a creative writing practice of literature, the launching of *Shigarami zōshi* in 1889 is especially noteworthy because this journal identified itself as a space of *hihyō*, entirely dedicated to the critical reading of literature. When Mori Ōgai Rintarō (hereafter referred to as "Ōgai" based on the scholarly convention), a young elite who was at once a literatus and a medical doctor, founded *Shigarami zōshi*, he was very clear about what this journal would be: From its first issue, it carried the idiosyncratic epithet *"bungaku hyōron"* (evaluative discussions of literature), indicating that it would not include *hihyō* about general topics but only the *hihyō* about the specialized subject matter of literature. Note the difference from the epithet of *Kokumin no tomo*: *Seiji, shakai, keizai, oyobi bungaku no hyōron* or "evaluative discussions of politics, society, economy, and literature," which includes discussions about a variety of topics beyond literature. *Shigarami zōshi*'s intervention also stands out in contrast to *Shuppan geppyō*. While *Shuppan geppyō* was groundbreaking as a *hihyō*-centric journal, *Shigarami zōshi* went a step further by focusing exclusively on *hihyō* of the literary field. This was a *hihyō* with a concentration, a clear manifestation of more specialized work within the practice.

In *Shigarami zōshi*'s mission statement, Ōgai laments the "chaotic" state in which the "world of literature" found itself in late nineteenth-century Japan: "There are an extremely large number of foreign elements in the world of literature in Japan. . . . Multiple aesthetic factors of our own, those of China, and those of the West are scattered around."[8] If the differences in writing styles are the source of the chaos, what can untangle it and solve the problem is *hihyō*. Ōgai continues: "This chaotic state should not be endured for a long time. We are aware that the time to clear this up is nearing. What helps this chaos be cleared is nothing other than *hihyō*."[9] With the guide of *hihyō*, Ōgai anticipates a "moment of catharsis" in the scene of literature.[10] This journal thus designates itself as a platform where "writings in the world are brought to be evaluated with aesthetic eyes, clarified for their authenticity and falseness, and stripped of their wrongs. In so doing, the journal wishes to assist the natural force of cleansing and expedite the effects of catharsis."[11] By thus appointing itself as a space of *hihyō*, that is, a forerunning guide in the "world of literature of this country," *Shigarami zōshi* articulates its special relationship to literature, one exclusively conceived as a linguistic, creative practice that would expect an "aesthetic" gaze from *hihyō*. Following *Shigarami zōshi*, more journals that specialized in *hihyō* of creative, literary production began to emerge, including *Waseda bungaku* (Waseda literature, established in 1891) as a bulletin for those who studied literature at Tokyo Senmon Gakkō, and *Bungakukai* (The world of literature, established in 1893) established by those who advocated the noninstrumentality of literature among the *Jogaku Zasshi* School (Society of *Jogaku zasshi* [Women's magazine]).[12] Before the turn of the century, *hihyō* was turning into a specialized practice that had to cater to a concentrated subject matter such as literature, and the new expectations for *hihyō* with expertise took a material shape in print media, providing stability.

    The motion to bifurcate *hihyō* to have specialization was part of a larger discursive trend, as the belief in the division of labor for efficient progress of the country was gaining traction in the intellectual discursive sphere. Sohō and his platform, *Kokumin no tomo*, represent the prevalence of this belief. As we saw in chapter 1, Sohō invested much effort in providing the evolutionist vista of Japan developing from "half-civilized" to "full civilization."[13] One of Sohō's essays, appearing in 1888 *Kokumin no tomo*, also promotes the idea of specialization of labor and reveals how that would bring Japan to "full civilization." In a leading article titled "Seijijō no bungyō" (The division of labor in politics), Sohō emphasizes the importance of the division of labor in civilized society: "When matters develop along with their progress, their organs naturally grow more minute and detailed, which leads to the enforcement of the law of division of labor."[14] Evolutionist thinking is clearly at work here. While there are organisms like the unicellular "protozoa," Sohō states, the "human race" consists of multiple, separate bodily functions. What differentiates these two groups is the level of "development."¹⁵ In the same way that simple organisms evolve and diverge into species with more complicated constituents, Sohō claims, by analogy the political system must follow the law of division of labor and subdivide its individual functions.¹⁶ To his regret, "there is enough evidence that in Japan, the division of labor in the political arena has never been put into practice."¹⁷ If individuation happens as Sohō wishes, each of the divided parts can engage in more specialized labor. Further specialization is imperative especially in anticipation of the upcoming opening of the Imperial Diet, promised for 1890 based on the 1881 imperial instructions. Sohō thus likens the specific case of Meiji Japan's twenty-year-old political system to the general process of evolution from the unicellular to multicellular organisms, positing development through the division of functions in politics as a natural, inevitable consequence of human civilization.

Indeed, Sohō's discourse can be contextualized in a larger historical force. As we saw with Nishi Amane's *Hyakugaku renkan*, thinking about how to organize knowledge in a different taxonomic order was an urgent, ongoing concern for Meiji intellectuals. The notion of dividing labor, especially intellectual labor, for specialized work was in tandem with Meiji Japan's aspiration to rework intellectualism and further classify disciplines for efficient transmission of knowledge. The heightened attention to *hihyō* as an independent practice owed itself to this trend. The interest in taxonomy and division further entered into the discussions about *hihyō*, prompting a call for concentration within the practice of *hihyō* and facilitating the formation of its specialized relationship with literature in print media.

In this climate, young elite Ōnishi Hajime composed his theory of *hihyō*, outlining the relationship between *hihyō* and creative work as its object. Ōnishi's 1888 essay "Hihyōron" (A theory of *hihyō*) will be the primary focus of my analysis for the remainder of this chapter. I pay attention to Ōnishi's discourse not simply because it was one of the earliest attempts to theorize *hihyō*'s workings in Meiji Japan, and because it addresses the *hihyō*–literature connection, but also because it includes a moment that radically breaks with the notion of the division of labor prevalent at the time and thereby enlarges the scope of *hihyō*. In short, I feature "Hihyōron" because it was predictive of the failures of *hihyō*—failures that were full of generative moments of critical reading.

The Structure of "Hihyōron"

Ōnishi was among the early generations of philosophy students studying at the University of Tokyo in the late 1880s. After graduation, he had the privilege of continuing his education in Germany. Despite the reputation that his exceptional educational background brought to him in his time, Ōnishi remains one of the underexamined intellectual figures from late nineteenth-century Japan. "Hihyōron" was written when Ōnishi was in his early twenties and attending school in Tokyo, and it was published in the "Special Contributions" section of *Kokumin no tomo*.[18] Intentionally or not, "Hihyōron" (pp. 25–30) is preceded by the aforementioned essay by Sohō, "Seijijō no bungyō" (pp. 1–6), in the twenty-first issue of this journal. This arrangement gives rise to an appearance that Sohō's attention to "division" prefaces "Hihyōron" and the latter's attempts to speculate *hihyō*'s relationship to creative work.

"Hihyōron" consists of seven sections:

- Creative Production (*sōsaku*) and *Hihyō*
- The Duty of *Hihyō*
- The Range of *Hihyō*
- What to Evaluate in *Hihyō*
- The Realm of Thought in Our Country
- That Which Requires *Hihyō*
- Errors in Ventriloquism

The structure of Ōnishi's essay is clear, as it can be broadly divided in two parts. At first, the essay deliberates on a general theory on how *hihyō* should proceed in front of an object, and then it goes on to identify problems with what circulates as *hihyō* in present-day Japan and prescribe solutions. The first three segments explain what *hihyō* is supposed to be and how it should conduct itself; the focus here is not the *hihyō* in the specific historical context of late nineteenth-century Japan, but critical reading conceived on a universal scale. The essay takes a distinct turn in the fourth section, "What to Evaluate in *Hihyō*," where Ōnishi refocuses attention on the particular case of Japan and what he finds to be the poor quality of *hihyō* produced in it. The rest of the essay is spent on the discussion of what needs to happen in the specific scene of late nineteenth-century Japanese *hihyō* so that *hihyō* can achieve its ideal state. This structure indicates that the second half provides the specifics against which the universal theory presented in the first half retroactively comes into relief. Thus in the following section, I begin with the examination of the latter half of "Hihyōron" to investigate Ōnishi's immediate concerns and suggestions.

Hihyō's "Should-Be"

In the second half of "Hihyōron," ranging from the fourth to the seventh section, Ōnishi discusses at least two registers of *hihyō*. One is what circulates as *hihyō* in his time, the manifestations of *hihyō* that contemporary intellectuals practice daily in print media. In his view, none of this qualifies for the title of critical reading: It is a "should-not-be" of *hihyō*. The other register of *hihyō* is a speculative kind, an elaboration of what needs to be done to remedy the current "should-not-be": It is *hihyō*'s "should-be." Yet importantly this "should-be" assumes a transcendental quality such that it also points to *hihyō*'s "cannot-be." Among the various ideal visions of *hihyō* that Meiji intellectuals proposed, Ōnishi's emerges as the most ambitious one.

The fourth section, "What to Evaluate in *Hihyō*," focuses on the current situation of *hihyō* practice in Japan. Ōnishi's writing here assumes satirical overtones, as he laments:

> Among the changes that took place in papers and journals in the past couple of years, nothing compares "hihyō" even remotely.... With the recent prevalence of *hihyō*, there are people who cast a magical spell upon themselves to transform into *hihyō*-practitioners.... Yet it seems that they only want to pronounce perfunctory *hihyō* upon every recent publication that differs in range from politics, economy, poetic writing, fiction, history, to philosophy, and, as if to say those books were not enough, they even try to evaluate books on mathematics. Those practitioners are indeed versatile, and it makes sense that they earn a great reputation as "eight-handed multitaskers." Perhaps their *hihyō* may have some folk medicine–like efficacy. But the practitioners of that sort are not what I call *hihyō*-practitioners.[19]

According to Ōnishi, those who currently exercise *hihyō* are not respectable practitioners, because they are not specialists in what they read, and therefore cannot adequately select "what to evaluate" in their *hihyō* among many publications. The peculiar description of pseudo-practitioners in Ōnishi's prose in fact singles out one actual figure, Takahashi Gorō (1856–1935), a prolific contributor of *hihyō* to *Kokumin no tomo* evaluating recent publications. Since the second issue of *Kokumin no tomo* (March 15, 1887), Takahashi's *hihyō* pieces constantly appeared in this journal; in some issues the entire *hihyō* section was filled with Takahashi's writings alone.[20] By the time Ōnishi's "Hihyōron" was published, Takahashi's *hihyō* covered an enormous range of intellectual writings that varied in topic from "politics, economy, poetic writing, fiction, history, philosophy," through law and religion, to "mathematics." Scanning Takahashi's publication record, Ōnishi sarcastically insinuates that an "eight-handed multitasker" like Takahashi, for his very "versatility," cannot make specialized enough selection in the contemporary scene of *hihyō* practice.

Ōnishi's finger pointing was so obvious that it triggered a direct, personal response from Takahashi himself. About a month after Ōnishi's "Hihyōron" appeared in *Kokumin no tomo*, Takahashi wrote a ten-page essay in another intellectual journal, *Rikugō zasshi*, to refute Ōnishi. Takahashi begins his refutation with a passive-aggressive disclaimer: "I am not a *hihyō* practitioner by any means. I am not someone who wants to be a *hihyō* practitioner. I am not fond of practicing *hihyō*. And yet when I encounter an extremely conceited *hihyō* practitioner who brings a blanket accusation to other contemporary *hihyō* practitioners, I must conduct *hihyō* upon that person."[21] From then on, Takahashi crafts a detailed, point-by-point response to Ōnishi's discussion.[22]

A particularly interesting motion Takahashi makes is his attempts to attribute the weakness of his own *hihyō* writings to structural limitations imposed upon him and, in so doing, condemn Ōnishi as a mere worshiper of the West. First, Takahashi stresses practical reasons why his prolific *hihyō* writings have been produced in the way they were. That one piece of *hihyō* is generally given a limited material space (a page or two), Takahashi writes, makes it difficult to compose a *hihyō* that is "broad in scale, grand in discussion."[23] He then expands this point by noting that there are different types of *hihyō* in the world:

> Ōnishi wrongly assumes and incessantly repeats that any *hihyō* would be rigorous *"kurichishizumu"* [criticism] or *"rebyū"* [review]. And yet the short pieces of *hihyō* that are half-page, one to two pages long are the kinds similar to so-called *"bukku nōchisu"* [book notice] attached at the end of Western journals, or similar to "books or current literature" that appear at the end of weekly journals such as *The Spectator*. When new books are out, publishers send them out to newspaper and magazine companies for advertisement.

Those companies skim through what types of books they are and help advertise them. To be honest, "detailed evaluations" that we write are no different from those short "book notices." Basically, the term "criticism" can refer to brief *hihyō*, as well as perfunctory evaluation of an artwork. Of course, these types of *hihyō* must be different from a rigorous type of *hihyō* that people like Thomas Macaulay composed.[24]

Laying out the type difference of *hihyō*, Takahashi acknowledges that the *hihyō* he writes leans toward briefing the nature of new publications for the purpose of "advertisement."[25] In so saying, Takahashi admits that what he produces cannot compare to a "rigorous type of *hihyō*" like Thomas Macaulay's, one that Ōnishi would endorse without reservation.[26]

Takahashi's response illuminates the ways in which he perceives what Ōnishi approves as *hihyō*. As his reference to British thinker Macaulay demonstrates, Takahashi underlines that the author of "Hihyōron" may "worship anything made in the West," hence showing a symptom of "Western epilepsy."[27] Takahashi's accusation is not groundless because in the fifth section of "Hihyōron," "The Realm of Thought in Our Country," Ōnishi underlines how an "isolated island in the Orient has been assailed by Western thought," to an unprecedented degree in recent years.[28] The awareness of civilization hierarchy is clearly present in Ōnishi's writing. Many of Ōnishi's exemplary writers, either in the category of *hihyō* or in that of creative writing, are of Anglo-European origins: William Shakespeare, Johann Wolfgang von Goethe, and Lord Byron. The frequent juxtaposition of the East and the West, with Japan positioned as a pursuer of the latter's intellectual genealogies, also suggests that Ōnishi believes in an order of civilization. As such, like many of his contemporaries, Ōnishi to some extent affirms the dynamics of influencer and receiver, Western predecessor and Eastern follower. Takahashi is clearly referencing this aspect of Ōnishi's discussion.

Nevertheless, "Hihyōron" does not simply argue for the necessity of following the intellectualism developed by Anglo-European thinkers; at least, appropriation of Western knowledge is not regarded as an ultimate goal for Japan in Ōnishi's account. As far as his rhetoric is concerned, Ōnishi seems to be interested in the antithesis, as well as the synthesis, that would occur among various modes of thought rooted in different lands: the West, China, and India. Ōnishi writes, "Perhaps these three [the West, China, and India] are able to harmonize with each other in the end. Or they might clash completely. Their antagonism and their harmony will become the history of the realm of thought in Japan's future."[29] According to Ōnishi, the genealogies of Eastern thought are "those which have already developed in the past," whereas Western intellectual movements "have grown in the past, are still growing in the present, and will continue to grow in the future."[30] It is necessary to recognize that Ōnishi's point here is not to affirm a civilizational hierarchy but to identify what is most needed in contemporary Japan: Different levels of intellectual development are not about who is more civilized but rather who is familiar with what.

This is where Ōnishi begins to paint a picture of *hihyō*'s "should-be." Ōnishi states that Japan already developed a sufficient degree of understanding of Eastern thought because it has long been exposed to Chinese and Indian traditions. Therefore, it is now in need of mastering an intellectualism that is less familiar to the country, namely, the Western kind. Having expertise in Western thought that "parallels Western intellectuals' competence" is vital, not because Western thought is the most advanced but because Japanese intellectuals are yet to be well-versed in it.[31] Western thought in Ōnishi's logic thus becomes one out of many genealogies of knowledge that needs to be learned. Self-identified "scholars" in contemporary Japan merely "ventriloquize Western thought" without being able to evaluate it, writes Ōnishi in the final section of the essay, and in their faulty ventriloquism they spread misconception. Ōnishi argues that studying Western thought, currently underexamined, prepares Japanese intellectuals to be better rounded thinkers. If we follow Ōnishi's thinking, the primacy that initially appeared to be given to the West is relativized: All intellectual genealogies, Eastern or Western, are equally necessary for Japan to further enrich its reading practices. Read this way, "Hihyōron" argues for an all-encompassing, transcendental position of a critical reader, a position that goes far beyond a mere worshiper of the West. As the final passage of the seventh section witnesses:

> In order to understand the contemporary period, one must transcend it. In order to transcend it, first one must pierce advanced Western thought. Anyone who wishes to transcend the time, understand it, and become its instructor must master Western thought in fine detail with clarity, and then conduct *hihyō* upon it. I believe this is a worthy guiding principle in the realm of thought in today's Japan.[32]

If Japan should aim at cultivating the broadest scope of thought possible, the West alone cannot be a model. Ōnishi expects practitioners to have an advanced command in various genealogies of knowledge even to the extent of relativizing the powerful West. They must seek every form of intellectualism with which to produce *hihyō*, and their *hihyō* has to transcend the time and place of composition.

The orientation toward transcendentalism in Ōnishi's vision has been underexamined in scholarship. In the same way that Takahashi positioned Ōnishi as a worshiper of the West, the limited number of existing studies on Ōnishi's work tend to consider him primarily as an introducer of Immanuel Kant and Matthew Arnold to Japan.[33] Such positioning is certainly grounded in textual evidence, as Ōnishi makes references to and relies on both figures in his writings, including "Hihyōron." For instance, Ōnishi's exposure to Kant is undeniable as he quotes the *Critique of Pure Reason* (1781) in his work.[34] Furthermore, "Hihyōron" would not have taken the shape that it did without Arnold's seminal essay, "The Function of Criticism at the Present Time" (1865).[35] Yet I mention Ōnishi's relationship with Western intellectual giants not to rehash a "Western influence upon Japan" model and reenact a civilizational hierarchy in my discussion. The point is that out of a vast body of Western knowledge, Ōnishi read and "selected" their discourses. Kant asserts, "Our age is the genuine age of criticism, to which everything must submit."[36] Arnold claims, "Criticism first; a time of true creative activity, perhaps,—which, as I have said, must inevitably be preceded amongst us by a time of criticism,—hereafter, when criticism has done its work."[37] Throughout his work, Ōnishi highlighted these particular ideas to make them relevant to a Japanese readership. The questions that we need to ask then have less to do with who influenced Ōnishi but more to do with what in his Western predecessors' accounts, Ōnishi found worth recreating and, more important, what his selections brought about.

Ōnishi's selections of Kant and Arnold, and their idea of criticism's importance, highlight the essentiality of critical reading in late nineteenth-century Japan, while simultaneously relativizing the particularity of the Japanese case. His discourse as a whole points to *hihyō*'s "should-be," a transcendental quality that it needs to assume to be successful. Studying the intellectual genealogies about critical reading that arose outside Japan, Ōnishi developed an affinity for those Western thinkers and mobilized their rhetoric to grasp the circumstances of contemporary Japan. In so doing, he also situated Japan in the lineage of historical moments at which being critical was passionately pursued for varied reasons. Yet the mobility of the rhetoric of "criticism now," its applicability to different contexts, also limits the specificities of each instance. The very fact that the rhetoric was effectively transferred across time and space cancels the necessity of identifying the "age of *hihyō*" with late nineteenth-century Japan alone. If the need for critical reading is not exclusive to this context, then it is not just the putative degree of civilization that determines if a given place requires critical reading. Regardless of whether or not he was aware of what he set in motion, Ōnishi's selections pointed to the dislocation of a civilization hierarchy prevalently imagined between the West and the rest. As if to reinforce such a hierarchy-invalidating motion, "Hihyōron" seeks the highest degree of critical judgment, in front of which every historical manifestation, Western or not, is leveled.

Ōnishi's vision of *hihyō* is impossibly lofty, and, as such, the *hihyō*'s "should-be" is also its "cannot-be." His theory is unique, however, not only because it posits the highest possible incarnation of *hihyō* but also because it expects this ideal form of *hihyō* to make a strange, "creative" turn. In the first half of "Hihyōron," Ōnishi paints a picture of a universal model of *hihyō* and elaborates on what should happen when *hihyō* engages with a creative piece of work for critical assessment. There he claims the necessity of *hihyō*'s self-erasure at the height of its action, that is to say, *hihyō* necessarily becoming one with what it reads to be critical to its fullest capacity. By insisting on a temporary elision of the distance between *hihyō* and its object, Ōnishi ends up suspending the totality of *hihyō*. Needless to say, such a claim diverges from the contemporary discourses, including his own, that promoted the independence of *hihyō* as a "foregoing guide to the culture of this country."[38] Yet I consider this moment of apparent divergence far from invalidating Ōnishi's theory. This is because *hihyō*'s divergence theorized by Ōnishi constitutes grounds for a utopian vision of critical reading, one that is at once critical and creative, a vision that anticipated its generative failures in the ensuing years.

Hihyō's Creative Turn

Hihyō, as a "foregoing guide," must exercise its expertise upon highly concentrated subject matter like literature. It is a very difficult task, thus acknowledges Ōnishi. The first section of the essay "Creative Production and *Hihyō*" begins by arguing that the difficulty of obtaining "a great work of *hihyō*" matches the unlikeliness of coming by "a great work of creative production."³⁹ Indeed, *hihyō* and creative work are not the same. The distinction is spelled out in this section, explicitly and repeatedly: "Poets seize beauty by intuition, while *hihyō* practitioners logically understand it"; "Poets take beauty and make it intrinsic to their work," while "*hihyō* practitioners interpret the reason behind beauty"; "Poets understand nature, while *hihyō* practitioners understand poets"; "In the world of literature, creators receive the highest decoration, while it is *hihyō* practitioners who award it to them."⁴⁰ In addition, *hihyō* holds an exceptional status over creative writing activities:

> Practitioners of *hihyō* are positioned to bring up the rear of creators, though at the same time the former also entertains the pleasure of serving as the lead of the latter. It is not that a great work of *hihyō* comes only after a great work of creation. Great *hihyō* not only arrives after a masterpiece but also induces a masterpiece in the future. *Hihyō* not only reflects on things past but also directs things yet to come.⁴¹

Echoing Arnold, Ōnishi states that creative production's efflorescence or decay in any given time and context hinges upon how effectively *hihyō* accomplishes its mission. In this way, Ōnishi envisions that *hihyō* as an independent entity fluidly precedes and succeeds creative production and, in so doing, contributes to the success of creativity yet to come.

It is possible to read a parallel between Ōnishi's "Hihyōron" and Sohō's "Seijijō no bungyō," in that both of them demonstrate an awareness of the necessary division of intellectual labor. As discussed, the correlation between their discourses is brought into relief with Sohō's claim preceding and prefacing Ōnishi's in the same issue of *Kokumin no tomo*. In fact Takahashi Gorō took issue with "Hihyōron" partially on this point about the division of labor: "That Ōnishi is so extreme as to say that poets and *hihyō* practitioners are distinct from each other is far beyond the reality.... The horizons in which poets allow themselves to be are quite broad."⁴² Yet Takahashi's reading of "Hihyōron" and, by implication, the comparability of Ōnishi's discourse to Sohō's, is not entirely verifiable because while it insists upon the division of *hihyō* from creative production, "Hihyōron" also stresses a temporary union to be formed between the two. This means that Ōnishi's theory of *hihyō* contains a moment rather disagreeable to the contemporary zeitgeist.

Furthermore, "Hihyōron" posits this union as a constitutive duty of *hihyō*: The greatest incarnation of *hihyō* as depicted in this theory is thus at once critical and creative. Ōnishi brings up this point in the second

CHAPTER 2

section, "The Duty of *Hihyō*." According to Ōnishi, *hihyō*'s essential duty in relation to creative production is to "see existing objects as the way they exist" and to "recognize the visible form of matters without a blur or unevenness, in the same way that mirrors reflect things."[43] The immediate task assigned to *hihyō* is therefore to "elucidate the truth and penetrate the exquisiteness" of a given creative work.[44] In order to undertake that task, however, practitioners of *hihyō* must abandon their exceptional status and edge closer to the object under assessment:

> Those who exercise *hihyō* must first place themselves in the position of creators, think further about creators' thoughts themselves, feel further creators' feelings themselves, and become mentally one with creators in their entirety. In other words, the practitioners of *hihyō* must for once not be differentiated from creators. Only by merging with creators can the practitioners locate the secret of creators' thoughts and feelings and reach a state of no regret. Nevertheless, once they position themselves in the creators' place, they must flap their wings to rise up to the land of ideals and conduct absolute *hihyō* upon creators' bearings in the light of the highest standards. That is to say, *hihyō* practitioners must bring themselves close to creators for a time and distance themselves from them for another. They must once become the best friends of creators and then turn into genuine strangers.[45]

The task of *hihyō* is to pave the way for creative production to arrive: Such a task is obviously premised upon its differentiability from a creative work that it examines. But the steps that Ōnishi describes here entail *hihyō* temporarily canceling itself; in the very attempt to complete the task, *hihyō* is requested to undergo a phase of discarding its own position and privilege and uniting with its target. This indicates that in order for *hihyō* to remain itself, its independence necessarily comes to a halt, as it has to concede itself to and rely on creative production, the very thing from which it must be severed. Puzzling as this may sound, *hihyō* has to become non-*hihyō*, a creative object in particular, in order to achieve its highest status as critical reading.

Ōnishi's theory of *hihyō* is peculiar. In his vision, the uniting process of *hihyō* and creative production, which necessitates the self-cancelation of *hihyō*, is crucial for it to be "fully acquainted with what exists inside, hidden and muted," or the "truth," of its object.[46] The peculiarity of "Hihyōron" further intensifies because in spite of the centrality of this uniting process in this theory, the author speaks little about how such a union may take place and what steps need be taken for the union to ensue. Ōnishi presents his writing as a theory, and he explains the problems of current *hihyō* in detail. Nevertheless, such an elucidatory demeanor of a theorist is nowhere to be found in this section of the essay and, as a result, his theory is left void of what enables *hihyō* to realize itself as *hihyō*. Without delineation of the core workings of *hihyō*, what Ōnishi calls "absolute *hihyō*" remains inscrutable and impracticable. "Hihyōron" at this point is failing as a *hihyō* theory.

It is possible to understand the lack of elucidation here as Ōnishi's dismissiveness for his focus of the essay is elsewhere, as Komori Yōichi suggests. Taking note of the amount of textual space that Ōnishi devotes to each section, Komori concludes that the goal of "Hihyōron" is not to deliberate on the proceedings of the union, how it takes place in critical reading practice, in the first half, but to assert the necessity of seeking the "highest standards" possible for *hihyō* in the second half.[47] While Komori's reasoning is quantitatively substantiated by the actual line and word count spared to spell out *hihyō*'s "highest standards," however, I maintain that the reverse is also conceivable: That Ōnishi mobilizes almost no word to account for how to accomplish the essential union between *hihyō* and creative production gives rise to a haunting and at the same time amplifying effect in his theory. I propose we linger in such an effect because this is where I consider "Hihyōron" is the most suggestive about *hihyō*'s trajectories and, by implication, taking the most creative turn.

While the self-effacement of *hihyō* poses a challenge to its alleged integrity as an independent reading practice, when *hihyō* needs to cancel itself, it is not simply that it has to give itself up, but that it has to surrender itself to alterations and transfigurations specifically into creative work. What ensues from *hihyō*'s self-cancelation, in other words, is its total submission to creativity. In this moment, critical endeavor and creative endeavor become one and the same. Instead of forcibly spelling out *hihyō*'s creative bearings, "Hihyōron" lends itself, perhaps unwittingly, to a failure to do so at all and, in so doing, unlocks unlimited possibilities of what creative form *hihyō* may take when it is at its height. Where Ōnishi says nothing, he leaves open a number of paths for *hihyō*'s creative transformation. Read this way, the failure in Ōnishi's theory can be recast as the most creative gesture that his critical language makes in its attempt to theorize *hihyō*.

To conclude the examination of Ōnishi's theory proposed in the age of *hihyō*, it helps to reflect on Arnold, whom Ōnishi (and Sohō) admired.

Interestingly, what happens in Ōnishi's theory seems to enact Arnold's vision of criticism's creative turn. In "The Function of Criticism at the Present Time," from which "Hihyōron" borrows many ideas, Arnold remarks, "To have the sense of creative activity is the great happiness and the great proof of being alive, and it is not denied to criticism to have it; but then criticism must be sincere, simple, flexible, ardent, ever widening its knowledge."[48] While initially predicating criticism independently of creative activity, Arnold's essay acknowledges that criticism is still "not denied" creative capacity.[49] In the context of "Hihyōron," Arnold's remark reveals a new twist by Ōnishi: For Ōnishi, it is not that *hihyō* is "not denied" access to creative activity, but rather that it is required to be creative to sustain itself as such. Put differently, while being creative is an option for Arnold's criticism, it is a necessity for Ōnishi's *hihyō*. Ōnishi's twist points to an aspiration, perhaps one that is stronger than Arnold's, for an unprecedented mode of reading: One must be creative to read in a newly critical way. If the creative turn is programmed into critical reading as suggestively presented in "Hihyōron," I contend that it did take place in many cases of critical reading that emerged in late nineteenth-century Japan. Indeed, *hihyō*'s creative turn manifests most strongly when *hihyō* fails to perform the essential task of reading and engaging with a given object. In part 2, I will examine four cases of such unprescribed, felicitous incarnations of *hihyō*'s creative turn, one that came with its failure.

Part II

Practices of Critical Reading

CHAPTER 3

On Dividing
The "Literature and Nature" Debate

> Literature, in effect, is instituted as a division
> and as such its institutional status is never fully
> assured. This lack of assurance measures the risk
> of its possible disappearance, but also and at the
> same time the possibility that something else, a
> new catachresis, has always begun to divide its
> name into the future.
>
> —Peggy Kamuf

Literature is an instituted, hence unstable division in the system of knowledge, says Peggy Kamuf.[1] While her account primarily addresses higher education in the Anglo-European context, we can observe a manifestation of the same idea in late nineteenth-century Japan where the deliberate reorganization of knowledge, the knowledge divorced from the Sinosphere, was initiated. "Literature" or *bungaku* was a division of knowledge that fin de siècle Japan attempted to establish anew as an aesthetic, as well as national, property, and many discussions took place to both conceptualize and materialize the dividing line between literature and its exterior, that is, what literature is *not*. The "Literature and Nature" debate, the subject of the *hihyō* case study undertaken in this chapter, is one example of such modern discourses that revolved around the idea of individuating literature.

The 1889 "Literature and Nature" debate was trailblazing in a unique way: It was one of the earliest instances in which print media publicly staged a dispute by means of exchanges of *hihyō*; furthermore, it was one of the first public debates specifically to contest the boundaries of literature. In the debate, two intellectuals, Mori Ōgai and Iwamoto Yoshiharu (1863-1942), disputed the essential quality of literature and its divisibility from "nature." Iwamoto posited "nature" as a key component of literature, yet the vagueness of his initial use of the term

81

triggered Ōgai's censure. Considering Iwamoto's terminology and logic to lack rigor, Ōgai argued for the division of "nature" from "literature," the inadequacy of the former as a categorical component of the latter. In response, Iwamoto tried to clarify what he meant by "nature" as less a matter of tangible objects but rather of spirituality. Ōgai, however, continued to misread Iwamoto's explanation and forced a completely different meaning of "science" upon Iwamoto's "nature." With their exchanges continuously unlatched thus, the debate was unable to achieve the fundamental premise of *hihyō*, that is, as a reading practice tasked to make legible the value of what it reads.

Despite failing to engage with their object, however, the pieces of *hihyō* produced during this debate ended up staging the topic of division uniquely in late nineteenth-century Japanese discourses surrounding literature. I am particularly interested in the ways in which Ōgai's *hihyō* disabled the logical progression of exchange with his opponent. Ōgai's writings aggressively ripped apart Iwamoto's discourse to the extent that there was no room for a dialogic relationship to be formed between the two. Rather than engaging with Iwamoto in a reasonable manner, Ōgai dissected his writing into minute pieces, examined each component for its validity, removed defects, and replaced them. As a result, his *hihyō* enacted "disconnect" on the contextual, semantic, and stylistic levels in this debate. This disconnect, as I see it, is key to understanding the performative effect of Ōgai's *hihyō*. His method of composing *hihyō* began to resemble the theory of scientific observation and experiment proposed in French writer Émile Zola's "The Experimental Novel", a theory that Ōgai elsewhere attempted to reject from the realm of aesthetic literature. Ōgai's scientifically choreographed *hihyō* in the debate thus ended up approximating in form his own claim about the division that has to be made between literature and science, hence making the dividing line visible. Such a style of crafting *hihyō*, relying less on content than on form, marked a radical break with contemporaneous discourses. Put differently, no one had written *hihyō* like Ōgai.

If, as Kamuf says, literature is a division infinitely haunted by insecurity in the current institution of knowledge, the same goes for critical reading practice that surround literature. As *hihyō* began to be instituted in late nineteenth-century Japan, it struggled to invent itself differently from existing critical reading conventions, even as it did not know how it would do what it was expected to do. *Hihyō* was troubled by its own uncertainty from its inception. Yet, if we follow Kamuf and believe that such hauntedness is simultaneously inhabited by a moment for something else to emerge, we may think that Ōgai's misreading, or "catachresis," of Iwamoto's discourse entails exactly that possibility. Through its failure to engage with Iwamoto, Ōgai's *hihyō* opens an alternative possibility for envisioning critical reading, pointing toward the future; we who live in the current century are its recipients. In this case study, I intend to examine Ōgai's *hihyō* as a reference point from which to entertain potential shapes that critical reading might be able to take.

The Doctor–Writer

In the beginning of 1889, one Japanese medical doctor wrote a prescription—a prescription not for drugs, but to explain to writers and writers-to-be in fin de siècle Japan how to write a novel. The doctor first introduces Zola's theory, one that proposes the application of peculiar methods to the production of the novel:

> You may have already heard of Émile Zola. Zola is from Provence, France. Fictional work of so-called naturalism (*naturalisme*) is what Zola produces. The term, "experimental novel" (*Le Roman expérimental*), that he coined met with a favorable reception in the enlightened world. Zola used this term as the title of the first chapter of his theory of the novel, but it came originally from theories of experimental medicine presented by the famous French physiologist Claude Bernard. Bernard said that contemporary scholarship was based on two methods, observation (*observation*) and experimentation (*expérimentation*). . . . Zola immediately took Bernard's words and applied them to novel production.[2]

The doctor of this prescription, however, immediately negates Zola's perspective on naturalist writing as nonliterary:

> Although analysis and dissection can certainly be used for the production of the novel, many found it inappropriate that Zola presented the results of analysis and dissection directly as his novel. The result of experimentation is fact. Doctors like me are satisfied with pursuing fact, but would that be the same for novel writers? . . . Indeed, the outcomes of analysis and dissection offer good ingredients for writers, but effective ways of mobilizing them must be obtained solely by intuition (*intuition*).[3]

In this prescription, Zola's "nature" is posited as a synonym for "fact," or that which becomes available through scientific methodologies of "observation and experimentation." Yet such "nature qua fact" should not constitute the novel itself, because, for this doctor, the quintessential component of the novel is "ideal" (*idéal*), an intangible, yet universal aesthetic quality that only authorial "intuition" can reach. This prescription was titled "Shōsetsuron" (The theory of the novel), and was written by "Medical Doctor, Mori Rintarō." Needless to say, this doctor is one of the most canonical writers in modern Japanese literature, now best known as Mori Ōgai.

Ōgai was many things at once: army surgeon, researcher, editor, translator, essayist, poet, and fiction writer, among others. His prescription for the novel, published soon after he returned from a government-sponsored four-year research trip in Germany as a military hygienist, and written in the name of a medical practitioner, launched his writerly career. It is essential to be attentive to the hybridity with which the doctor-writer produced his works. Whether intentionally or not, he suppressed his own hybridity by insisting upon the dividing line between literature and what it is not and, by implication, that between "Mori Ōgai" and "Mori Rintarō." Referring to this doctor-writer figure as "Ōgai" has long been the norm in scholarship; there are however some scholars who choose not to do so, as the name "Ōgai" might reinforce the predominance of his single profile as a fiction writer.[4] While I am aware of the risk, I will continue to identify this figure as "Ōgai" in this book. In part, this is a matter of clarity and consistency. At the same time, I wish through this choice to emphasize that this figure is the same person who acts as Aizawa Kenkichi (chapter 4) and pretends to be Eduard von Hartmann (chapter 5). While these names infinitely divide the doctor-writer "Mori," they still reference the indivisible individual. I will continue to use "Ōgai" to be reminded of his divided, yet indivisible existence.

Ōgai resubmitted his prescription for the novel a few months later when, again identifying himself as a medical doctor, he challenged his contemporary Iwamoto's opinion essay "Bungaku to shizen" (hereafter "Literature and Nature"). Framed anew as a theory of the constitutive, autonomous quality of literature, Ōgai's writing combatively contradicted Iwamoto's claim of an inevitable correlation between "literature" and "nature" and invited an immediate response from Iwamoto. Their confrontation was construed as the "Literature and Nature" debate based on the title of Iwamoto's essay. In the following I begin by tracking the exchange to establish the facts, who said what, in order to contemplate what their interaction, especially doctor-writer Ōgai's out-of-the-ordinary writings, instantiates.

The Conflict, Staged

In April 1889, Iwamoto, a leading promoter of women's education and teacher at a women's school, contributed his opinion essay, "Literature and Nature," to *Jogaku zasshi* (The women's magazine), a journal dedicated to the improvement of women's status through education, of which Iwamoto served as a lead editor.[5] The appearance of Iwamoto's essay in this medium, in particular that he used his own platform to publish the piece, indicates his investment in this topic. "Literature and Nature" begins with the author's expressing his "pent-up frustration toward the matter of 'literature and nature,' a grievance against the recent world of literature," and makes two counterclaims pertaining to what literature is and what it should not be as a type of fine arts:

> The greatest literature [*saidai no bungaku*] is that which transcribes nature [*shizen*] the way it is.
>
> The most beautiful fine arts [*kyokubi no bijutsu*] would never be accompanied by immorality.[6]

As he clarifies in the beginning of the essay, Iwamoto's account certainly did not come into being out of the blue; he formulated these aphoristic statements to participate in contemporary discourses on expressive activities, such as fiction writing and theater performance, that were at the end of the nineteenth century on the verge of collective institutionalization as fine arts.[7]

There are at least two specific intellectuals toward whom Iwamoto's essay was directed. First, Tokutomi Sohō, the founder and chief editor of *Kokumin no tomo*, had in a recent editorial essay argued, "Where does subtle and euphemistic language come from? The restrictions on free speech must be the cause of it. And if we consider subtlety and euphemism to be markers of elegance in writing, we must admit such elegance was manufactured by the restrictions on free speech."[8] Iwamoto rejects Sohō's association between literary writing and manufacturing, separating the former from any notion of artificiality or fictionality evoked by the term "manufacture." In addition to Sohō, Iwamoto also addresses Ishibashi Ningetsu, who contributed a short opinion piece to the same issue of *Kokumin no tomo* in which Sohō's essay appeared; in it, Ningetsu claimed that artistic performance and reality needed to be separated, noting that the role of a prostitute in theater need not correspond to the actor's own morals in reality. Addressing Iwamoto and others who claim such an equation, Ningetsu asserts that "you know what fine art is, but are you nonetheless pushing fine art into the narrow confinements of religion and morals and extinguishing it?"[9] Iwamoto argues against Ningetsu's rhetorical question, stating that things that are not beautiful in actuality do not turn into beauty when expressed in an alternative form. Published five days after the appearance of Sohō and Ningetsu's essays in *Kokumin no tomo*, Iwamoto's "Literature and Nature" clearly attempted to engage with the evolving discussions of the relation between literary or theatrical expressions and real life.

Although neither Sohō nor Ningetsu pursued active confrontation against Iwamoto, "Literature and Nature" invited an unexpected, unusually combative reaction from Ōgai. Two weeks after the publication of Iwamoto's piece, Ōgai contributed to *Kokumin no tomo* an elaborate essay titled "'Bungaku to shizen' o yomu" (Reading "Literature and Nature") as a rebuttal. "Reading Iwamoto's 'Literature and Nature,' I was totally dumbfounded," he begins—"dumbfounded" not because he was impressed, but because he found Iwamoto's claims "so easily refutable that it could be done with one breath."[10] After thoroughly negating Iwamoto's two theses, Ōgai ultimately provides modified versions of them:

> The most beautiful fine arts may sometimes be accompanied by immorality.[11]

> The most beautiful aesthetic literature does not generally transcribe nature the way it is.[12]

In rejecting Iwamoto's formulae, Ōgai submits an alternative conception of literature, one rooted in the idea of "beauty" (written *"bi"* with a Chinese character, accompanied by *"shōne"* in katakana, that is, Ōgai's phonetic transcription of the German *Schöne*. Hereafter for terms Ōgai provides more than one rendering, I provide the English translation in my discussion, followed by the Chinese and Japanese renderings in Ōgai's original usage and German translation in parentheses.), as against Iwamoto's choice of "nature" (*"shizen"* [Chinese characters]; *"natsūru"* [katakana] = *Natur* [German]). "Beauty" is not identical to "nature," Ōgai maintains, because "'beauty' becomes materialized, not when 'nature' is reflected in the 'spirit' (*"seishin"* [Chinese characters]; *"gaisuto"* [katakana] = *Geist* [German]) as the way it is, but when the fire of 'idea' (*"sō"* [Chinese character]; *"idē"* [katakana] = *Idee* [German]) burns off bits of dust attached to 'nature,'" through the process called "transubstantiation" (*"tenka"* [Chinese characters]; *"toransuzubusutanchiachion"* [katakana] = *Transsubstantiation* [German]).[13] According to Ōgai, aesthetic literary production (*"bibungaku"* [Chinese characters]; *"shōne riteratsūru"* [katakana] = *schöne Literatur* [German]), which should pursue the materialization of "beauty," cannot equate such unprocessed things as "nature"; literature, in other words, requires not "mimesis" (*"mohō"* [Chinese characters]; *"nahāmungu"* [katakana] = *Nachahmung* [German]) but the human intervention of "manufacturing" (*"seizō"* [Chinese characters]; *"shaffen"* [katakana] = *schaffen* [German]) and delineation of "beauty" in relief.

Iwamoto responded promptly to Ōgai. Within a week after receiving the revised theses from Ōgai, Iwamoto used his platform *Jogaku zasshi* again to argue that the disagreement was concerned less with the idea of literature than with the definition of the term, "nature" (*shizen*):

> The philosophy that Dr. Mori believes in and the one that I do have different bases, and the words that Dr. Mori understands and the ones that I do have different meanings. . . . What I call nature includes the natural spirit. Consider these: Facial looks in physiognomy are regarded as divine manifestations; spirits can be seen in nature; *Geist* [written *"gaisuto"* in katakana] can be recognized in *Natur* [written *"natsūru"* in katakana]. These examples agree with my position, although some disputers from a certain school of philosophy may still not.[14]

Iwamoto thus restates what he means by "nature" in hopes of dispelling Ōgai's misunderstanding.[15] Repeating that what he takes issue with is the ways in which Sohō and Ningetsu had characterized expressive activities, be they literary or dramatic, Iwamoto argues that Ōgai's explication of "nature" in the scientific sense—and by extension the aesthetic quality of literature—are "irrelevant" to what he had initially advocated in "Literature and Nature."[16]

Iwamoto's explanation might have sufficed to end the exchange, but the discussion continued. Ōgai replied to Iwamoto in the following issue of *Kokumin no tomo*, only to neglect Iwamoto's clarification in its entirety. Quickly dismissing his opponent as "delusional," Ōgai simply repeats, "beauty in nature, *Das Naturs chöne* [sic], might include dust, and what helps the dust burn off and makes artistic beauty, *Das Kunsts chöne* [sic], out of nature is the talent of poets and artists. Nature as it is, which includes dust, cannot possibly be beautiful."[17] As the correspondence between them was completely broken, the rift was unbridgeable at this point. To the surprising rebuttal from Ōgai, Iwamoto returned a brief note defending his reasoning. In the note, Iwamoto nods at Ōgai and affirms the possibility of "beauty in nature that might include dust." Then quoting from Ralph Waldo Emerson's seminal essay, "Nature," he emphasizes his belief in a trinity essential to the production of literature: "Truth, and goodness, and beauty are but different faces of the same All."[18] Presumably, Iwamoto made these gestures to arrive at a compromise with Ōgai's insistence on the independent quality of beauty and its singular importance to literature. Without delving further into what constitutes literature and what to think of nature in relation to it, the debate came to an end.

The confrontation between Iwamoto and Ōgai marks a missed opportunity. It had a grand premise when initiated, as it revolved around intertwined questions about the nature of literature and the literature of nature, questions that could have enlightened us about the genealogies of verbal expressions. Despite this potential for enlightenment, for a breakthrough in conceiving literature, the exchange quickly became stuck in a mire, unable to present a coherent discussion to its audience. The pivotal ideas posed during the debate—Iwamoto's inquiry into what lies at the center of Ōgai's concept of beauty in literature, for instance—remained undeveloped.[19] In addition to the fact that their exchange saw an anticlimactic ending, their disjointed communication made later scholars almost unanimously dismiss the debate as a product of the immaturity of Japanese intellectualism at the time.[20]

I suggest, however, that this debate be reevaluated for what these intellectuals' muddled interaction brought to the fore. Ōgai's blatant disregard for where Iwamoto came from and what he had to say in "Literature and Nature" appears odd and disorients readers. Those effects, I propose, are the point of his rhetorical maneuvers and the focus of my investigation in the subsequent sections. In the appearance of disjointed bickering and failed critical engagement, this debate, specifically Ōgai's rhetorical moves within it, ultimately instantiates his claim, manifesting a dividing line that he claims needs to be drawn afresh between literature and what it is not. It is important to remember when this debate took place, Japan was in the middle of transforming the structure of knowledge to accommodate the country's desire for realizing a full civilization. When read against a backdrop of the shifting configuration of knowledge in the late nineteenth century, Ōgai's writings emerge as his attempt and struggle to break with the existing epistemological constellation, one that was all too familiar to him and his contemporaries. That Ōgai had to write in such strange, disorienting fashions may speak less of him as an individual writer but more of the time period, a formative moment of the new perceptions of knowledge, including that which is called "literature," in which he was caught. In that sense, this debate helps us bear witness to one of the "origins" of modern Japanese literature. Karatani Kōjin once underlined the significance of what he called the "discovery of landscape," or the rupture in epistemological framework, that facilitated the rise and prevalence of the concept of literature in the 1890s.[21] The "Literature and Nature" debate is inscribed with such rupture; when the boundaries of literature were contested in negotiation with those of what it is not, Ōgai's *hihyō* proceeded to clarify the dividing line between literature and nonliterature. My contention is that this division was written into existence in the form of contextual, semantic, and stylistic disconnect, marking his *hihyō*'s creative turn.

Ripping from the Context

One strange move Ōgai makes in contradicting Iwamoto is his decision to take no account of the context of Iwamoto's "Literature and Nature." Iwamoto's essay was initially conceived as a refutation of Sohō and Ningetsu and their ideas as presented in *Kokumin no tomo*. In the essay, Iwamoto mobilized the specific terms Sohō and Ningetsu used— "manufacture" and "immorality," respectively—and thereby fairly clearly indicated his targets. Furthermore, there was a history of conflict in the late 1880s between Iwamoto and Sohō, and by extension Sohō's ally Ningetsu at *Kokumin no tomo*, which involved two schools of thought: the *Jogaku Zasshi* School represented by Iwamoto, and the Min'yūsha School led by Sohō. This intramural conflict over beliefs and priorities had become constant at the time "Literature and Nature" appeared; in short, the piece unambiguously contributed to an ongoing fight between rival schools. In his response to Iwamoto, however, Ōgai reframed "Literature and Nature" exclusively as a theory of literature, causing all contextual factors to be pushed aside throughout the debate. To make sense of Ōgai's disregard for the context, I begin by explicating the situation with which Iwamoto grappled, in order subsequently to underline how Ōgai, who must have been aware of the situation, abruptly severed the discourse from its context.

Biographical notes are helpful here to illustrate where Iwamoto was coming from when he presented "Literature and Nature." Both Iwamoto and Sohō were born into the samurai class in 1863 (Ōgai, born 1862), amid massive political upheavals which ultimately amounted to the collapse of the Tokugawa shogunate and the rise of the Meiji monarchy in

1868. That they were born in the early 1860s meant that they were too young to become active participants in political movements during the Meiji Restoration and its immediate aftermath; they could be neither "patriotic samurai" (*shishi*) of the pre–Meiji Restoration nor "stalwart youth" (*sōshi*) of early Meiji Freedom and People's Rights Movement that sought broader implementation of democracy.[22]

As the Meiji period unfolded, for many youths direct participation in politics became unrealistic. As noted in the introduction to this book, the shift in the regime brought about drastic restructuring of the socioeconomic order. The shogunate's rigid class hierarchy—samurai at the top, followed respectively by farmers, artisans, and merchants—was virtually nullified in the beginning of the Meiji period, destabilizing the social standing of many newly "former" samurai. For the Iwamoto-Sohō generation, being born a samurai no longer guaranteed a secure career in the political arena. Iwamoto, whose birthplace did not have tight connections with the winning team of the Meiji Restoration (the Satsuma, Chōshū, Tosa, and Hizen domains), enjoyed even less chance of a career in the central government.[23] In this sense of needing a different outlet besides politics, Iwamoto and Sohō had much in common: As youths of the former samurai class, they had to reclaim their standing in society actively.

The late 1880s thus marked a historical moment at which young latecomers to the restoration began to construct their own ground, apart from direct participation in politics, through reading, writing, and expressing ideas, in print media. In this project of building and structuring an alternative field to politics, both Iwamoto and Sohō attempted to use their cultural capital, that is, the disciplinary training in reading and writing afforded by their class privileges. Both had recourse to the newly emerging print industry to solicit readers and foster an intellectual community within and upon which they could further stabilize their position. Iwamoto established *Jogaku zasshi*, a journal promoting education for women, in July 1885; Meiji Jogakkō (Meiji Women's School) in October; and the *Jogaku Zasshi* School as the journal's publishing base in December of the same year. Similarly, Sohō orchestrated the founding of the Min'yūsha School and the publication of *Kokumin no tomo* in February 1887. For both Iwamoto and Sohō, launching these journals was inherently a construction of a field, to borrow Pierre Bourdieu's term, in which the former samurai youth of high literacy and educational training could reinscribe themselves in Meiji Japan's changing social order.[24]

Yet despite their similarities, they did not seek their goals or establish themselves in Meiji Japan in the same fashion. For Iwamoto and his fellow Christian intellectuals at the *Jogaku Zasshi* School, the struggle to carve out space for "position takings" in still unstable, postshogunate Japan manifested as an investment in women's education.[25] For Sohō and members of *Kokumin no tomo* at the Min'yūsha School, however, it meant taking a stand as journalists, presenting themselves as a progressive, highly male-centric intellectual community that would intervene in politics through speech and the press. In other words, Iwamoto and Sohō took different routes in their attempts to reinvent themselves in Meiji Japan.

The difference between the two schools manifested itself against the backdrop of Japan's nation-building process in the 1880s. Over a decade into the Meiji period, the configuration of the country's ministerial system—who would lead the country, and by what means—was still unfixed, inviting political unrest.[26] In 1881, the imperial edict to open the Imperial Diet in 1890 sought to rectify the situation. In the years leading up to the issuing of the constitution in 1889, therefore, Japanese elites needed to formulate plans for realizing a new form of "Japan" that would replace the Tokugawa shogunate and engaging with the chaos of the early Meiji period. The forthcoming Imperial Diet prompted many elite youth to sketch blueprints for a Japan yet to come. Those who gathered at the *Jogaku Zasshi* School together with Iwamoto, like those affiliated with the Min'yūsha School led by Sohō, saw that Meiji Japan was in the midst of producing a new form of the nation, and they sought to participate in their own ways.[27] Yet their visions of this new Japan diverged, notably with regard to women's position, and this split manifested legibly in their print platforms.

If the ways in which *Jogaku zasshi* responded to the construction of the nation-form differed conspicuously from those of *Kokumin no tomo*, the Imperial Constitution of Meiji Japan, issued in February 1889, marked a clear defeat for the *Jogaku Zasshi* School: The new constitution granted neither suffrage nor eligibility for election to women. Somewhat surprisingly, then, the 149th issue of *Jogaku zasshi*, published five days after the promulgation of the constitution, did not explicitly verbalize its dismay. In fact, Iwamoto and the editorial team openly celebrated the arrival of the new legal order.[28] It is likely that under censorship, print media could not overtly attack the government or anything to do with imperial orders. Yet while applauding Meiji Japan's constitutional milestone, *Jogaku zasshi* did not forget to make brief reference to the clear gender disparity inscribed in the new legal codes. A small column included toward the end of that issue raises a concern: "Nowhere in the constitution is mentioned a difference based on male–female gender," and yet the election laws and many others are applicable to "men only."[29] The anonymous columnist then remarks that they need to "wait until the time is ripe" to have further discussion on gender-based inequality.[30] The rhetoric of "untimeliness" mobilized in this small section of *Jogaku zasshi* is in striking contrast to the phrase "a once-in-a-lifetime chance," with which a *Kokumin no tomo* headline celebrated the promulgation of the constitution.[31] The new constitution and subsequent legal order was a victory for Sohō, his platform *Kokumin no tomo*, its majority male readers, and by and large the Min'yūsha School. For Iwamoto, *Jogaku zasshi*, its readership, many of them women, and the *Jogaku Zasshi* School, however, it was another hurdle to overcome.

Note the timing of "Literature and Nature." It was published in April 1889, a few months after the constitution, and it appeared in *Jogaku zasshi* as a negative response to texts written by Sohō and Ningetsu, members of *Kokumin no tomo*. As such, Iwamoto's confrontation with the writers at *Kokumin no tomo* in "Literature and Nature" was part of the larger, ongoing struggle between the *Jogaku Zasshi* School and the Min'yūsha School. Iwamoto essentially asks whether members of *Kokumin no tomo* are really "the nation's friends" as they claim—because they do not seem to act accordingly. In other words, embedded in "Literature and Nature" was a skepticism toward the Min'yūsha School's agenda, which seemed to cater exclusively to young, educated male readers.

The two schools' conflict was not limited to the issue of women's right to participate in politics; intertwined with this were two concurrent matters: licensed prostitution, on the one hand, and a series of moral corruption scandals surrounding women's schools on the other. The first concern on prostitution manifests clearly in "Literature and Nature." Not long before "Literature and Nature," Iwamoto in *Jogaku zasshi* insisted on the "total eradication of brothels" from Japan.[32] Then, when Kabuki actor Ichikawa Danjūrō refused to play the role of a prostitute in theater, Iwamoto sided with the actor and supported *Jiji shinpō* (News on current events), a daily periodical that favorably presented Ichikawa's stand.[33] Ningetsu's opinion piece in *Kokumin no tomo* advocated the independence of expressive activities from reality and, in so doing, rejected Iwamoto and others who supported the Kabuki performer. Iwamoto's problematization of Ningetsu in "Literature and Nature" thus extended the ongoing debate over the pros and cons of licensed prostitution.

For advocates of women's status, no less urgent was the progressing campaign against young women in the academic settings, albeit this point is less visible in "Literature and Nature." In the late 1880s into the early 1890s, multiple print media, including *Kokumin no tomo*, featured scandals regarding female students and teachers. Various media spaces, fiction and nonfiction alike, repeated the same narratives about the moral corruption of those involved in women's education. Fictional works, such as Ozaki Kōyō's *Fūryū kyōningyō* (Elegant Kyoto doll, serialized in literary coterie magazine *Garakuta bunko* from May 1888 to March 1889) and Saganoya Omuro's *Kusaretamago* (Rotten egg, featured in literary journal *Miyako no hana* in February 1889), thematized troubling, sexually charged affairs of young women.³⁴ As if to resonate with such repetitive, fictional depictions of problematic young women, journalists too initiated a negative campaign against female students and women's education.³⁵ The daily newspaper *Yomiuri shinbun*, for instance, published multiple articles presenting "rumors" surrounding women's schools as if those rumors had been "facts."³⁶ The final few years of the 1880s thus saw a moment in which both fiction and news reports reproduced the narrative of moral deterioration on the scene of women's education, a moment that *Kokumin no tomo* referred to as the "shock of women's education."³⁷

Various media outlets supplemented each other, actively undermining the *Jogaku Zasshi* School's efforts to solidify the social ground for women's education. To Iwamoto and his cohorts, whose social standing could be seriously damaged by the conflation of fiction and nonfiction that depicted young female figures, Ningetsu's belief that performance and reality were independent of and separable from each other was too optimistic. Iwamoto's contradiction of Ningetsu reflected the former's frustration that literary devices such as gender- and age-based scandals could easily slip into popular imagination, likely encouraging confusion of the real and the fabricated. Similarly, when scandals were forged and circulated among readers as plausible stories, members of the *Jogaku Zasshi* School did not welcome Sohō's rhetoric of "manufacturing" literary expressions, nor the favorable tones he attached to it. For the *Jogaku Zasshi* School, factors enabling slippage between fiction and fact were nothing but threatening.

As a group of Christian intellectuals who intended to reestablish their position in society by advocating for women, the *Jogaku Zasshi* School and its leading member Iwamoto had to take an active role in these contemporary discussions. When addressing the problems, it was particularly important for them to do it publicly through print media, because countering those negative forces in journals would potentially, if they handled it well, increase the chances of raising public support for women's education and, by implication, fortify their own social standing. As social historian Okada Akiko rightly observes, by actively engaging with counterforces and discussing women-related issues widely in print media, the *Jogaku Zasshi* School could advertise and spread their agenda in the public sphere.[38] With all this at stake, Iwamoto crafted "Literature and Nature."

If contextualizing Iwamoto's essay helps us understand the stakes, it makes Ōgai's choice to rip the essay from its context all the more puzzling. Ōgai was quite aware that "Literature and Nature" was Iwamoto's intervention in existing discussions about women. In fact, Ōgai participated in the dispute about licensed prostitution as public health expert "Mori Rintarō" in the medical journal *Eisei shinshi* (New journal of hygiene, established by Ōgai himself in 1889)—only to sneer at Iwamoto's idealistic blindness to the "actual state of society."[39] It seems likely that Ōgai was tracking "who said what in which medium" concerning women-related issues, and yet instead of acknowledging Iwamoto's struggles and treating "Literature and Nature" as part of a larger discursive network surrounding women's status, Ōgai read the essay purely as a discourse on literary writing. After Ōgai's initial reaction to "Literature and Nature," the correspondence between Ōgai and Iwamoto proceeded as a debate primarily about the essential quality of literature, what it should and should not be. Their interaction said almost nothing about women, dragging "Literature and Nature" ever further from its initial context.

Given that Ōgai was familiar with Iwamoto's background as an advocate of women's status in Meiji Japan, his move to sever "Literature and Nature" from those issues transpires as a conscious maneuver. Moreover, Ōgai introduced another level of disconnect, one concerned with semantics, into the debate. While isolating "Literature and Nature" from the surrounding discussions on women, Ōgai read Iwamoto's key term, "nature" (*shizen*), in a way violently divergent from Iwamoto's usage. Even as the dispute revolved around this term, the ways in which Ōgai mobilized "nature" actually had little to do with what Iwamoto's "nature" pointed to. With Ōgai aware of Iwamoto's line of thinking and rhetoric, I consider Ōgai's handling of Iwamoto's "nature" to be a deliberate misreading. Yet my intention is not to blame Ōgai for manipulating "nature" but to evaluate the creativity of his misreading. One might remember Harold Bloom's note on creative misreading, and how strong poets must read their predecessors inaccurately in order to acquire their own poetic strength.[40] Through deliberate, creative misreading of Iwamoto, Ōgai, as if to substantiate Bloom's claim, mapped the stakes of his own discourse.

Remolding the Word

Ōgai's "nature" was incompatible with Iwamoto's. It is tempting to attribute the grave rift between the two instances of "nature" to philological differences in background: Ōgai and Iwamoto received different types of linguistic education, with the former versatile in German after many years in that country, the latter studying English through involvement in domestic Christian communities; as such, their vocabularies were dissimilar. That said, what prompted the disconnect between Ōgai's "nature" and Iwamoto's was not so straightforward: Ōgai deliberately bent the semantics of Iwamoto's "nature." We need to ask how he did it, and to what effect.

Natur, wissenschaftliche Literatur, schöne Literatur, poetischer Naturalismus, Ideal, Idee, Geist, Tatsache, Transsubstantiation: Ōgai's initial refutation against "Literature and Nature" is oversaturated with these German terms. Indeed, Ōgai was fluent in German: He studied in Germany as a military surgeon on the governmental mission between 1884 and 1888, participating in Japan's nation-building project. While Japan had begun to send young elites to various European and Anglo-American countries to determine its own nation form in the 1870s (remember the Iwakura mission initiated in 1871), the years nearing the inauguration of the Imperial Diet in 1890 felt a more intensified need to solidify the shape of the nation. Among many places, Germany became a popular destination for studying abroad in the early 1880s, indicating Meiji Japan's strong interest in establishing a constitutional monarchy modeled after the German Empire. Ōgai's exposure to German was a product of Japan's infatuation with rising Germany in the fin de siècle, and the frequent references to German in his writings produced at the end of the 1880s reflect such a background.

While flaunting his expertise in German, Ōgai makes gestures at accessibility for his Japanese readers. Most obviously, almost all of the German words are rendered in phonetic katakana to replicate the original German pronunciation, translated into Chinese compound words that approximate the meanings, or both at once. By showing possible linguistic expressions in different languages, Ōgai's writing creates vocabularies with which to discuss unfamiliar things. His text, in other words, assumes a translingual quality: As with Nishi Amane's *Hyakugaku renkan*, it is informative in a way, but also confusing and even intimidating at times.

The ways in which Ōgai's refutation is written thus gave rise to an appearance that the Ōgai-Iwamoto dispute revolved around their different ways of using "nature," with Ōgai harshly problematizing Iwamoto because his own conception, derived from the German *"Natur,"* was incompatible with the latter's usage. Such an understanding of the debate is also facilitated by a historical situation in late nineteenth-century Japan in which translingual practice was ubiquitous. As philologist Yanabu Akira notes, although many intellectuals attempted to transplant new concepts to Japanese usage during the 1870s and 1880s, a general consensus about the semantics of many terms, including *shizen* or "nature," did not come into being immediately.[41] As people with different educational backgrounds began to use certain signifiers in a not necessarily universal fashion, disagreements as to what term to use in what way became prevalent in the intellectual communities.

And yet, what the debate represented was not so simple as a clash between Iwamoto's Emersonian "nature" and Ōgai's German *"Natur."* Nor can the confrontation be schematized as Iwamoto's lack of rigor falling before Ōgai's linguistic versatility. Throughout the exchange there was little sensible correspondence because Ōgai behaved as though with utter disregard for the ways in which Iwamoto discussed the topic.

In "Literature and Nature," Iwamoto clearly does not posit "nature" solely in the sense of tangible objects and perceptible phenomena. Iwamoto's "nature" is rendered a distinct trait that is at once ethical and aesthetic. "Nature," in his formulation, emerges as a realm in which "virtue" and "beauty" are nurtured in a "spiritual" manner. When the most "beautiful" essence of "nature" is captured in writing, Iwamoto explains, "divine poesy" arises as a result, and this poesy remains untouched by "immorality."[42] Iwamoto's conception of "transcribing nature" thus does not entail a mere description of exteriority, but rather points to transcription of a kind of nature premised upon intangible qualities, ones that he believes are innate in exterior appearance. His evocation of "spirit" and *"Geist"* in "nature," his rephrasing of "nature" as "great teacher" and "enormous ideal," his recourse to Emerson to underline the trinity of truth, goodness, and beauty—all confirm how this "nature" has little to do with what Ōgai calls "fact" ("*jijitsu*" [Chinese characters]; "*tātozahhe*" [katakana] = *Tatsache* [German]).[43]

The harmonious unity of truth, goodness, and beauty is an inevitable, "natural" phenomenon, and "literature" needs to entail a linguistic incarnation of such "nature," posits Iwamoto. The validity of his conception of "literature and nature" is not a question in my analysis. The point is that Iwamoto uses the term "nature" in a specific way, which Ōgai suppresses. Refuting "Literature and Nature," Ōgai delineates divisions between truth, goodness, and beauty, and associates them with the disciplines of science, ethics, and poetics, respectively. In this process, Iwamoto's "nature" is swiftly rephrased by another term, "fact," and placed in connection with "scientific literature" ("*kabungaku*" [Chinese characters]; "*vissenshafutorihhe riteratsūru*" [katakana] = *wissenschaftliche Literatur* [German]).[44] In spite of such an elaborate explanation, what Ōgai presents reveals very little about Iwamoto's "nature." Ōgai's rhetoric thus generates a schism, not a dialogic relationship, vis-à-vis what it contradicts. As a result, their interaction quickly falls out of joint. The sense of disconnect activated in Ōgai's account is thus at least twofold: While it dissociates "Literature and Nature" from a particular context in which Iwamoto had to defend the emerging field of women's education, it also abstracts from Iwamoto's "nature" a specific signification, turns the term into an empty signifier, and then replenishes it with a different meaning. By disregarding the semantic configuration of Iwamoto's wording, Ōgai's writing shifts the stakes of "Literature and Nature"; what was once an attempt to defend a field promoting women's status and, by implication, affiliated members' social standing in Meiji Japan's new order are reframed into a theory of literature that waits to be challenged. With Ōgai's aggressive intervention, Iwamoto's essay is forcibly transformed into a narrative that fails to adequately portray the relationship between empirical fact and ideal beauty, and science and fine arts.

The path through which Ōgai remodels Iwamoto's "nature" is noteworthy because his misreading does not simply bend the definition of Iwamoto's term but also reaches Zola's theory of the novel. While imposing an utterly different meaning upon Iwamoto's "nature," Ōgai characterizes Iwamoto's formulation of "transcription of 'nature' the way it is" as the "poetic naturalism" (*shigakuteki no shizenshugi* [two sets of Chinese characters connected with a Japanese case particle *no* in the middle]; *poēchisseru natsurarisumusu* [katakana] = *poetischer Naturalismus* [German]) prevalent in Europe; likens Iwamoto to Zola, the French promoter of naturalist writing; and condemns such "nature" in the sense of mimesis (*mohō* [Chinese characters]; *nahāmungu* [katakana] = *Nachahmung*) as unable to accomplish "aesthetic literature" (*bibungaku* [Chinese characters]; *shōne riteratsūru* [katakana] = *schöne Literatur* [German]).[45] Referring to his early writing condemning Zola, Ōgai explains:

> Zola turned to the scientific methods that pursued "nature" by means of observation and experimentation, and he applied them to aesthetic literature. The details are described in my essay, "Shōsetsuron," that appeared in the first issue of this year's *Yomiuri shinbun*. . . . However, the "nature" that is sought by observation and experimentation is "fact." Satisfaction with acquiring "fact" points to science, not fine arts.[46]

In Ōgai's rhetoric, "nature" is grouped together with "observation," "experimentation," "fact," and "science." These terms are then positioned separately from "beauty," "ideal," "aesthetic literature," and "fine arts." There is an obvious discrepancy between Iwamoto's "nature" and what Ōgai says about "nature." Despite that, the former is fused with "poetic naturalism," which, according to Ōgai, is exemplified by Zola's "scientific methods" of literary production. Ōgai maintains that Zolaist naturalism became indistinguishable from science while still circulating as a type of fine arts in Europe, and that such conflation must not happen. Ōgai thus raises a strong objection to the situation unfolding overseas in relation to the case of Iwamoto's discourse produced in Japan. Yet, given that Iwamoto's "nature" is at odds with what Ōgai says about "nature," Ōgai's problem with the "poetic naturalism" of European origin has nothing to do with the literature envisaged by Iwamoto.

In fact, Ōgai's rhetorical acrobatics are doubly suppressive: In addition to undermining Iwamoto's discourse, Ōgai also brings an injustice to Zola's. When "Shōsetsuron" offered a prescriptive account for writing novels a few months prior to the publication of Iwamoto's "Literature and Nature," Ōgai accomplished the task of prescription specifically by positing Zola's 1880 essay, "The Experimental Novel," as a counterexample not to be followed. That is to say, Ōgai's theory of the novel is negatively formulated as what novel writers should *not* do, in opposition to Zola's proposal for the application of physiological methods to the production of the novel. What is important is that Ōgai's presentation of Zola's methods is partial, leaving out the crucial segment of "The Experimental Novel" that Zola himself cared to clarify.

Indeed, Zola advocated what he called the experimental novel and its fundamental reliance on the physiological model of "observation" and "experimentation." Zola writes: "We should operate on the characters, the passions, on the human and social data, in the same way that the chemist and the physicist operate on inanimate beings, and as the physiologist operates on living beings."[47] There is no doubt that the French writer invested in "scientific" approaches to recreate in writing physical semblance of objects and phenomena. Such recourse to "scientific" approaches was exactly what Ōgai attempted to reject from the realm of "literature." When "science," "fact," and "nature" are considered synonymous, as in Ōgai's postulation, Zola's theory appears to advocate mimetic, descriptive writing, produced in the least mediated manner writerly possible. More important, however, while speaking favorably about physiologically designed investigation, Zola did not give ultimate primacy to "science," a discipline that Ōgai flatly equated to the acquisition of unmediated facts, in the production of novels.

What Zola found particularly useful as writing techniques in the realm of science involves human intervention. Zola's "The Experimental Novel" draws heavily on Claude Bernard's *An Introduction to the Study of Experimental Medicine*. As these titles suggest, Zola places significant emphasis on "experimentation," that is, "experimenting" upon the information acquired through "observation," and, "observing" what ensues from "experimentation." "Experiment" is, according to Zola's presentation of Bernard's theory, "but *provoked* observation," and therefore, "the experimentalist is a man who ... *institutes* an experiment in such a way that ... it will furnish a result which will serve to confirm the hypothesis or preconceived idea" (emphasis added).[48] Note that what Zola calls "experiment" does not take place spontaneously but needs to be externally induced with an experimental intent. Taking up Honoré de Balzac, Zola further explains how a writer introduces an experiment in their writing practice:

> As Balzac does not remain satisfied with photographing the facts collected by him, but *interferes in a direct way* to place his character in certain conditions, and of these he remains the master. ..., the whole operation consists in taking facts in nature, then in studying the mechanism of these facts, *acting upon them*, by the *modification of circumstances and surroundings*, without deviating from the laws of nature. Finally, you possess knowledge of the man, scientific knowledge of him, in both his individual and social relations [emphasis added].[49]

Experimental writers, as painted by Zola, are not expected to simply reproduce physical likeness of the world in the linguistic form; they must exert their intent upon what exists out there and alter it within the range of order of phenomena. They must do so actively so as to build and confirm their hypotheses. Zola's reference to photography in the passage is counterintuitive. The photographic lens captures what falls in its framing capacity indiscriminately. Contrary to the general assumption, including Ōgai's, that Zola exclusively attempted to practice photographic, in other words, mimetic description, Zola's "scientific knowledge" deviates from the mechanically acquired, nonselective information that an optical device may reproduce. The acquisition of "scientific knowledge," according to Zola, requires human intervention, a subjective eye that sets a photographic lens in a specific position, an experiment calculated on purpose, for the sake of successfully describing "relations" that are not necessarily externalized. "To describe is no longer our end," Zola writes, because description should serve as an "account of the environment which determines and completes man."[50] In other words, description of "scientifically" obtained information needs to take place not for the sake of describing but in the interests of revealing "the causes or the consequence in his [man's] surroundings."[51] Zola thus clarifies the instrumental use of description, the importance of observing and writing down the results of intentional experiments upon human relations, in the production of the novel. Ōgai never mentions this part of Zola's account when he makes reference to "naturalism." The picture of the French writer that Ōgai presents—Zola as an ardent advocate of "naturalism" solely satisfied with fact-based description—is thus reductive.

In "Shōsetsuron," Ōgai took a firm stand against Zola's reliance on "science" in literary writing, arguing that "science" alone would never give rise to a defining quality of "aesthetic literature" and, by extension, "fine arts." A few months later, Ōgai mobilized Zola again to reprimand Iwamoto and rearticulate the incompatibility of "science" and "aesthetics." Ōgai's attack against Iwamoto is premised upon the comparability of Zola's proposal to Iwamoto's view, while there is in fact no viable connection between Zola and Iwamoto other than that both of them employ the rhetoric of "nature" to elaborate on their ideas of literary production. In short, Ōgai bunches together two independent manifestations of "nature," only to misread both.

Importantly, those instances of misreading bring to the fore Ōgai's vision of literature and the processes through which he paints his vision in the form of writing. While bending both Zola's idea of description and Iwamoto's conception of literature, Ōgai's account repudiates the discourses of literature that revolve around the term, "nature," irrespective of what each instance of "nature" points to. Ōgai singles out the rhetoric of "nature" even at the cost of reductionism and, in so doing, stages his own discourse in contrast. "Nature" as a signifier is emptied and abstracted into a point of counter-reference, in opposition to which Ōgai starts presenting his theory of literature, one that is supposed to be a linguistic incarnation of "beauty" and its unparalleled importance in the scene of literary writing. Therefore, when Ōgai suppresses the texts that he is supposed to read critically, thereby failing in his reading practice, what ensues from his failure is the further solidification of the dividing line between literature—a kind that he promotes—and what it is not. In other words, Ōgai labors to delineate literature's boundaries and by extension those of aesthetics specifically by foregrounding "nature" and its ultimate incompatibility with them.

Ōgai's misreading needs to be contextualized especially against the changing system of knowledge in fin de siècle Japan. As discussed previously, in the late nineteenth century a constellation of knowledge underwent a massive reorganization in Japan, the processes of which involved distancing from the Sinosphere and installing alternative models from Euro-Anglo-American counterparts. Where to draw a line within a corpus of knowledge and how to behave as intellectuals to represent that line were not as obvious as they had been, and precisely because of this the division of intellectual labor was actively pursued. Produced in that context, Ōgai's response to Iwamoto uniquely addresses the historically conditioned, confusing situation about intellectualism and his own standing in it.

Division and Indivisibility

While ripping Iwamoto's discourse from the original context and reinventing the semantics of Iwamoto's "nature," Ōgai's account underlines the inevitability of separating the aesthetic realm from the scientific one. The division is proposed to advocate for the autonomy of beauty and its primacy as a quality of literary writing. There is no inherent necessity to sever aesthetics from science, and Ōgai's behavior in the debate was unnecessarily aggressive. Yet Ōgai's claim on the division was at least not an isolated attempt in late nineteenth-century Japan.

As discussed in part 1, the urge to divide labor, especially an intellectual type of labor, was a historical phenomenon in late nineteenth-century

Japan: To a heightened degree, dividing things into smaller, more specialized units was considered synonymous with understanding them better and being enlightened by the new taxonomic order. The individuation of the space of *hihyō* in print media was itself premised upon the logic of separating critical language from other forms of intellectual writing practice. The call for further bifurcation, especially branching off intellectual labor, was shared by many of Ōgai's contemporaries. In addition to Sohō, who campaigned for the division of labor in the political arena in 1888, Hasegawa Tatsunosuke (aka Futabatei Shimei, the author of *Ukigumo* [The floating cloud, 1887–89]), for instance, translated Russian Schellingian scholar Mikhail G. Pavlov's essay and published it under the title "Gakujutsu to bijutsu no sabetsu" (On the distinction between sciences and fine arts) in 1888.[52] That both Futabatei's translation and Ōgai's initial response to Iwamoto's essay appeared in the same print medium, Sohō's *Kokumin no tomo*, exemplifies how the division of intellectual practices and, by extension, the reordering of knowledge itself, was of great concern to many young intellectuals at the time.

The inquiry into divisions of intellectual labor manifested saliently in the institution of knowledge, as Japan began to invest in higher education in the 1870s. The University of Tokyo, Meiji Japan's first public university, was established in 1877 with four major faculties—law, science, letters, and medicine—which over the following few decades led to further division and specialization of academic disciplines.[53] Such a formal, top-down decision on how to divide knowledge at this historical juncture had particularly strong implications for young intellectuals trained in the Chinese classics. Literature scholar Joseph Murphy offers useful insight here, in his survey of the inception phase of higher education in early Meiji Japan:

> Japanese intellectual space from roughly 1890 to 1945 is unique in that the disciplinary divisions of the modern university instituted in the space of a generation along contemporary European lines were inhabited by scholars who retained a corporate/corporeal memory of intellectual work under a different regime of knowledge in the form of Chinese studies. These scholars neither feared the formalization involved in math nor took for granted the immiscibility of knowledge produced by the humanities and the sciences.[54]

The Meiji elites' intellectual foundation was deeply rooted in the genealogies of classical Chinese studies, which consist of the "broad range of cultivated learning, including rhetoric, ethics, natural philosophy, metaphysics, poetry and music."⁵⁵ Because of that, Murphy argues, they typically showed less resistance to multidisciplinary work compared with their Euro-Anglo-American counterparts. To some, however, the very fact that they were susceptible to the nondivision of knowledge posed a serious challenge.

For middle to upper-class families in the 1880s, exposing their children to Chinese studies at an early age was still a common practice, and as such, the generation of youth, including Ōgai (born 1862), Sohō (born 1863), and Iwamoto (born 1863), who had been already schooled before the institutionalization of higher education was initiated by the Meiji state, did not necessarily consider Chinese studies and the breadth of its disciplinary scope a relic of the past. Precisely because those traditions were deeply inculcated and internalized in their mindset, what Meiji youth experienced in the late nineteenth century constituted a "lived contradiction" between what they had been taught and what was beginning to be institutionalized.⁵⁶ For readers of Ōgai's generation, the range of learning that Chinese studies afforded was not heterogeneous or multidisciplinary in itself: It only began to emerge as such retroactively when the division of disciplines materialized in higher education. To participate in Meiji Japan as elites, especially as nonpoliticians, meant that they had to question, if not negate, their lived, foundational learning experiences. What was imposed upon them was a drastic shift in ways of perceiving things, a kind of shift that would not be reversed once taken. It became crucial for them to actively censor undivided intellectual activities within their own practices so as to align themselves with the emerging order.

In this climate, where breaking things down was immediately linked to the formation of new educational institutions, Iwamoto's essay, which unambiguously presented the indivisibility of qualities—truth, goodness, beauty—in literary writing, emerged as that which had to be reprimanded.⁵⁷ To be sure, Iwamoto was not invoking the genealogies of Chinese classics, as he clearly drew on Emerson. Still, coming from a Japanese intellectual of a specific generation who had to be extra cautious about the "immiscibility of knowledge," a picture of literature that is at once true, good, and beautiful, was irreconcilable with the logic of division, hence unacceptable. This is not to say that Iwamoto had no part in the shared call for division of labor, nor that he actively resisted the zeitgeist of the late nineteenth century. He was a participant in the same force, a salient example of which was the individuation of the *hihyō* section in his primary platform *Jogaku zasshi*. The point is rather that the multidisciplinary conception of writing practice—what Meiji youth had internalized and hence had to resist—surfaced in Iwamoto's discourse, regardless of the writer's intention. "Literature and Nature," in other words, conjured what had been acceptable before the idea of dividing intellectual labor gained traction, and was directed at Sohō and Ningetsu, who were strong advocates of dividing intellectual labor. Accidentally or not, Iwamoto's motion questioned the validity of division, revealed the possible irreducibility of intellectual practice to the clean scheme, and thereby posed a threat to the contemporaneously shared belief in division.

Ōgai's reaction to Iwamoto, the former's insistence on separating "science" from "aesthetics" in the debate, was thus in direct correlation with the shifting constellation of knowledge in late nineteenth-century Japan. Ōgai, who bore witness to the moment at which the system of knowledge was revamped, underlined in "Shōsetsuron" the incommensurability of literary, aesthetic writing with science. He then used "Literature and Nature" as another point of reference against which the primacy of the emerging system of knowledge could be iterated. By attacking Iwamoto and misreading his "nature," Ōgai spotlighted Iwamoto's view of literature as outdated for its failure to conceive the dividing line adequately and, in so doing, rearticulated his position as an advocate of the separation of disciplines. Ōgai's exceptionally aggressive maneuver indicates in reverse that dividing intellectual practice into more specialized categories was not a universal model, but rather a historically conditioned phenomenon that had to be consciously enforced. Ōgai's confrontation with Iwamoto was, in that sense, a manifestation of a "lived contradiction" of late nineteenth-century Japan, when many intellectuals believed that the new order of knowledge must prevail over the other forms of intellectualism.

Ōgai was certainly not the only young elite who championed the individuation of intellectual labor, and yet the ways in which he handled the situation were outstandingly acrobatic in his time. During the debate, he did not just explicate and defend the disciplinary division in content, but also substantiated the dividing line stylistically in form. That is to say, Ōgai delivered his *hihyō* of Iwamoto in such a distinct fashion that his writing ended up staging what it argued. By presenting itself in an unparalleled style, Ōgai's writing diagnostically revealed the dividing line between intellectual practices that may be unfamiliar to his contemporaries and pressed them to understand how to conceptualize their relationship with things yet to be reorganized in the realm of knowledge. Irrespective of Ōgai's intention, the *hihyō* he produced in this debate transfigured from a practice of reading and evaluating what other writings say into a performative process of bringing into existence what it promotes.

Making Visible the Dividing Line

Recall that the initial *hihyō* of "Literature and Nature" was submitted under the name of "Mori Rintarō," Ōgai's birthname that he used as a medical doctor. This piece of writing is produced as a medical doctor's intervention in the discourse on literature. In fact, as if to reflect the scientific quality of medicine, Ōgai mobilized a "scientific" methodology, specifically a kind that Zola proposed in association with physiological observation and experimentation, to refute his opponent. This means that Ōgai relied on "science," an association with which he tried to expel from the realm of "aesthetic literature," in order to negate Iwamoto's proposition of "nature"-based "literature."

Such a style of writing broke with the conventions of expository writing with which Iwamoto's essay and other contemporary discourses about literature were composed. The "Literature and Nature" debate was therefore not just about what the debaters said about the definition of "nature" in relation to "literature," but also about how they presented the topic at hand. Intellectual historian Julia Thomas suggests that "nature" was the "changing, contested matrix within which the political possibilities of modernity were explored" during the transitional period from the Tokugawa shogunate to the Meiji regime.[58] If, as Thomas states, "nature" was a site from which the "possibilities of modernity" were sought in fin de siècle Japan, Ōgai's handling of Iwamoto's "nature" is one manifestation of such seeking. It is so, however, not simply because Ōgai problematized Iwamoto's usage of "nature," as Thomas seems to suggest in her brief note on the debate, but also because Ōgai used Iwamoto's "nature" as a springboard from which to make legible the modern division of intellectual labor.[59] Taking advantage of Iwamoto's discourse, Ōgai constructed and presented his logic to delineate the importance of dividing knowledge, and he did so by choreographing his writing as "scientific" discourse. Among the many contemporaries who participated in discussions about literature and published their work in the intellectual communities as *hihyō*, no one else rendered a discernible form to the dividing line between literature and what it is not in the way that Ōgai did. In short, Ōgai's critical (mis)reading of Iwamoto's "nature" was in and of itself his creative endeavor.

To initiate his refutation, Ōgai restates Iwamoto's two theses. When doing so, he does not quote them directly but slightly modifies them by assigning each one a numeric indicator:

(1) The greatest literature is that which transcribes nature the way it is.
(2) The most beautiful fine arts would never be accompanied by immorality [emphasis added].[60]

The numerical identification, marked in italics, appears subtle, and yet its effect is crucial, in that the numbers generate a sense of anticipation of development, both chronological and logical, that should ensue from (1) to (2) to the next. This numbering marks the beginning of Ōgai's stylistic legerdemain. Departing from these two theses, now assigned numbers, Ōgai spotlights the slipperiness of the terms in Iwamoto's writing. Ōgai writes: "Beauty" is a distinctive characteristic of "fine arts," while "greatness" is merely an accidental and hence not a determining feature of "literature." As against the appearance of the parallelism in Iwamoto's account, according to Ōgai, there is no correspondence between "the greatest literature" and "the most beautiful fine arts." This is because, Ōgai explains, the realm of "literature" needs to be separated into two independent categories: "aesthetic literature" and "scientific literature." Therefore, Ōgai reasons, what corresponds to the "most beautiful, aesthetic literature" must be the "most truthful, scientific literature." As a logical consequence, a revised hypothesis arises:

(3) The most *truthful, scientific* literature is that which transcribes nature the way it is [emphasis added].[61]

The "greatest literature" in the first statement presented in Iwamoto's essay is rephrased as the "most truthful, scientific literature." This rewrite is framed as a logical clarification of an ambiguity underlying in Iwamoto's usage. To further solidify the hypothesis, Ōgai substitutes "nature" with "fact" and proposes a fourth, conclusive hypothesis:

(4) The most truthful, scientific literature is that which transcribes *fact* the way it is [emphasis added].[62]

As a result of Ōgai's rhetorical operation, what was originally a statement about a triadic quality of "literature" is gradually, but forcefully converted into an explication of "science" and its relationship to "fact."

Ōgai approaches Iwamoto's second remark on "fine arts" in the same, forcefully revisionist manner. Reasoning that "beauty" requires no verification, unlike "truth" or "goodness," Ōgai rejects Iwamoto's association between "fine arts" and "immorality." "Beauty" is autonomous, and that is what needs to be materialized in an art form. Based on this notion, Ōgai rewrites Iwamoto's second thesis into a somewhat compromised form:

(5) The most beautiful fine arts *may sometimes* be accompanied by immorality [emphasis added].⁶³

Using this as a foothold, Ōgai develops another hypothesis to inspect the relationship between "aesthetic literature" and "nature":

(6) The most *beautiful aesthetic* literature is that which transcribes nature the way it is [emphasis added].⁶⁴

Ōgai's sixth hypothesis appears to resemble Iwamoto's first. Nevertheless, positioned after the clear separation of "aesthetic literature" from "scientific literature," and "beauty" from "truth" and "goodness," Ōgai's formulation has little in common with Iwamoto's. In other words, Ōgai's logic attempts to disprove a hypothesis that never belonged to his opponent. He concludes:

(7) The most beautiful aesthetic literature *does not generally* transcribe nature the way it is [emphasis added].⁶⁵

Throughout Ōgai's debunking of the association between "literature" and "nature," Iwamoto's original statements are taken apart into empty words, challenged, and then reassembled in another order. The revised statements resemble the original formulae rhetorically, but utterly diverge from Iwamoto's versions in content.

Ōgai's handling of Iwamoto's account employs a distinctively "scientific" method of assessment. His evaluation unfolds as if it were a process of probing and testing of given subjects, and his writing presents the rationale behind each step that he takes one by one. Iwamoto's statements are treated as hypotheses to be verified or disproven; they are inspected and dissected into pieces, and each one is then tried for its viability. When the trial fails, inoperative pieces are removed and supplanted by new ones. Ōgai conducts close observations of his opponent's rhetoric and experiments intentionally upon it in order to reach a claim that appears more rigorous.

As strange as it may sound, Ōgai's manner of argumentation closely resembles what Zola advocated in "The Experimental Novel." As we have seen, Ōgai took issue with Zola's theory of the experimental novel in his "Shōsetsuron," while leaving out a foundational aspect of Zola's naturalism—the importance of active human intervention in the "scientific" production of the novel—in his *hihyō*. Knowingly or not, Ōgai brings back what he had suppressed previously in "Shōsetsuron" when engaging with "Literature and Nature," this time as a method of evaluation: He contradicts Iwamoto's theory not simply by stating what it is and how it is inaccurate, but also by purposefully observing and experimenting on it. In that sense, Ōgai puts into practice Zolaist "science," that which he had not acknowledged when problematizing Zola's naturalism. More important, he does so not to produce a novel but to write a piece of *hihyō*, and specifically to divorce "science" from "aesthetics." As such, Ōgai's move marks an unexpected mobilization of Zola's theory in the production of *hihyō*. To assess Iwamoto's discourse, Ōgai proceeds as if he were a physiologist operating on trial subjects. Indeed, he identified himself as medical practitioner "Mori Rintarō" when confronting Iwamoto. By indicating that he read his opponent's accounts as a "scientist," he positioned his critical reading as "scientific" discourse on literature and its divisibility from other "nonliterary" disciplines. Ōgai's rhetorical moves in this debate thus uniquely practice what he preaches.

In Ōgai's refutation, "science" makes a surprise appearance as a mode of examination, one that on the content level is ejected from the realm of "aesthetics." The intricacy of Ōgai's discourse has a series of implications. If Ōgai "scientifically" makes his case about the necessity of segregating "science" from "aesthetics," then Ōgai's discussion of "aesthetics" may rely on what it estranges. Alternatively, if "aesthetic literature" is independent of "fact" obtained through "scientific" methods, as Ōgai states, then perhaps his own "scientifically" composed writing has no interest in being "aesthetic." When Ōgai's *hihyō* argues for the primacy of "aesthetics" by mobilizing a "scientific" mode of evaluation, we are ultimately unable to characterize what his *hihyō* is, that is, whether "science" or "aesthetics." And indeed, the doctor-writer never directly speaks of how he conceives the relationship between "science" and "aesthetics" (or the lack thereof) in his own writings.

That said, it is significant that this apparent discrepancy in Ōgai's writing—a "scientific" discourse on "aesthetics"—arises only if we follow his schema of separating "science" from "aesthetics." Instead of simply accepting his dividing line, however, we can dwell on it as an effect of his writing. In considering Ōgai's rhetorical move, Thomas LaMarre has helpfully observed that many of Ōgai's writings reveal the opposite of what he says:

> In fact, despite his insistence on modern divisions, it is possible to see the real work of Mori Rintarō/Ōgai in terms of a mixture of scientific, social, and literary effects on an unimaginable scale. . . . If we temporarily forestall the urge to assign a hierarchy to these mixes in terms of foreground and background, or dominant and subordinate modes, it is evident that, despite their claims to the contrary, his works are far from separating science, society, and literature. The result is an intensely hybridized mix of facts, power plays, and fictions.[66]

If with LaMarre we acknowledge the hybridity of *what* Ōgai writes, we can also recognize it in *how* he writes. That is to say, Ōgai's writing is an "intensely hybridized mix" not simply because of the diverse subjects addressed, but also because of the multiplicity of "effects" his writing style generates. His response to "Literature and Nature" embodies such a "mix," in that it emerges as a "scientific" discourse about "aesthetic literature" composed by a medical doctor, and that it turns to "scientific" methodologies to present its take on "aesthetic literature" in a unique, unprecedented fashion. With its unambiguously "scientific" turn, Ōgai's writing self-referentially exhibits what "science" writes and what "aesthetics" does not, thereby demonstrating the very idea of dividing knowledge. The apparent anomaly of a "scientist" deliberating on "aesthetics" is a prominent example of the "effects" produced by the creative composition of Ōgai's writing.

Ōgai's *hihyō* wrote the division into existence, clarifying the boundaries of "science" and "aesthetics." When there was a collective call for the division of intellectual labor among opinion leaders, his writing showed how to draw a line to separate disciplines and, in so doing, afforded a space for comprehension of the division. The line between what had been practiced until then and what needed to be done from then on was put on display for readers to see. His *hihyō*, in that sense, was directed not merely at the undivided form of knowledge, but also at existing forms of critical reading that could not assist in understanding the dividing line of knowledge. Among his contemporaries, no one performed critical reading like this doctor-writer; his move was extraordinary and exceptionally innovative within late nineteenth-century discourses on literature.

Critical Invention, Creative Intervention

About two decades prior to Ōgai's confrontation with Iwamoto, Nishi, in fact a distant relative of Ōgai, interpreted the encyclopedic system of knowledge as "*hyakugaku renkan*, the circular relations of one hundred learnings" (see chapter 1).[67] As contemporary intellectual Yamamoto Takamitsu notes, Nishi made an effort to grasp a "[systemic] whole," not "parts," of knowledge as established and practiced in foreign lands.[68] Nishi did not entirely negate the categorization and individuation of intellectual labor, as he clearly elaborated on disciplinary segments and each of their significance, but as his neologism *hyakugaku renkan* indicates, Nishi's focus was ultimately on delineating relations among parts of a system of knowledge, which he comprehended as linked in a circle. But when Ōgai's generation came of age during the 1880s, most young intellectuals were preoccupied with a radically different conception. For them, the circular interrelation of learnings as conceived by Nishi was superseded by their divisibility.

The "Literature and Nature" debate was fought when the realm of knowledge had moved irrevocably toward further compartmentalization, with each section mutually independent. Throughout the confrontation, Ōgai one-sidedly distorted Iwamoto's "nature" and foreclosed a possibility of dialogue. As contradictory as it may sound, what appears to be Ōgai's intellectual inflexibility—his persistent misreading of Iwamoto— also marked his intellectual creativity. By inventing a stylistic means to engage with the topic at hand, his *hihyō* uniquely intervened in the urge for dividing. His writing divided what had been conceived as indivisible, or what had not even been examined in relation to divisibility, in a timely, innovative manner and, in so doing, engendered hybrid effects. In chapter 2, we saw Ōnishi Hajime, who says nothing about how his lofty *hihyō*—at once critical and creative—operates in actuality. I suggest that Ōgai's rhetorical move in the "Literature and Nature" debate was one incarnation of such *hihyō*, conjured into being out of the very amorphousness of the critical reading practice.

I have discussed in this chapter that in the proceedings of this debate, we can observe the invention of a new style of writerly expression as *hihyō*. If we approach the debate as merely a clash between the concept of "nature" originated in the West and that of *"shizen"* fostered in Japan, which is to say, as a conflict between modernist Ōgai and outmoded Iwamoto, we end up limiting our scope of understanding; we also risk diminishing a historical moment pregnant with *hihyō*'s various potentials. Consider, instead, Ōgai's acrobatic moves as the traces of his struggle to address the epistemological shift in the conventions of knowledge, ones that performatively foregrounded the topic at hand. Ōgai made those moves as *hihyō*, a new mode of critical reading, in the way that no others had expected. When we are in search of different ways of reading and being critical in our times, Ōgai's practice, his creative failure in reading his opponent, affords a useful point of reference for us to reflect on ours. The next chapter takes up another debate on literature, one that illuminates the limitations and possibilities of critical reading in relation to fictional prose.

CHAPTER 4

Knowing the Dancer from the Dance
The "Dancing Girl" Debate

> Labour is blossoming or dancing where
> The body is not bruised to pleasure soul,
> Nor beauty born out of its own despair,
> Nor blear-eyed wisdom out of midnight oil.
> O chestnut tree, great rooted blossomer,
> Are you the leaf, the blossom or the bole?
> O body swayed to music, O brightening glance,
> How can we know the dancer from the dance?
>
> —W. B. Yeats

Would it be possible to separate the dancer from the dance?[1] I will reformulate Yeats's question and ask if it would be possible to know when, and where, the dance begins and ends. Taking this question as my point of departure, I examine one manifestation of the failure of *hihyō*, that is, its inability to identify when and where it begins and ends.[2]

The focus of my investigation is a dispute prompted by Mori Ōgai's 1890 story, "Maihime," hereafter "The Dancing Girl." In this well-known story, Ōta Toyotarō, a young Japanese elite, is sent to Germany on a governmental mission to study law, and while there becomes romantically involved with a young, beautiful, but impoverished German dancer, Elise. Elise eventually becomes pregnant, and yet, upon the intervention of his friend Aizawa Kenkichi, Ōta leaves her to go back to Japan and take a job as a bureaucrat. Soon after the publication of "The Dancing Girl," then-leading intellectual Ishibashi Ningetsu criticized Ōgai's work, pointing out several inconsistencies in the story. Ningetsu's *hihyō* invited a strong response from Ōgai. As the critic reacted to the author in turn, their exchanges developed into a debate, taking place primarily in the media space created for the practice of *hihyō*. Oddly, the exchanges of *hihyō* between Ningetsu and Ōgai maintained a façade of fiction—both writers assumed the personae of fictional characters from their own writings—and furthermore, the debate ended up providing alternative endings to "The Dancing Girl." When contemporaneous discourses about critical reading unanimously insisted upon the necessity of objective distance between *hihyō* and its object, including fiction itself, the "Dancing Girl" debate shows another moment of *hihyō*'s failure: Here *hihyō* can no longer claim authority over fiction because the division between the two is disturbed. Contrary to the expectation of the dividing line, we cannot be sure where "The Dancing Girl" ends and its *hihyō* begins.

Using this dispute as a case study, I will illuminate how the division was promoted, and how it failed to be observed, in the actual practice of *hihyō*. In examining implications of *hihyō*'s failure here, I revisit the notion of dividing intellectual labor, of distinguishing critical language from other manifestations of language (see chapter 2). While the "Dancing Girl" debate failed to maintain the proposed distance between critical language and literary production, the collapse of the categorical distinction also brings to light the arbitrariness of classifying what language is appropriate for critical reading practice. As such, this debate opens the possibility of less confined, perhaps more creative ways to express reading experiences in writing.

"The Dancing Girl" first appeared on January 3, 1890, in the prestigious intellectual journal *Kokumin no tomo*.[3] Since its publication, scholarly work on the story has been extensive; indeed, "The Dancing Girl" is among the most studied literary works written during the Meiji period (1868–1912). Until the 1980s, there were two major trends in scholarship: an "I-novelistic" approach that considered "The Dancing Girl" to be Ōgai's autobiographical confession, and another that situated the work as an example of the emergence of modern subjectivity (*kindai jiga*) in Japanese narratives. In the 1980s and 1990s, several scholars undertook different analytical approaches such as semiotics, as with Komori Yōichi's narratological reading and Masao Miyoshi's analysis of the novelistic form of the work.[4] More recent studies by Christopher Hill and Tomiko Yoda have closely examined the story's mode of narration in relation to the rise of a modern, national subject.[5]

By contrast, Ningetsu's *hihyō* and the debate that ensued did not attract much scholarly attention until the 1950s. Following a study by Usui Yoshimi that historicized literary debates during and since the Meiji period, scholars such as Hasegawa Izumi, Sasabuchi Tomoichi, and Kobori Keiichirō examined the "Dancing Girl" debate for its historical significance—or rather, for its unimportance and unproductivity.[6]

Their studies primarily emphasized how Ōgai skillfully and cunningly defeated his opponent.[7] In a more recent study, Saitō Mareshi intervened in this Ōgai-centric scholarly narrative, elucidating the broader sociohistorical implications of the debate by situating the discourses surrounding "The Dancing Girl" within the larger context of the Sinographic sphere.[8]

The focus of this chapter is on the failed relationship between *hihyō* and fiction, "failed" in the sense that Ōgai's creative work and the subsequent exchange of *hihyō* became inseparable. I want to think about this failure in light of classical sociological studies of field formation, which suggest that fields come into existence by being placed in networks of multiple concurrent forces, such as critics, publishers, educators, awards, and so on.[9] Works of literature need to be recognized as such by being evaluated, and the act of evaluation simultaneously sustains and valorizes itself by purposefully engaging with works of literature. The examination of the debate illuminates contemporaneous reception of "The Dancing Girl," which undoubtedly contributed to the configuration of the field of literature at that time, and thus helps to reveal the intricate process of field formation. By reading the story and the debate side by side, we can trace how the two were entangled and informed one another. In the sense that literary production and critical reading valorize each other and hence are mutually dependent, I share the sociological perspective on the discussions surrounding "The Dancing Girl."

At the same time, reading "The Dancing Girl" and the "Dancing Girl" debate in relation to one another complicates the idea of field formation because it poses a question about the divisibility of the literary work from the critical reading, and by extension, of writers from critics. To say that literature is constructed as a field through criticism (and other forces) risks presuming the ultimate divisibility of these constituents. The case of the "Dancing Girl" debate presses us to rethink the process of a field's emergence and calls the putative divisibility into question. If the alleged distance between literature and critical reading ceased to hold, and if the debate continued to unfold as an extension of the story, as I will demonstrate, the model of field formation that presumes the divisibility of literary production and critical reading needs to be reconfigured. "How can we know the dancer from the dance?": Yeats's question, with which Paul de Man famously grappled, is still pressing.[10] If we cannot fully distinguish the language of critical reading from that of literary work, as shown by de Man's constitutive confusion of the literal and the rhetorical, then we cannot know for sure that critical reading is a separate, independent force that helps establish literature from the outside. The case of "The Dancing Girl" and the debate surrounding it suggests a fluid relationship formed by critical and creative language. In this chapter I intend to stay with such fluidity, in hopes of envisioning unpredictable, freer ways of composing critical language.

Great Story, But . . .

"The Dancing Girl" received immediate recognition from contemporary readers, in part because of the wide circulation of *Kokumin no tomo*—the journal in which the story was published—and also because of Ōgai's reputation as an up-and-coming introducer of European writing traditions. A variety of commentaries appeared soon after the publication, revealing the multifaceted ways in which contemporary readers interpreted "The Dancing Girl."[11]

Just a month after the story appeared, Ningetsu published a two-page essay evaluating the piece in the same journal.[12] While Ōgai did not respond to most of the contemporaries' comments, Ningetsu's *hihyō* triggered an intense reaction. In his *hihyō*, Ningetsu first acknowledged that "The Dancing Girl" was the "masterpiece among all the works" that had appeared in that issue of the journal. Having said so, he immediately changed course and listed five problems he detected in the story, ranging from structural to trivial, beginning as follows:

> [1] The plot of "The Dancing Girl" is about circumstances in life where romance and fame become incompatible. The work sets up an individual who is timid, cowardly, while merciful, uncourageous, and lacking an independent mind, and it makes this character confront such circumstances. In so doing, the work reveals the relationship between his standing and the circumstances he finds himself in. . . . I cannot help thinking that, in Ōta Toyotarō's act, that is, in the part about his abandoning Elise and returning to Japan, the relationship between the character's personality, circumstances, and actions becomes incoherent. . . . I believe that he [Ōta] needs to be someone who would abandon fame and choose romance. . . . The author is aware of the difference between the realm of poetry and that of human affairs, and yet he ultimately forgot about this difference in his actual creative practice.[13]

In addition, Ningetsu identified four other issues: 2. the work's failure to depict the protagonist as a consistent character; 3. the overly detailed description of the protagonist's biographical information; 4. an inappropriate title; and 5. the improper mixture of a German proverb and Japanese language.

Ningetsu spends most of his essay elaborating on the first point, that is, why protagonist Ōta takes a job in Japan and leaves his young, beautiful German lover Elise, who is pregnant with his child.[14] While Ningetsu's point here is often interpreted as an indication of his morally driven romanticism, in fact his objection has little to do with either ethical treatment of women or romanticization of love.[15] Rather, Ningetsu takes issue with what appears to be the discrepancy between Ōta's personality as described earlier in the story and the action he takes toward the end: Ōta, "who is timid, cowardly, while merciful, uncourageous, and lacking an independent mind," needs to "abandon fame and choose romance." According to Ningetsu, such incoherence prevents "The Dancing Girl" from reaching "the realm of poetry," which Ningetsu elsewhere defines as a fundamental source of beauty.[16]

After two months of silence, Ōgai offered his official response to Ningetsu on April 25 in "Kidori Hannojō ni atauru sho" (Letter to Kidori Hannojō).[17] The debate quickly progressed when Ningetsu replied on April 27 with "Maihime saihyō" (Second evaluation of "The Dancing Girl").[18] Despite the appearance of a heated exchange, however, the debate was disjointed because of the strange ways in which Ōgai structured his refutations. Instead of answering Ningetsu's points in the presented order, Ōgai rearranged them. If we follow the numbering of Ningetsu's five points mentioned earlier, the reorganized order proceeds 4, 3, 2, 1, 5. As such, the title of the story is recast as the first point of contention, although Ningetsu had spent little time on this issue. Irrespective of how seriously Ōgai took this question about the title, he made it his point of departure. Clearly the debaters did not agree on priorities, at least at the level of presentation. When Ningetsu responded to Ōgai, however, he accepted the rearranged order and began with whether "The Dancing Girl" was a proper title.[19]

In addition, Ōgai did not treat with equal gravity Ningetsu's primary concern regarding the personality-action incoherence of Ōta. Ōgai remarks:

> If choosing a person with such a personality as poetic material was the same as disregarding the difference between the realm of poetry and that of human affairs, Shakespeare, who created "Hamlet," would be counted as someone who did not understand the

difference between the realm of poetry and that of human affairs. Let alone Goethe who created "Werther.". . . . Why couldn't two minds coexist: one mind that respects virginity and the other that leaves a woman with irremediable mental illness after asking her mother to take care of her and providing living expenses?[20]

Ōgai's reordering of Ningetsu's five problems, together with his flat rejection of what Ningetsu had called incoherence, resulted in a disjointed exchange. The subsequent interaction focused exclusively on the story's title, leaving Ningetsu's primary concern unattended.

Ningetsu's April 27 response was incomplete and indicated that a second part would follow.[21] But Ōgai did not wait, publishing a new piece of *hihyō* on April 28 with more questions: "Futatabi, Kidori Hannojō ni atauru sho" (Second letter to Kidori Hannojō).[22] Published so soon after Ningetsu's response, Ōgai's new piece created the appearance that he was driving Ningetsu into a corner. Indeed, it seems likely that Ōgai's aggressive responses kept Ningetsu from prevailing in the end. Eventually Ningetsu withdrew from the battle after his "Maihime sanhyō" (Third evaluation of "The Dancing Girl"), ending the debate abruptly and without any clear conclusion.[23] What remained was an impression that Ōgai's rigor and speed had overwhelmed his opponent. And yet, as noted previously, Ningetsu's most urgent question was pushed aside: whether "The Dancing Girl" achieved "the realm of poetry" as a representative work of literature was never actually discussed.

The Consensus on the Dividing Line

Before delving further into the implications of the "Dancing Girl" debate, I want to revisit the discursive trend of late nineteenth-century Japan, that is, the importance attached to the division of intellectual labor. As discussed previously, among many forms of labor for those equipped with high literacy was a critical reading practice. This practice, in being formulated as an independent one, needed to be exercised differently from other intellectual activities that dealt with language.

The divisibility of critical language from literary language was commonly claimed and sometimes actively promoted in this period. The two main actors in the debate, Ōgai and Ningetsu, themselves advocated the importance of *hihyō* in Japan, especially *hihyō* as a precursor to the cultivation of Japan's own literature. Regardless of what they ended up enacting through their interactions in the debate, the ways in which they conceptualized the relationship between critical reading practice and literary production reveal the primacy they placed upon *hihyō*. As discussed in chapter 2, the exceptionalism of *hihyō* was strongly articulated in the mission statement of Ōgai's journal *Bungaku hyōron: Shigarami zōshi* (Evaluative discussions of literature: The weir), which asserted that nothing other than *hihyō* could help Japan establish and advance its own literature.[24] Upon receiving news of this new journal, Ningetsu expressed his appreciation for Ōgai's endeavors:

> When I look at our literary world now, it is reaching the extreme of confusion and turbidity. Nonetheless, we are lacking ways to bring this up to a level of fairness and clarity. It is at this point that I feel the necessity of *hihyō* most keenly. In this age, I encountered the birth of *Bungaku hyōron: Shigarami zōshi*. I am not a big drinker, but I cannot help but empty my glass to celebrate it.... Indeed, *Shigarami zōshi* began discussions at the very right moment.[25]

Although they would engage in battle just a few months later, Ningetsu and Ōgai agreed with one another on the urgent necessity of *hihyō* if literature were to flourish in contemporary Japan. Positing *hihyō* as a driving force for the literature yet to come, both considered practicing *hihyō* as an activity separate from the production of literature. The conception of the relationship between *hihyō* and literature was thus premised on the divisibility of the two—a premise of divisibility entertained by no means unique to Ningetsu and Ōgai. As I showed in part 1 of this book, contemporary intellectuals were enthusiastic about the stratification of intellectual labor; it was posited as a necessity for the efficient progression of the nation into a full civilization. It was in this climate that "The Dancing Girl" appeared in *Kokumin no tomo* as a literary work, prompting the heated exchange of *hihyō*. How, then, did such *hihyō* come to disregard that stratification and become indistinguishable from what it evaluated?

Fiction Becoming *Hihyō*, *Hihyō* Becoming Fiction

Ōgai's responses and rhetorical acrobatics in the debate generated an appearance of him forestalling further objections from Ningetsu. While scholarship on the debate is scarce, existing studies often examine the material solely to underscore Ōgai's unreasonable belligerence. Against such an interpretation, I read the exchange between Ōgai and Ningetsu as a manifestation of critical reading, one that failed to execute what it was expected to do, but was still full of generative energy. Their disjointed correspondence, self-consciously practiced as *hihyō*, turned into a forum through which *hihyō*'s alleged independence from what it evaluates—here pointing to literary work—faltered. I contend that out of the fusion of *hihyō* with its object arises possibilities of conceiving varied forms of critical language.

While my discussion has thus far presented the debate over "The Dancing Girl" as the battle between Ōgai and Ningetsu, I have already noted that, strictly speaking, this formulation is not accurate; both writers disguised themselves by assuming fictional names and personae for the confrontation. Ningetsu's first piece of *hihyō* was issued under the name of Kidori Hannojō, a character in his novel *Tsuyuko hime* (Lady Tsuyuko).[26] In the novel, Kidori is a wealthy young man who is imprudent and insensitive; although in love with the heroine, he cannot take a hint of rejection and is held up to public ridicule from the beginning to the end. Condemned by this comic character, Ōgai responded under the name of a fictional character of his own: Aizawa, who in "The Dancing Girl" defends his friend, the protagonist Ōta. Throughout the debate, both discussants remained "in character." The debate was fought, in other words, on two levels at once: Ningetsu versus Ōgai and Kidori versus Aizawa.

To be clear, there is nothing unusual in writers using pen names, a common practice in many literary fields to this day, including during the Meiji period. Both Ōgai and Ningetsu used multiple names over the course of their writing careers, and indeed the names for which they are best known today, "Mori Ōgai" and "Ishibashi Ningetsu," were not their legal names.[27] Neither of them explained why they assumed fictional personae for the debate—they may have begun so merely on a whim. Nevertheless, writing incognito in this debate yielded remarkable effects unlike those usual in the employment of pseudonyms. That their identities were obvious to readers, and why they disguised themselves are not at issue here.[28] The point is that, regardless of whether the debaters were conscious of what they were enacting, they introduced Kidori and Aizawa into the space of *hihyō*, thereby causing the exchange of *hihyō* between Ningetsu and Ōgai to trespass in the world constructed of fiction. The confusion of *hihyō* and what it criticized, a conflation of critical assessment and fictional production, ensued. The words and deeds of these fictional characters in the end conjured up room that cannot be accounted for as either *hihyō* or literature.

I take seriously the fact that Ningetsu's initial essay was issued under the name of Kidori Hannojō, because Kidori's presence poses a threat to the authority of what is said within Ningetsu's *hihyō* from the onset. In *Tsuyuko hime*, Kidori plays the role of an oblivious fool who has no clue what is happening around him and his love interest. Having *hihyō* issued under the name of such a comically inept figure risks turning the whole discussion into a farce. Imagine a clown, looking all serious, writing *hihyō*, and intruding into a space where he does not belong; the sheer appearance of this clown may render null and void all that takes place in the space. Seemingly aware of the threat, after contradicting Kidori/Ningetsu's evaluation of "The Dancing Girl" at length, Aizawa/Ōgai asserts that it is ultimately pointless to explain emotions to clumsy Kidori, who clearly did not understand them in the world of *Tsuyuko hime*.[29] Yet the degree to which Kidori in *Tsuyuko hime* is mocked is such that Kidori's name alone puts Ōgai in a double bind. The author of "The Dancing Girl" cannot dismiss Ningetsu because his questions could undermine the work's reputation. At the same time, the author cannot respond to Kidori in a serious tone because the latter is a comical fool. By presenting a piece of *hihyō* with his name on it, the mocked Kidori gazes derisively back at what lies beyond the story world within which he is confined. Regardless of what Ōgai does, the possibility remains that the mockery does not stay with Kidori alone but extends toward Ōgai. While Ōgai's intention in responding as Aizawa Kenkichi remains inaccessible to us, this move helped to break the double bind: As Aizawa, Ōgai could engage with Kidori/Ningetsu without fully exposing himself.

What is more important about the introduction of Aizawa into the debate is that this character, who plays a crucial part in the narrative of Ōta, became a hinge between "The Dancing Girl" and what lies beyond the story world, specifically, that of *hihyō* in reality. With the participation of Aizawa, the correspondence between Kidori/Ningetsu and Aizawa/Ōgai unfolded *as if* it had been an extension of the story of "The Dancing Girl." Recast as the first-person respondent, Aizawa began to assert himself without being narrativized by Ōta, *as if* he had departed the world enclosed in "The Dancing Girl." It is this *as if* that needs further consideration.

In the beginning of his first response to Kidori/Ningetsu, Ōgai assumes Aizawa's persona and writes:

> I'm not somebody who is literate in poetic writings. Because of that, when I read my friend Ōta Toyotarō's account that he wrote on the ship, I was simply moved by it and didn't think about

whether or not I should pass his writing forward for possible publication. Recently I heard that someone called Ōgai titled Toyotarō's account "The Dancing Girl" and published it in *Kokumin no tomo*.[30]

Note that Aizawa in this passage distances himself from Ōgai, stressing that Ōgai is the one who made Ōta's writing public, while Aizawa himself was a mere observer. The portrayal of Aizawa in "The Dancing Girl" strongly works in favor of Ōgai in the debate. While Ōta is described as someone unable to exercise his agency at any decisive moment in the story, Aizawa, in Ōta's recollection, serves as the ultimate decision maker on Ōta's behalf. Aizawa dares to play the role of the villain in order to save his friend from adverse circumstances; he secures a job as a foreign correspondent for Ōta in Berlin, escorts Ōta to Count Amakata, arranges Ōta's homecoming, and helps Ōta restore his public reputation as a bureaucrat in the Meiji government. Most memorably, Aizawa is the one who tells Elise about Ōta's departure from Germany, while Ōta avoids confronting her by making himself sick and falling unconscious. Aizawa is thus painted as Ōta's protective friend throughout the world of "The Dancing Girl." The mobilization of Aizawa in the debate thus creates the appearance of the long-time friend coming once again to Ōta's defense.

As already noted, Aizawa/Ōgai's initial response, "The Letter to Kidori Hannojō," is written in a disorderly manner, reorganizing and even dismissing the questions that Kidori/Ningetsu raised. Yet its flaws become powerful, specifically because Aizawa is portrayed as beholden to Ōta in the story world. Consider the conclusion of "The Dancing Girl": Despite all his pragmatic support, Aizawa is blamed by Ōta for "spiritually killing Elise."[31] The story famously ends with Ōta's ambivalent remark: "A great friend like Aizawa Kenkichi cannot be easily obtained in this world, and yet there still remains even today a part of my mind that bears a grudge against him."[32] In the voice of Aizawa, who is held accountable for the tragedy that marks the end of Ōta's recollection, the letter to Kidori carries considerable weight. Although directed to Kidori, Aizawa's words also serve as his belated response to, if not expression of responsibility for, Ōta's resentment.

Furthermore, the casting of Aizawa as respondent to Kidori/Ningetsu camouflages potential weaknesses in Ōgai, the actual debater. If the letter were regarded as coming from the writer Ōgai, his behavior might have worked against him to undermine the clarity and conviction of his arguments. However, when presented as from Aizawa, the unreasonable moves conversely work in his favor. That is to say, the very abruptness of the letter functions as proof of Aizawa's desperate attempt to defend Ōta and justify his actions. Aizawa's signature thus helps to stage a scenario in which Aizawa is so desperate that he even sacrifices the coherence of his account. With Aizawa's name on it, the crux shifts from the validity of the writer Ōgai's rebuttal to the sincerity of Aizawa's friendship. As such, the appearance of Aizawa directly speaking to Kidori lessens the chance of Ōgai's being called out for his outlandish rhetorical moves.

When Aizawa and Kidori began to respond to each other's discourse and exchange *hihyō*, the border that separated the fictional realm of "The Dancing Girl" from the external world also began to topple. The boundaries became further disturbed because of the venues in which their correspondence appeared. Whereas "The Dancing Girl" was included in the literary writing section of *Kokumin no tomo*, Kidori/Ningetsu's initial *hihyō* came out in the *hihyō* section of the same journal. Similarly, Aizawa/Ōgai's first letter to Kidori/Ningetsu was published in *Shigarami zōshi*, whose space, according to founder Ōgai, was dedicated to *bungaku hyōron*, the "evaluative discussions of literature." Reading the dispute thus requires constant back-and-forth movements between form and content. In investigating the debate, we may look at the physical space in which the exchange took place. The space in print media that features *hihyō*, a space to nurture literary production from a distance, appears to confirm *hihyō*'s independence from what it evaluates. Still, the appearance of personal letters to and from fictional characters problematizes this alleged distance that *hihyō* must maintain from its object. The actual contents of *hihyō* extend to and trespass on the world constructed in "The Dancing Girl," further reinforcing the discrepancy between form and content. Indeed, though removed from the frontline, Ōgai and Ningetsu as actual *hihyō* practitioners are present inseparably from Aizawa and Kidori throughout.

While these accounts appear to be *hihyō* written by real-life individuals they belong at the same time in the fictional world, redirecting readers back to "The Dancing Girl." As if to reveal the arbitrariness of dividing critical language and literary language, the pieces of *hihyō* do not remain independent of what they criticize; they are no longer contained in a distant, privileged space. As noted previously, both Ōgai's launching of *Shigarami zōshi* and Ningetsu's prolific writings on other writers' works exemplify their shared interest in putting *hihyō* on a stable basis as a precursor to national literature. Nevertheless, their practices of *hihyō* contradict their claims about *hihyō*'s detachment from its object, encroaching upon *hihyō*'s exceptionalism. By introducing fictional characters as contributors in a space reserved for *hihyō*, the exchange ended up revealing the impossibility of drawing a clear dividing line between *hihyō* and literature, and critical language and creative work.

Fiction, Reality, Luck

As the mutual infiltration of critical language and fictional production proceeded, the "Dancing Girl" debate invited another threat to the space of *hihyō*. When one of the debaters introduced the rhetoric of "luck" into the discussion, the debate began to jeopardize the certitude of the real world in which it was taking place. If the general assumption is that fiction confirms the nonfictional reality that encapsulates fiction, the "Dancing Girl" debate gives rise to a moment at which reality, which fiction is supposed to assure, becomes eroded by fiction. The primacy of reality over fiction is overturned in that reality no longer simply acts upon fiction because it begins to be acted upon by fiction. What we consider the world of the real to which *hihyō* belongs, as a result, no longer appears to be an absolute, turning into a variant of fiction.

The troubled relationship between fiction and reality is foregrounded when Aizawa/Ōgai strangely remarks, in response to Kidori/Ningetu's first point, that Ōta's respect for virginity and his return to Japan are not mutually exclusive. In order to explain this further, Aizawa/Ōgai offers hypothetical scenarios for what might have happened if the story had not developed as it originally did:

> You might argue that Ōta had abandoned Elise before she went mad and that he had already given up his original intention of respecting virginity. But you can say so only because you do not understand the state of a weak person who is driven by certain circumstances. Ōta is weak. It is a fact that he accepted the count's offer. However, if he had never fallen ill to the degree that he could not remain conscious of what was happening around him after he went back home, and, if Elise had never gone mad and had a chance to converse with Ōta, Ōta might have relinquished the thought of returning to Japan. How would we ever know? If he had given up returning to Japan and lost face in relation to the count, perhaps he would have felt deeply ashamed and even killed

himself. How would we ever know? Even slaves would be capable of terminating their lives, and certainly Ōta would.[33]

In this passage, the inclusion of hypothetical endings is peculiar, given that "The Dancing Girl" was already written and published. Suggesting alternative endings after the fact would potentially undermine the reputation that the piece had begun to garner and also put the author in a disadvantageous position in the debate. To be sure, Aizawa's name lessens the negative effect of such hypotheticals. That is to say, since Aizawa was blamed for the devastating fate imposed upon Elise, his proposal of other endings demonstrates the degree to which he took Ōta's final remarks seriously. The what-ifs here further reinforce the appearance of Aizawa shielding Ōta from Kidori/Ningetsu's accusation, blurring any sense of the original architect of "The Dancing Girl" insinuating his own writerly inadequacy.

More important, however, the introduction of hypotheticals into the debate adds another layer of fictionality to this already fiction-full correspondence. The character Aizawa extracts hypothetical probabilities from the story world. As though departing from the confinement of "The Dancing Girl," to which he originally belongs, Aizawa mobilizes his imagination and entertains alternative fictional endings. What we encounter here is fiction offering interpretations of what would have been possible besides what actually happened. The moment that the Aizawa/Ōgai duo introduces the what-ifs, in other words, fiction begins to weave fiction.

Aizawa/Ōgai's account further complicates the relationship between fiction and reality by stripping reality of privilege. After mentioning the different ending scenarios, Aizawa/Ōgai remarks, "It depended purely on luck that things actually did not go in those directions."[34] The implication of "luck" here is that whether or not a hypothetical possibility develops into reality is not necessarily determined by logic. What concretizes as reality is accidental, and, therefore, there can be no a priori reason or necessity for reality to exist as such. According to this line of thinking, reality is necessarily a posteriori, preinhabited by multiple other possibilities that might or might not be realized.

Such a notion of "luck" works in favor of Aizawa/Ōgai when it enters the debate at hand. Regardless of whether or not such an effect is calculated, the thought that fiction and reality are mediated by luck serves as a powerful counterargument against Kidori/Ningetsu's primary concern about the personality-action incoherence. Kidori/Ningetsu objected "that, in Ōta Toyotarō's act, . . . in the part about his abandoning Elise and returning to Japan, the relationship between the character's personality, circumstances, and actions becomes incoherent."[35] But if what takes place depends on luck, the disconnect between Ōta's action, personality, and the situation suggest that reality is not dictated by logic but by luck. Contrary to the negative nature of Kidori/Ningetsu's comment, his objection to Ōta's behavior as unreasonable turns into a support for Aizawa/Ōgai's conception of the accidentally realized version of the story.

At the same time, "luck" undermines the certainty of reality; it encroaches not simply on the reality of the debate but also on the existential reality of Aizawa and, by extension, Ōgai. For Aizawa, the world of "The Dancing Girl" is not fiction: It is the reality in which he resides. He reassures readers that the reality he experiences is indeed the realized one. And yet positing "luck" as a crucial determinant of reality implies that Aizawa's reality is not the only conceivable one. Aizawa's remarks on hypothetical scenarios reflect, self-referentially, back onto his reality, revealing the contingency of his own existence, which we know is fictional. Aizawa's version of reality and his being in it belong to the constructed story world of "The Dancing Girl," which inevitably evokes the fact that they are fictionalized by author Ōgai. By the same token, the idea of existential contingency goes for the reality where Ōgai stands. If this theory of luck is to be believed, then the reality in which Ōgai exists must also be conceived as merely accidental, governed by chance. Reality as generally understood as something legitimate suddenly becomes uncertain, open to multiple other hypothetical probabilities. As a chain of fictions overlaps with a chain of realities, the border between fiction and reality cannot be sustained.[36]

The "Dancing Girl" debate foregrounds the impossibility of distinguishing critical language from creative expression, and the unsustainability of the division between reality and fiction—and this despite that Ōgai's and Ningetsu's insistence on the necessity of individuating *hihyō* from other forms of linguistic activities and intellectual labor. The failure to maintain *hihyō*'s independence is key, as I consider this failure to be a productive one. While defying the postulated boundaries of *hihyō* that they were painstakingly establishing themselves, the correspondence between Aizawa/Ōgai and Kidori/Ningetsu further calls into question the scope of *hihyō*, particularly *hihyō* as a constructive precursor to a new

Japan. In so doing, their *hihyō* helps us imagine the possibility of *hihyō* that is not bound by preset categories and broadens the horizons of *hihyō*.

Luck, Intervening

I now revisit the rhetoric of "luck" (*gyōkō*), the trickster of the debate, mobilized by Aizawa/Ōgai. In fact this rhetoric sets in motion more than just a canceling of the putative categorical divisions, due to the unfavorable overtones it carried in the intellectual discourses of late nineteenth-century Japan. When Japan believed it must rebuild itself, and that critical reading must function to lead the country in an orderly manner, the unpredictable effects of luck emerged only as obstacles to be suppressed. Its sudden appearance in the debate therefore gave rise to an especially uncomfortable discordance with the zeitgeist. That this luck was mobilized against a piece of *hihyō* that was published in *Kokumin no tomo* magnifies the discordance. This influential journal, in which both Ōgai's story and Ningetsu's initial *hihyō* appeared, was one of the major forums actively negating the idea of luck in favor of logical, causal development (of Japan) at the time. Indeed, this position had much to do with the ways in which this journal strategically carved out its niche and cultivated its readership: young, educated males.

Intellectual historian Kimura Naoe's 1998 study *Seinen no tanjō* (The birth of youth) details the processes through which *Kokumin no tomo* rhetorically fabricated different types of politicized—or, rather, depoliticized—youth, thereby having a profound impact not only on young people's daily practices but also on their thought formation.[37] According to Kimura, the journal painted the figure of "stalwart youth" (*sōshi*) as a bunch of "barbaric," "uncivilized," "visionless" activists associated with the overtly political, often violent, activism seen in the Freedom and People's Rights Movement; the journal, in so doing, rejected this activist figure as myopic, ineffective, and ultimately detrimental to the construction of a new Japan. Against the negated "stalwart youth" came the production of an alternative, and much preferable, "youth" (*seinen*). By distancing itself from the "stalwart youth," Kimura continues, *Kokumin no tomo* called forth a sophisticated "youth" who would not engage in political activism in the present but would rather take charge of building a new Japan in the future. Note the temporal aspect inscribed in the dichotomy between "stalwart youth" and "youth"; while the former is depicted as someone who aspires to immediate change and acts at the present time, the latter looks ahead and, from the point of the envisioned future, determines retroactively what is important now. In the youth's vision, a future is believed to be a linear, logical extension of the present.

The idea of how youth should behave now to support the arrival of a new Japan in the future is exemplified in Tokutomi Sohō's New Year's address of 1890, a set of opening remarks that appeared in the same issue as Ōgai's "The Dancing Girl." In the address, Sohō reminds his readers: "This year is the year that holds the first Imperial Diet. It is the year that combines the natural development of the past twenty-something years of the Meiji period and the human promises. We must surrender and submit all sorts of human affairs to this year."[38] Underlining the significance of that year, Sohō exhorts readers to prepare for the year's monumental event of the opening of the first Imperial Diet: "Now I entered the twenty-third year of the Meiji period with hope and fear.... If Heaven's Creator ever came down to our country, I wish he would make me pass through this eventful, difficult year of the twenty-third year in victory and peace."[39] Interestingly, while Sohō repeats the necessity of preparation, his rhetoric only revolves around mental states—"deep consideration" (*fukaku omonpakaru*), "determination" (*kakugo*), "aspiration" (*setsubō*), and "deliberation" (*jukukō*)—and ignores physical action.[40] In short, Sohō does not describe what exactly this preparation involves. Immediate, tangible forms of preparation remain unidentified, and for that reason, action is infinitely deferred into the future. The vagueness of Sohō's remarks, and particularly his avoidance of language evoking direct participation in politics, communicates a certain message: Readers are essential constituents of a new Japan yet to come, yet they are allowed to take part in the nation-building project only insofar as they are not involved in "stalwart youth"-esque political activism in the present moment. It makes sense that Ōgai's "The Dancing Girl" appeared in this venue as a piece of literary work catering to such a readership, to the "youth" willing to imagine a future participation in the "new Japan" that was supposed to await them, just like the protagonist Ōta.

Kimura offers a vital observation about the ways in which *Kokumin no tomo* produced these two figures in relation to each other. According to Kimura, around the late 1880s, the journal explicitly prioritized the law of causality as an essential attribute of a figure of youth.[41] In his aforementioned New Year's remarks, for example, Sohō exhorts: "An event necessarily becomes a result in relation to what came before it, and a cause in connection with what will arrive after it.... and that is why we must carefully take this year into consideration."[42] Under the presumption that youth's daily practices, intellectual but not overtly political ones, would necessarily lead to the building of a more civilized Japan in the future, *Kokumin no tomo* strongly favored logic, reason, knowability, and predictability, as well as a linear, continuous, and inevitable progression. It then rejected illogicality, unreason, unknowability, unpredictability, and chance disturbing linear, logical progress. Needless to say, the former list is associated with "youth," and the latter with "stalwart youth."

A key term used frequently to represent the latter category in *Kokumin no tomo*, according to Kimura, was none other than "luck":

> In order to describe such circumstances [of "stalwart youth"], the rhetoric of "luck" [*gyōkō*] was commonly used, with a contemptuous tone. The very fact that this rhetoric could only have a negative register demonstrates one gravely important characteristic of the "youth" discourses. What does it mean to have a mind for luck? It points to an egoistic thinking that practices must bring about remarkable results no matter what, even when there are no efforts to organize them effectively and constructively. It indicates the immediate linking of action with result, which was considered inherent in the very behavioral principles of "stalwart youth." . . . Seen from the perspective of "youth," "luck" must not occur, nor would it possibly take place. It goes against the law of "causality."[43]

This view of "luck" against "causality" clearly manifests in Sohō's representative work of the time, *Shin Nihon no seinen* (The youth of new Japan): "There is nobody who wishes for luck, as there is no such a thing as luck. . . . There is only the law of causality in a democratic society."[44] In order for Japan to make steady progress, "causality" needed to be prioritized, and "luck" eliminated. The belief in causality, as paired with aversion to luck, penetrated *Kokumin no tomo* and its surroundings in the late nineteenth century.

The conviction was clearly shared by Ningetsu, a major contributor to *Kokumin no tomo*. While confronting Aizawa/Ōgai in the "Dancing Girl" debate, Ningetsu concurrently serialized "Zaika ron" (Theory of causality) from April 1 to 3, 1890, in the daily paper *Kōko shinbun* (The public paper).[45] In this theory, Ningetsu repeats the significance of causality as follows:

> Causality is a motive (cause) that drives characters in tragic drama into the edge of misery. . . . causality means, namely, cause for effect, foreshadowing the end.[46]
>
> Characters would never fall into the edge of unhappiness and misery by chance if it were not for a motive (cause).[47]
>
> There are no events in the world that happen by chance. How could there be an effect without cause? . . . In sum, the novel without cause is not a novel.[48]

Ningetsu expresses his serious discomfort with the concept of "chance" (gūzen) and denies the possibility of "chance" developing into a determinant of any result. The law of causality in his theory governs every happening, not only inside but also outside literary production, and therefore there is no space for "chance" to interrupt the linearly predictable, logically acceptable flow of events, fictional or not.

The effect must be known in advance, and its relationship with the cause is necessarily explicit. "Chance" in Ningetsu's theory is thus placed in an antagonistic juxtaposition to causality, similar to how "luck" is rejected as an antithesis to causality in *Kokumin no tomo*. Irrespective of Ningetsu's self-awareness, "Zaika ron" demonstrates his conceptual affiliation with *Kokumin no tomo* by asserting that accident and coincidence need to be excluded from both reality and fiction. That the publication of Ningetsu's theory of causality coincided with the "Dancing Girl" debate revolving around *Kokumin no tomo* thus explains why Ningetsu problematized the inconsistency between Ōta's personality and his behavior (Ningetsu's first point). According to the law of causality, whatever Ōta does has to be logically explicable. It is not unrelated that the piece of *hihyō* in which Kidori/Ningetsu raised the question about the character's contradictory behavior appeared in Sohō's journal; indeed, because of its publication venue, Kidori/Ningetsu's discussion of what he saw as the story's divergence from logical development further underlined the primacy he attached to the law of causality. The character of Ōta, who in Ningetsu's understanding represents the lack of consistency and resists logical explanation, should have never surfaced in this opinion-leading journal.

Given the interplay among the rhetoric of luck, the law of causality, Ningetsu, and *Kokumin no tomo*, Kidori/Ningetsu's claim that Ōta should have chosen romance over career success emerges as ironic.

Recall that the very issue of *Kokumin no tomo* in which "The Dancing Girl" was published urged readers to develop greater political awareness in anticipation of the opening of the first Imperial Diet. If we borrow Kidori/Ningetsu's formulation of career versus romance, "The Dancing Girl," written by a young Japanese elite, in a sense highlighted the importance of "youth"-esque political awareness by ending with Ōta's ultimate siding with bureaucratic career over romance. Regardless of whether or not it is causally explainable, or of the sentiment it conjures, this ending alone is aligned with the journal's agenda of focusing readers' attention to politics; it also demonstrates a way to participate in the building of a new nation, not as a political stalwart, but as an educated youth. Yet in Kidori/Ningetsu's reading, Ōta's taking up a career path in the governmental arena raises a problem; the law of causality that permeated *Kokumin no tomo* and his own work entails that Ōta should put aside professional goals and, by implication, nation, and prioritize romance. This means that Kidori/Ningetsu's concern potentially conflicts with the ideological principles of both *Kokumin no tomo* and the youths who contribute to it, though inadvertently so. Kidori/Ningetsu's critical reading of "The Dancing Girl," in short, ends up imploding the time and space within which it is confined, precisely when Ningetsu follows his own theory supported by the zeitgeist. The rhetoric of "luck," thus, not only digresses from the dominant discursive force of the time but also brings into relief the disconcerting implications of Kidori/Ningetsu's *hihyō*. In so doing, "luck" hints that causality may not necessarily be a valid parameter for contemporary *hihyō* and, by implication, a vista for the nation in the making.

It is important to note that the notion of luck is mobilized by fictional character Aizawa (Ōgai in disguise). Recall the beginning of Aizawa/Ōgai's first rebuttal, in which Aizawa tells how he learned about Ōta's account published in *Kokumin no tomo*, insinuating that he is a reader of the journal.[49] Given that he is a promising young bureaucrat who, with his expertise in diplomacy, facilitates Japan's progression into a more civilized nation, his familiarity with the journal is reasonable. Yet what is extraordinary is that this fictional character, who reads *hihyō* in *Kokumin no tomo* and writes his own in return, introduces "luck" into the debate. Aizawa brings back "luck" as an essential component of its critical reading to explain why Ōta behaved as he did; Aizawa's gesture here serves as a critical evaluator not only of its immediate opponent Kidori/Ningetsu but also of *Kokumin no tomo* and, by extension, of the defining rationale of the time, at once. As if "luck" asserted its own promise, the fictional world of the story, hovering around its narrative and formal confinements, *accidentally* overflows into the outside, the space of *hihyō*, and offers a critical reading of what initially constituted itself. In this moment, fiction, the convention excluded from the vision of a new mode of critical reading, and luck, the idea suppressed in favor of the causality-based linear progression of events, are reinstated as *hihyō*. When *hihyō*'s independence no longer prevails, and all the logical, forward-moving constructions of and for it comes to a halt, its failure presents what critical reading can be, instead of what it must not be.

As the "Dancing Girl" debate proceeded, the language used for literary work and that for critical reading began to infiltrate each other. Unable to be grounded in either fiction or reality, the words were left to drift around. Out of this drifting state arose room for "luck." The logical unfolding of the debate, as well as the positive coming together of *hihyō*, was forced to trip over this "luck." This debate reveals the dynamic effect of "luck," introduced specifically by way of fiction, at work in the realm of *hihyō*: It divulges the arbitrariness of dividing the usage of language and, in so doing, foregrounds the possibility of conceptualizing critical reading practices not bound by rigid categories. It is easy to dismiss the Ōgai–Ningetsu interactions in the "Dancing Girl" debate as "unproductive," as we often do when we encounter what appears absurd. If we disregard their practice of *hihyō* simply because they did not reach a conclusion or because they made no sense, however, we risk limiting the range of what we can say and do in the practice of *hihyō*.[50] This is certainly not to suggest that we must begin writing fiction when we criticize our object of study. Rather, I consider the failure of *hihyō* in the "Dancing Girl" debate to be an open invitation to reimagine our own use of critical language. Let us dwell on *hihyō*'s failure in the "Dancing Girl" debate; it affords one example of how to practice critical reading without suppressing various possibilities for weaving critical language. Another case of such possibilities, such creative weavings of critical language manifested as *hihyō*, will be the focus of the next chapter.

CHAPTER 5

Against Interpretation
The Submerged-Ideal Debate

> In most modern instances, interpretation amounts to the philistine refusal to leave the work of art alone. Real art has the capacity to make us nervous. By reducing the work of art to its content and then interpreting *that*, one tames the work of art. Interpretation makes art manageable, conformable.
>
> —Susan Sontag

Susan Sontag's 1964 meditation was preceded by more than half a century, when in 1891 Japanese Shakespearean scholar Tsubouchi Shōyō confessed his powerlessness as a reader in front of *Macbeth* and revealed his ultimate incapacity to interpret the masterpiece.[1] Upon publishing his lecture notes on *Macbeth*, Shōyō stated that he would not offer an interpretation of the text, but would instead "explain the meaning of words and grammatical constructions just as they appear in the text."[2] The reasoning behind this decision, he says, was that due to its abysmal, all-encompassing nature, William Shakespeare's work would reject being reduced to a singular meaning that interpretation usually generates. Shōyō's attitude triggered a strong reaction from Mori Ōgai, who rejected the former's not offering interpretation as irresponsible. This chapter analyzes the interaction between Ōgai and Shōyō that ensued from their disagreement in reading methodologies in the early 1890s, the so-called submerged-ideal debate, and reflects on what their disjointed correspondence ultimately enacted.

To read for interpretation or not: The submerged-ideal debate stands out among other discourses revolving around *hihyō* and literature in late nineteenth-century Japan because it was one of the earliest instances in which the stakes of literary interpretation as a critical reading method were publicly contested. While the content of the exchange remained highly abstract, as the debaters primarily discussed reading methodology without providing many concrete examples and references, the debate helped to stage two different streams of *hihyō*: interpretation-driven, meaning-seeking *hihyō* on the one hand, and *a*-interpretative, descriptive *hihyō* on the other. With or without interpretation: The difference of the types of critical reading methodology is particularly relevant to us twenty-first-century scholars of literature, as we are becoming ever more aware of the bounds of our approaches to what we read. When our reading practices still tend to rely on "'depth' interpretation—the hapless and hopeless pursuit of an ultimate meaning," as Rita Felski puts out, the submerged-ideal debate presents itself as a refreshing opportunity through which to contemplate our own practices, what we do in the name of critical reading.[3]

The Ōgai–Shōyō exchange took an intriguing turn; as was the case with other debates featured in this book, this debate was out of joint, never unraveling the point of contention. When the discussion did not proceed in a problem-solving direction because of (again) Ōgai's misreading and manipulation of his opponent's discourse, Shōyō suddenly changed his style of writing from sober prose to a playful mode known as *gibun* (戯文): an allegorical, parodic, witty, exaggerated, and satirical style of writing that had been developed and exercised prolifically toward the late Edo period. Shōyō's move entailed the introduction of literary devices and writing conventions that were supposed to be suppressed as "outmoded" in Meiji Japan's *hihyō* practices. Moreover, due to its playful nature, Shōyō's *gibun* digressed from what *hihyō* needed to accomplish and betrayed expectations for the new and objective style of critical language. The unexpected resurgence of playful writing, the supposedly regressive, hence unfit writing conventions for *hihyō*, dislocated the tension of the dispute, foreclosed the possibility of Ōgai fighting back seriously, and brought Ōgai's pen to a halt. The debate soon came to an end without a palpable resolution on the pros and cons of interpretation in the practice of critical reading. As we have observed, establishing *hihyō* by separating it from other forms of specialized, linguistic activities was of great concern to late nineteenth-century Japanese intellectuals. Both Shōyō and Ōgai were aware of the pressing need to institute *hihyō*, its codes of conduct, and a distinct form of language for the practice at the time. Despite their contemporaneous claims about *hihyō*'s exceptionalism, the submerged-ideal debate, with its incorporation of the playful writing traditions in critical reading practice, foregrounded a moment at which *hihyō* could not maintain the appearance of seriousness. As such, this case marks yet another manifestation of *hihyō*'s failure, its inability to substantiate its independence as modern Japan's new critical language.

The submerged-ideal debate has typically been examined through the scope of "why" Ōgai took issue so excessively with Shōyō's method of *hihyō*, an a-interpretative reading presented as a brief disclaimer about his lecture notes, and "why" Shōyō had recourse to playful writing. Several scholars have sought to discover the answers by identifying differences between Shōyō and Ōgai: their upbringing, education, and/or inherited cultural assets.[4] While these findings afford valuable information, the "why" approach inevitably searches for a fixed point of reference or "meaning" in the debaters' biographies.[5] This scholarly search has often resulted in the depiction of Shōyō, who cleaved to writing traditions that had developed in Japan before the Meiji period, in direct opposition to Ōgai, who blindly invested in the intellectual genealogies from Europe, only to fortify the stark antagonism between them. While I too think about "why," necessarily so in my investigation into this debate, my goal is not to rearticulate the opposition between Shōyō and Ōgai, but to observe and embrace what flashed out of their disjointed exchange of *hihyō*.

I pay special attention to Shōyō's use of *gibun*. While the rationale behind Shōyō's turn to the *gibun* style is out of reach, the writer's mobilization of it as yet another form of critical language deserves serious scrutiny. The debaters' contemporaries and almost all the scholarship from the later period flatly discounted the resurgence of *gibun* in this debate either as mere anachronism or as Shōyō's passive attempt to dodge Ōgai's attack.[6] Against these scholarly tendencies, I intend to recast what happened during the submerged-ideal debate as a flashed moment in which *hihyō* reflected on itself, on the possibility of it developing a more fluid relationship vis-à-vis preceding styles of critical practice. Reading Shōyō's playful writings, I am reminded of Mikhail Bakhtin's discussion on carnivalistic laughter: Directed toward dominant forces, be they state or religious authorities, carnivalistic laughter throws given hierarchies and orders off balance, "deals with the very process of change, with *crisis* itself," and exercises "[e]normous creative, and therefore genre-shaping, power."[7] If we draw on this Bakhtinian formula, the playfulness of Shōyō's *gibun* emerges as an embodiment of such laughter, one that informed a "process of change," even a "*crisis* itself," with its "creative" power, in the rather forced production of critical reading practice in late nineteenth-century Japan. By disrupting the space of *hihyō* in a seemingly nonsensical, "outmoded" way, Shōyō's writings brought into being a felicitous, carnivalesque incarnation of the languages reserved for humor, parody, and satire. In so doing, his *gibun* disclosed, even ridiculed, the arbitrary, prescriptive nature of what Meiji intellectuals conceived for the practice of *hihyō*.

Furthermore, the allegorical narrative that Shōyō composed in the playful writing style ended up presenting a worldview in which the chances of interpretation, here understood as identification of a single locus of meaning in the text, were preempted. Accidentally or not, while failing to embody the exceptional status attributed to *hihyō*, Shōyō's *gibun* writings enacted a-interpretation, the very reading method that he initially promoted in reading Shakespeare. Sidestepping interpretation, his *gibun* proceeded with laughter, a laughter that even laughed itself off, and gave rise to an alternative perspective on *hihyō*. The movements of Shōyō's *gibun* thus push open the limits of *hihyō*'s language and thereby help to unbind us from what we think we know as critical reading practice. Tracking the intricate exchange between Shōyō and Ōgai, in particular what Shōyō's *gibun* sets in motion, this chapter demonstrates one potential path to unfastening the constraints of critical reading, and imagining a freer, livelier, yet still critical, expression of reading.

Ambiguous Rhetoric

The neologism "submerged-ideal" (*botsurisō*) was coined by Shōyō around 1890. The term is mystifying and catchy, but from the very start what it involved was ambiguous; it is the term's amorphousness that triggered the convoluted unfolding of the debate. I begin, therefore, by unpacking Shōyō's neologism, quoting him extensively to situate us in the ambiguity of his wording, the slipperiness of which presumably contributed to Ōgai's intense reaction. In the introductory note to his commentary on *Macbeth*, Shōyō states:

> There are two methods of textual commentary. The first is to explain the meaning of words and grammatical constructions just as they appear in the text, and this includes commenting on rhetorical strategies. The other form consists of exposing the writer's true intentions, or the ideals that can be seen in the work. At first, I thought I would mainly employ the second type of commentary, but then I reconsidered and decided to use the first type. Here is

the reason. The second form of commentary, that is to say, "interpretation," may be deeply moving and beneficial for the reader when it is carried out by someone highly insightful. Yet there is the danger that someone of lesser discernment may, for example, take a cat and carefully interpret it as a tiger, conveying a misconception to the unwary reader. This may happen because Shakespeare's works are extremely similar to nature. . . . I say that Shakespeare's works look extremely like nature, not because the events and characters that he describes are the same as the ones existing in reality, but because the ways in which his works can be interpreted in every possible way in the reader's mind are exactly like God's creation. . . . The divine creation thoroughly accepts myriads of interpretation of all and still has much room. . . . Shakespeare's masterpieces appear as though there were still much room after containing almost any kind of ideals, and this is where his works come to look like the true character of the divine creation.[8]

Shōyō repeats the importance of not imposing a single "ideal" onto masterpieces and not delimiting possibilities of reading because great works such as Shakespeare's can be received in any number of ways, depending on who is reading, when, and in what location. Therefore, Shōyō concludes, "there is absolutely no call for analyzing works of submerged-ideals by mobilizing ideals."[9]

Scanning Shōyō's passage and rhetoric, we notice that the submerged-ideal carries at least two aspects and oscillates between them. On the one hand, it is an attribute of certain works of literature, ones that accept unlimited possibilities of reading. At the same time, it is a methodology of engaging with great works, a readerly attitude that refuses to commit to and enforce a single perspective upon them. Because these usages are not clearly differentiated in Shōyō's account, the term requires a readerly labor of contextualization when it appears. Furthermore, the semantic versatility of the Chinese character *botsu* (没) also contributes to the ambiguity of the term. While the character etymologically denotes "submerging underwater," it also indicates "nonexistence" in the common usage. Shōyō rather casually began using his neologism without clarifying what the submerged-ideal meant for him when he launched the *Macbeth* annotation project. The absence of clear explanation likely served as a source of confusion among his contemporaries as to what the writer attempted to communicate by this term. Shōyō's statement incited various reactions as a result. Iwamoto Yoshiharu, for instance, understood the submerged-ideal as the complete absence of the ideal in a given piece of literature, and rejected what he considered to be the theory of the submerged-ideal.[10] Terayama Seisen, on the other hand, explained the submerged-ideal as a type of "realism" accomplished by "observation" and "experiments,"[11] even stretching the theory of the submerged-ideal to mean the "essential body of the universe."[12] As these reactions from contemporary intellectuals demonstrate, Shōyō's coinage was understood in varied ways for its initial amorphousness.

Shōyō began to reference ideas akin to the submerged-ideal before he set about annotating *Macbeth* in 1891.[13] In fact, many of Shōyō's writings from the late 1880s into the early 1890s emphasize the necessity of impersonal and impartial *hihyō* that would not lessen possibilities of reading. What he calls "inductive criticism" (*kinō hihyō*) is supposed to prioritize description over interpretation, which according to Shōyō is one promising way to practice impersonal and impartial *hihyō*.[14] *Hihyō* is required to attain such an attitude, especially when it confronts a masterwork that would swallow any readerly approaches as if it were a "lake that would never reach its bottom."[15] If any hermeneutic move would inevitably lead to drowning in the "bottomless lake," Shōyō explains, the only option left for the reader is to describe, from a distance, what appears on the surface of the water without diving in.[16] Shōyō's precursory discussions of how to read thus paved the way for his proposal of the submerged-ideal theory.

Clearly, the submerged-ideal did not emerge from a vacuum. Yet its appearance is scattered across several writings of Shōyō's, who never seemed to present it in a comprehensive fashion. In order for us to grasp the contours of the submerged-ideal, therefore, we must assemble various manifestations of similar ideas to reconstruct it. This means that unless the reader is well familiar with Shōyō's general semantics, only the ambiguity of his rhetoric prevails. This aspect worked in Ōgai's favor; he was able to attack Shōyō's submerged-ideal theory in the public space because of the term's lack of clarity. Ōgai's *hihyō*, however, proceeded in an unexpected direction because instead of asking for further explanation from the inventor of the term, Ōgai began to fabricate his own semantics independently—and furthermore did so only to negate what he reinvented as Shōyō's submerged-ideal, an idea that was never held by Shōyō. The debate was thus disorienting not only because it involved an ambiguous neologism but also because the discussion continued to unfold without ever reaching a consensus of what the key term meant.

The Battle of the Submerged-Ideal

Among the varied responses that Shōyō received from his contemporaries, Ōgai's negation of the submerged-ideal theory was the fiercest one. Ōgai began by setting up a disguised figure called "Uyū-sensei," later identified as nineteenth-century German philosopher Eduard von Hartmann, and presented a rebuttal of Shōyō as though relaying Uyū-sensei's message.[17] Uyū-sensei became a "logician," Ōgai's writing explains, because he was "tired of describing facts," "wished to make every being and every mind return to a monistic state," and decided to seek the "reason for beauty" instead of "describing beauty."[18] From the monist standpoint, Ōgai as Uyū-sensei states:

> The world is not only filled with the real (*Reale*) but also full of the idea (*Ideen*). Shōyō sees the realm of submerged reason (*Wille*), not that of reason (*Vernunft*). He observes the sphere of consciousness (*Bewusstsein*), not that of unconsciousness. His thought never reaches the ways in which consciousness comes into existence and slightly diverges into subject and object. . . . The wings of peacocks' stem from the same nutrients. And yet each feather varies in color. The different colors come together and make patterns as a whole. Would that be because there is an innate ideal?[19]

Immediately noticeable is Ōgai's distinct choices of language, the way the passage is studded with German words, which are semantically translated in Chinese characters and accompanied by phonetic katakana transcriptions. Moreover, while Ōgai mobilizes those unfamiliar words to interrogate Shōyō's theory, there is a disconnect between what Ōgai presents here and what Shōyō himself says about the submerged-ideal; the former does not quite latch onto the latter. As far as the prefatory note to *Macbeth*'s annotation project is concerned, Shōyō never turns to such words as "reason" and "consciousness" to elaborate the submerged-ideal, nor does he thematize the "real" or the absence of the "ideal." Instead of following Shōyō's semantics, Ōgai as Uyū-sensei mobilizes quasi-Shōyō rhetoric to rewrite the submerged-ideal theory, only to contradict the reinvented version. In short, Ōgai/Uyū-sensei engages with ideas that do not belong to Shōyō, condemning them as invalid.

Ōgai's rhetorical acrobatics against Shōyō have a history. As early as 1889, Ōgai had already began to associate Shōyō's *Shōsetsu shinzui* (The essence of the novel, 1885–86) with "Émile Zola's naturalism" so as to reject "physiological observation" as the "end of the novel," even though *Shōsetsu shinzui*'s immediate concerns did not revolve around objective realism per se.[20] As Ōgai's forced reading of Shōyō continued into the succeeding years, Shōyō began to refer to Ōgai in his own writings, though in a jocular fashion. In one essay, for instance, Shōyō caricatures Ōgai as a "prestigious medical doctor" who could only drop "unintelligible German words" without offering a proper diagnosis.[21]

Shōyō had initially attempted to disperse the tension between the two and avoid direct confrontation. Nevertheless, Ōgai persistently redirected attention to his problems with Shōyō's writings. When Shōyō made a distinction between three different schools of the novel—the specific school (*koyū-ha*, also referred to as *shuji-ha* or *monogatari-ha*, which prioritizes plots and events); the eclectic school (*secchū-ha*, also described as *seijō-ha* or *ninjō-ha*, which highlights human emotions and characters); and the human school (*ningen-ha*, which elucidates connections between humans and events)—while emphasizing that no hierarchy obtained among them,[22] Ōgai countered:

> The specific, the eclectic, and the human, all of these notions exist in Hartmann's aesthetic theory. No need to quote from him extensively here; it will suffice to translate these schools using Hartmann's philosophical terms. Shōyō's "specific" is Hartmann's "generic idea" (*ruisō* or *Gattungsidee*), Shōyō's "eclectic" is Hartmann's "individual idea" (*kosō* or *Individualidee*), and Shōyō's "human" is Hartmann's "microcosmism" (*shōtenchisō* or *Mikrokosmismus*). . . . Shōyō and Hartmann make me weep at where they bifurcate.
>
> Hartmann's distinction between his three categories as three classes of beauty is rooted in his basic aesthetic philosophy. He attempted to reject the aesthetics of abstract idealism and to promote an aesthetics of concrete idealism. In his eyes, the road from a kind of unconscious formal beauty, pleasing only to the senses, to that secret and sublime realm of art, which is beyond the border of the microcosm, is the road from the abstract to the concrete. The generic idea and the individual idea (and the microcosmism) are merely mileposts on the way to that sublime capital.[23]

The passage shows yet another manifestation of the disengagement between the two intellectuals. To examine Shōyō's position, Ōgai introduces Hartmann, but offers no legitimate explanation of why it should be this German philosopher who has the authority, remarking only,

"Here, let me fetch Hartmann's glasses while looking into Shōyō's view of *hihyō*."[24] The reason why Ōgai privileges Hartmann as the aesthetic criteria is beyond our reach.[25] Ōgai's logic unfolds as follows: *Because* Shōyō's categories correspond to Hartmann's, and *because* Hartmann considered each class a "milepost" to the final, "sublime" stage of beauty, *therefore* Shōyō's three schools of the novel need to be hierarchized. While there is no necessity that Hartmann's schema and Shōyō's distinction be compared, Ōgai imposes (what he believes to be) Hartmann's view upon Shōyō's categorization. Without establishing the comparability of Shōyō to Hartmann, Ōgai poses a poignant question: "How would it be possible for Shōyō to say, 'see no hierarchy'?"[26]

Shōyō generally showed little interest in engaging in Ōgai's provocative moves. There were a few instances when Shōyō actually referenced Ōgai, but he made his addresses in a nonserious, caricatural way so as to deflect the attack. Shōyō's nonconfrontational demeanor lasted until Ōgai presented a much-stretched understanding of the submerged-ideal theory in response to Shōyō's preface to the *Macbeth* annotation project. Shōyō's change of attitude toward Ōgai's persistent provocation may have had something to do with the medium in which his *Macbeth* project was serialized: His annotations of Shakespeare, as well as his prefatory note, appeared in the first issue of *Waseda bungaku* (Waseda literature), a literature-focused journal launched under Shōyō's supervision when he was an instructor at Tokyo Senmon Gakkō (now known as Waseda University). The journal was established with the aim of serving as a platform especially for Tokyo Senmon Gakkō's literature majors guided by Shōyō. In other words, his writings here had a particular audience, that is, students of literature who expected to read them as supplemental notes that would help their studies.[27] Shōyō took up his pen to respond seriously to Ōgai when his prefatory note—most likely written with a specific body of students in mind, to demonstrate a method of annotation—was openly contradicted in an unreasonably twisted manner. When contextualized by the specificity of the journal, Shōyō's decision to confront his opponent emerges as less a conflictual than an educational move.

In multiple essays, all published in *Waseda bungaku*, Shōyō clarified the definition of the term "submerged-ideal," addressing directly and respectfully the disguised figure of Ōgai/Uyū-sensei. The essays attempted to elucidate where Ōgai's misunderstanding might have come from.[28] The extended explications, at times working sentence by sentence, indicate that Shōyō was conscious of his readership, that is, the students of literary studies who might benefit from reading the interactions between two contemporary intellectuals who specialized in literature. In unambiguous rhetoric, Shōyō repeats that Ōgai's reaction is based entirely on a misreading of the submerged-ideal theory. The "true intention of the prefatory note" of the *Macbeth* project is, Shōyō explains, to denote that in reading great works, "inconsistent 'interpretations' have little benefit and bring more harm."[29] The submerged-ideal does not at all mean the absence of the ideal but in fact points in reverse to the existence of the enormity of the ideal. Indeed, the submerged-ideal method was Shōyō's "desperate means," as he could never reach the enormous ideal of Shakespeare's masterpieces.[30]

Shōyō's elaborate explanation might have brought the skirmish to an end, but to his and other readers' surprise, it was met with another refutation from Ōgai. Not only did Ōgai completely disregard Shōyō's effort to eliminate ambiguity, but he also continued to bend Shōyō's words into something other than what Shōyō actually said. The rhetoric of the submerged-ideal (*botsu-risō*), for instance, was paraphrased by Ōgai as *botsu-shukan* (negation of subjectivity), *botsu-sōhyō* (negation of commentary), *botsu-ruisō* (negation of generic ideas), *botsu-seishin* (negation of preconception), and *bokkyaku-risō* (effacement of ideals)—none of which appear in Shōyō's writings.[31] Clearly, the list of words that Ōgai devised did not share the semantics of Shōyō's term. Shōyō pointed out this discrepancy many times, to no avail.[32] Shōyō even posed a sincere question to Ōgai, inquiring into Hartmann's aesthetic theory: "Is what you call the unconscious spirit an objective entity? What is its ultimate purpose for creating the universe? Why did it create consciousness? Uyū-sensei, I beg you to enlighten me."[33] Despite this straightforward language, Ōgai responded evasively: "If Uyū-sensei heard this, he would simply say, 'Read my *Philosophy of the Unconscious*.'"[34] Showing little interest in Shōyō's effort to straighten out the situation, Ōgai eventually likened Shōyō to a "masked Émile Zola," only to denounce him as a naturalist detrimental to literature.[35] The exchanges between Shōyō and Ōgai were out of joint throughout because the point of disagreement—where exactly they diverged from each other—remained obscure. The discussion was tautological: Shōyō repeated what he considered to be the source of disagreement and misunderstanding, while Ōgai continued to neglect Shōyō's reiteration. Ultimately, the debate was prolonged unnecessarily, ending with the appearance of irresolvability.

As if to break the deadlock, Shōyō produced a series of essays in *gibun*, the playful-writing style, allegorically reframing the confrontation as a medieval war tale.³⁶ Proposing a ceasefire within the allegorical narrative, Shōyō articulates why the battle needs to be suspended at this point:

> I cannot be convinced that Hartmann's philosophy is the sole, absolute truth. . . . As long as Ōgai offers no clear, positive proof that the visible ideal is the sole, absolute truth, and that this truth is worth rejecting other systems of new philosophy, . . . , Shōyō's theory of the submerged-ideal won't collapse.³⁷

> Now that I understand the real identity of Uyū-sensei, the main stronghold of my enemy is nothing other than Hartmann's great philosophy. When the time comes, I will lead hundreds of battleships, crossing the Indian Ocean and the Mediterranean Sea, and rush to the official domain in Germany in order to complete the final battle.³⁸

In the alternative narrative of Shōyō's playful writing, Ōgai is no longer an enemy, but merely a surrogate speaker for Hartmann. Thus informed of the end of the war out of the blue, and possibly exacerbated by the change in Shōyō's writing style and his adoption of *gibun* saturated with parodies and wordplays, Ōgai intensified his combative attitude. "When Shōyō stopped discussion just like that, how could I say anything at all?": In so saying, Ōgai still produced a twenty-six-page response, though only to find it not reciprocated.³⁹ The debate thus came abruptly to an end.

What Ōgai and Shōyō wrote to each other failed to form a dialogic relationship. In fact, the debate was a failure for more than one reason. Because of the absence of reasonable correspondence, their exchange, which originally pivoted on a question about reading methodology, did not develop further. The (non)viability of interpretation in critical reading practice, a pressing topic for Japanese intellectuals seeking to establish *hihyō*, did not get scrutinized; moreover, the serious, even vehement exchange of missives was interrupted and invalidated by the playfulness of *gibun*. Yet despite the seemingly unfruitful course of the debate, I consider that the failed dialogue deserves careful attention because it is inhabited by alternative possibilities of performing critical reading, possibilities that emerge from the workings of the submerged-ideal theory. Shōyō's proposal of a-interpretative reading is not only reminiscent of Sontag's 1964 claim, but also enriches our understanding of what going against and without interpretation allows us to do.

Against Interpretation

As we have already seen, Shōyō asserts that for his annotations of *Macbeth* he wishes only "to explain the meaning of words and grammatical constructions just as they appear in the text."[40] The submerged-ideal theory urges caution because "there is the danger that someone of lesser discernment may, for example, take a cat and carefully interpret it as a tiger, conveying a misconception to the unwary reader."[41] What accompanies this proposed methodology is the effacement of readerly "ideals" to be imposed upon the text, in other words, the removal of a readerly desire to make sense of the text. Despite Ōgai's tenacious attack, Shōyō did not modify his reliance on this theory; indeed, his determination to adhere to the submerged-ideal method shows that he hoped to accomplish critical reading precisely by submerging whatever ideals he entertained.

Present-day intellectual Karatani Kōjin offers a useful perspective on the submerged-ideal theory: "What Shōyō meant by an 'ideal' is nothing other than a meaning, or theme, that can be seen *through* the text."[42] As a methodology of reading, the submerged-ideal rejects interpretation and avoids foregrounding any meaning of the text as a whole because interpretation is less about explaining than constructing or even fabricating meaning. This implies that in the meaning-making process, interpretation might execute its task by doing an injustice to whatever material it engages with. Interpretation casts its gaze upon the material in front of it, moving toward its object, no matter how randomly that object has been initially put together and come into being, so as to make sense of it. To reach the meaning, the interpretive gaze moves to eliminate the uncontrollable and unknowable in its object. Pierced by this gaze, chance and entropy are brought to be rearranged in the causal order and begin to be understood in terms of necessity or telos. Once interpretation is in place and meaning takes place, whatever exists in the text but is not made into sense ends up being forced to recede into the background, as if it had never existed. It is also possible that whatever is nonexistent in the text is forged throughout the process, as if it were there from the start. Yet, given that the text always carries excess and lack, interpretation easily slips into readerly violence. The position of the submerged-ideal entertains skepticism about interpretation for fear of committing such vandalism and hence disengages interpretation from its putative scope.

Furthermore, the submerged-ideal theory doubts that interpretation adds anything new and beneficial to masterpieces. In his preface to the

Macbeth project, Shōyō compares Shakespeare's writing to a "mirror" that can "reflect every reader's face," suggesting the all-encompassing nature of the masterwork.[43] When a piece of work is already universal, in the sense of accepting any readings exercised in any given place at any given moment, it is impossible and unnecessary for a historically determined individual to come up with an interpretation that approximates the universality of the work interpreted. The rhetoric of the submerged-ideal at times resembles negative theology, especially when it references the "enormity of the ideal" or the "infinite, bottomless absolute."[44] And yet Shōyō's theory splits with the construction of the focal point in the negative: Showing no interest in encouraging the reader to search for the center, the submerged-ideal surrenders to a multitude of reader-text encounters no matter what those encounters look like or how they take place. The submerged-ideal method acknowledges the limits of interpretation and provides itself as a humble but responsible demeanor for the reader who is inevitably caught under historical restrictions.

If interpretation is of little use to validate why a certain literary work is great and capable of standing the test of time, there is nothing left for the reader to communicate, except to describe what they recognize in the work as it is. The submerged-ideal theory proposes description as an alternative mode of engaging with the text, as a more ethical methodology of *hihyō*, one that never suppresses or bends possibilities of reading. It is an attempt to bring back the text, which has been interpreted and hence manipulated, to its primary shape, that is, to words scattered on paper. The submerged-ideal seeks to lessen the impact of historical constraints that unavoidably accompany and condition interpretation. In so doing, it declines to foreground meaning and give rise to a focal point in the text. The submerged-ideal pushes aside interpretation, a reading method that seeks to homogenize the text, while accepting all the possibilities of reading to be embraced in the "bottomless lake." Insofar as every readerly encounter with the text becomes allowable, the submerged-ideal decentralizes the text and deactivates the interpretative gaze. As a result, the text becomes restored, remaining infinitely open.

Do not focus. Defocalize. In the workings of the submerged-ideal, the text cannot form a center or a singular meaning, and is treated as an agglomeration of words juxtaposed to one another. As such, the submerged-ideal as a reading method is programmed to be metonymic; it aims to register the intricate assemblage of words in their contiguity. Useful here is Roman Jakobson's examination on the structure of language. In his seminal essay Jakobson discusses two basic figures of speech—metaphor and metonymy—and links the former with the logic of similarity, the latter with that of contiguity.⁴⁵ Stressing that a competing dichotomy between metaphor and metonymy takes place in "any symbolic process," for "all verbal behavior and for human behavior in general," Jakobson productively stretches the scope of these rhetorical tropes into the semiotics of cognition.⁴⁶ Metaphoric cognition operates according to the logic of similarity, making connections between objects based on their qualitative affinities. Metonymic cognition, by contrast, registers contiguous relations between objects, based upon physical or spatial proximity. Metaphor arranges objects by evaluating their internal likeness, while metonymy engages with objects by listing what is located in the same vicinity. Whereas the metaphoric approach proceeds into the depth of objects so as to reach inner traits, the metonymic approach traces the surface of objects placed physically next to each other. Understood in this way, the two axes of language correlate with what the submerged-ideal theory demotes and promotes: The metaphoric corresponds to the rigid interpretive gaze that searches for internal meaning, while the metonymic, just as the submerged-ideal operates, disperses focus and prioritizes description.

Metonymy disables the metaphoric approach that searches for, if not generates, meaning. As an example of metonymic description, Jakobson references Russian writer Leo Tolstoy, stating that "in *War and Peace* the synecdoches 'hair on the upper lip' and 'bare shoulders' are used by the same writer to stand for the female characters to whom these features belong."⁴⁷ Here metonymy signifies the object by using a small physical feature, something distinct from what it points to but in material proximity to that thing, thereby using tangibility to render a connection to the referenced object. More important, because of its close attention to a small part, metonymic description is "physically unable to grasp the whole."⁴⁸ That is to say, description of an individual part cannot approximate the essence or entirety of the whole. In the metonymic vision, the total picture is often lost; rather, such totality is not intended at all from the beginning. Instead of diving into the depth of the object to disclose its internal essence, the metonymic touches the surface and proceeds no further than the parts.

The submerged-ideal as a reading method approaches the text with metonymic vision. It focuses on registering components of the text, refusing to excavate or reconstruct inner logic. The simple listing of words sidesteps the interpretative gaze and leaves behind the drive for meaning searching and sensemaking. Detailed descriptions accumulate in layers, yet those layers do not interact or interfere with each other. The submerged-ideal does not reassemble words described. Rather, each word, even as it is metonymically registered, stands alone and lives its own materiality. The whole remains ungraspable. If the interpretive gaze probes a thread that ties scattered words together into a whole, the metonymic vision of the submerged-ideal reading has no intention for that; it does not aspire to see a whole. By committing to metonymic description, the submerged-ideal opens up room to resuscitate the words, each one of them, that the metaphoric interpretation suppresses at the cost of the whole. It keeps its guard up against the search for meaning, which often results in the homogenization and, by implication, fabrication of the text. By decoupling reading from making sense of the text, this metonymic method revives possibilities of relating to the text without imposing any unified meaning afforded by interpretation.

What is noteworthy is that the theory of the submerged-ideal was conceived against the zeitgeist of the time. If we recall the discussion in part 1 about the emergence of *hihyō* in the late nineteenth century, "sensemaking" was an essential task for the new practice of critical reading, part of the necessary process of selecting things beneficial to contemporary Japan from among the influx of information. The submerged-ideal approach, with its call *not* to interpret but rather to *disperse* meaning, was therefore premised upon a logic incommensurable with what was being collectively proposed. Shōyō was indeed one of the many intellectuals who made an effort to legitimize *hihyō* in the late 1880s. To recapitulate, in 1887, his essay "Hihyō no hyōjun" in *Chūō gakujutsu zasshi* emphasized setting up "just criteria" for *hihyō* as necessary in contemporary Japan because such criteria enable "correct judgment."[49] Such an argument, however, presumes the existence of "that which is correct in the text," awaiting discovery and evaluation; in other words, the necessity of *hihyō*'s just criteria requires positing meaning innate in, and preceding any reading experience of, a text. And yet, with Shōyō's call to action regarding *hihyō*'s criteria still lingering in the air, he proposed the submerged-ideal theory. As if to invalidate his own claim, he declared the futility of seeking meaning in text and the ultimate impossibility of interpretation. The proposal of the submerged-ideal theory was thus not only incongruous with the contemporary zeitgeist but also a drastic departure from Shōyō's own position.

Seen in this context, Ōgai's strong reaction appears less unreasonable; it seems rather to reflect the primacy generally given to sensemaking in

AGAINST INTERPRETATION 147

the institutionalization of critical reading. Karatani's remarks on this debate and its performative framing are especially helpful in considering Ōgai's adverse attitude:

> What I want to point out is that it was Ōgai who took a position of opposition in this debate and who formulated the problem. He took all that coexisted as difference and diversity in the second decade of Meiji—all that Shōyō had affirmed in his conception of submerged-ideals—and out of it structured an opposition.[50]

Karatani's observation is indicative that variance, a mere difference of perspective, has no inherent necessity to be framed as antithesis until it is made so. Karatani's claim has some truth. In public debates, antithesis is often not a given but configured as such, staged by debaters themselves or by their readers. And indeed, Ōgai actively structured the interaction as conflict and created the appearance of antagonism, even though he was clearly not within Shōyō's intended student audience. That being the case, however, to read the disconnect between Shōyō and Ōgai as mere "difference and diversity" is reductive; that is to say, Karatani seems to disregard the radicalness of Shōyō's notion of not interpreting. Shōyō's a-interpretative demeanor marked a strange rupture with the contemporary discourses. Ōgai's belligerent reaction in a sense exhibits the intensity of discomfort that the submerged-ideal theory triggered among the intellectual community. In other words, Shōyō's theory was at odds with a general consensus of the time to such an extent that his fellow writer was compelled to restructure "difference and diversity" into an "opposition."

Beyond Karatani's observation, there is still a persistent scholarly tendency to emphasize Ōgai's manipulative and uncooperative behavior during the debate. While Shōyō's position in the debate has been underexamined, the length and hostility of Ōgai's writings, in addition to the insertion of Hartmann or Uyū-sensei as an ungrounded authority, have invited an approach which one might characterize as "Ōgai-bashing."[51] It is true that Ōgai makes multiple rhetorical, distracting detours throughout the debate without directly articulating his point. He sets up his own writings to work against him, ultimately driving the exchange into a mire. Yet however much the exchange between Shōyō and Ōgai appears disjointed, we must step back and pay attention to what their missives both revealed and obscured at once. To reiterate, the submerged-ideal theory, with its orientation toward a-interpretation, dislocation of the center, and refusal to focalize meaning, appeared to move in the opposite direction to the contemporaneously desired goals of *hihyō*. At the core of the Shōyō–Ōgai exchange lay the question of reading methodology, that is, the question of whether or not to read for interpretation, a mode that seeks to fix meaning in the text. When *hihyō* was posited as an examiner and creator of information value, tasked to select and determine what is important in written discourses for the sake of elevating Japan's status in the world, this question about interpretation of meaning loomed large.

In fact, throughout the debate Ōgai consistently insists on one problematic, the viability of the submerged-ideal theory as a new mode of critical reading: Shōyō needs to identify the theoretical foundation of the submerged-ideal to verify the ground of his reading method, one that comes *without* interpretation. Locating the foundational theory was crucial to Ōgai, especially because the submerged-ideal, while having rejected the necessity of *hihyō*'s criteria, refuses to supplant them. Already in his first response to Shōyō's preface, Ōgai poses a pressing question: Shōyō's description-based "inductive *hihyō*" is one way of engaging with great works, and yet "when one is about to make a judgment after completing observation and study, shouldn't there be ideals? Shouldn't there be some criteria?"[52] Ultimately, what is there to read if not for interpretation and sensemaking? Despite all the verbiage and aggression, Ōgai's primary concern is straightforward enough, and he returns to the same question constantly throughout the debate.

On this view, Ōgai's tone becomes increasingly aggressive, as Shōyō never addresses whether or not the submerged-ideal method is ultimately inconsistent with the call for new critical language of the time. Instead, Shōyō simply repeats the same idea, restating his own incapacity to validate a singular interpretative stand over others. "What Shōyō deprioritizes is partial logic, one that is swayed by personal likes and dislikes, one that is measured by narrow experiences," comments Ōgai.[53] And yet if Shōyō downplays logic as criterion, "even the words of great philosophers would not be able to escape being discounted, in which case, what is the remaining impartial logic that Shōyō would not deprioritize?"[54] If Shōyō insists that he stands with the submerged-ideal, espousing no criteria, does that not mean that "the submerged-ideal is itself a grand ideal that he acquired"?[55] These questions reveal Ōgai's frustration: If the submerged-ideal is one of many ideals, akin to logical thinking that functions as a criterion, it cannot evade the responsibility to clarify its own ground when undertaking critical reading. In the context of the late nineteenth century when identifying *hihyō*'s criteria for judgment, sensemaking, and interpretation was considered an urgent task, Ōgai's interrogation of Shōyō as a practitioner of *hihyō* was deeply rooted in the contemporaneously shared concern. Seen from that perspective, Shōyō's refusal to adopt interpretive criteria amounts to digression, even abdication of *hihyō*'s responsibility.

In the sense that Shōyō and Ōgai take the question of *hihyō*'s criteria very seriously, their contemplation demonstrates their closeness. Nevertheless, there is a vast distance between them in terms of where the practitioner of *hihyō* stands vis-à-vis the object of critical reading. Ōgai asks: What sort of "self" (*ga*) does Shōyō ultimately establish in his *hihyō*?[56] Ōgai's writings seek his opponent's "self" as a critical reader, the position from which Shōyō engages with, and makes a judgment of, a text in front of him. Shōyō, however, shows no interest in locating such a self in a legible manner. What Shōyō posits as his methodology of *hihyō* becomes possible precisely by effacing the self and, by extension, any criteria based upon which interpretation comes into being. In the *hihyō* deriving from the submerged-ideal theory, there is no space for a self to float up, nor is there any necessity for criteria to arise. Accordingly, interpretation, inevitably premised upon the ground of the self who interprets, must be submerged.

Shōyō's proposal for impersonal, a-interpretative description necessitates the annihilation of a self who interprets, thereby running the risk of jeopardizing his own self as critic, a self that has to be a responsible reader in the specific climate of late nineteenth-century Japan. The oddity of Shōyō's stance is only emphasized when he suddenly changes his writing style and begins to publish refutations in a conventional, satirical yet playful fashion that existed in Japan, namely, *gibun*. Where the contemporary consensus was that critical language in *hihyō* must be new, independent of existing genealogies of writing, Shōyō's mobilization of *gibun* to counter Ōgai, which itself was supposed to be part of critical reading practice (hence having to appear new), seems particularly inadequate to the purpose. Shōyō's performance in the debate was therefore, like his advocacy of a-interpretation, out of sync with the climate of the time. The submerged-ideal theory and, by extension, the debate revolving around it thus did not offer a refashioned mode of critical reading that was desired in late nineteenth-century Japan.

While Ōgai's vituperation and the peculiar, ungrounded positions taken by Shōyō contributed an additional layer of complication to the debate, reducing its chance of developing an enlightening dialogue for the advancement of *hihyō*, I contend that the debate was fruitful.

This is because, perhaps accidentally, the debate gave rise to a vision of what *hihyō* might look like if unbound by meaning, interpretation, or defined criteria. Specifically, Shōyō's *gibun* narrative unfolds to deny the existence of a focal point and, in so doing, affirm the nonexistence of the textual center, the main idea advocated in the submerged-ideal theory. Irrespective of Shōyō's intention, his *gibun* writings perform his proposed reading methodology, instantiating the possibility of critical reading that does not necessarily rely on identification of meaning via interpretation, albeit in a surprisingly unpredicted way. The remainder of this chapter focuses on a series of Shōyō's *gibun* writings and conjectures about what the sudden resurgence of the "outmoded" writing style in the submerged-ideal debate set in motion.

No Longer Playful

From the late Edo period into the early Meiji, humorous and often satirical writings, filled with wordplay, nonsense, and both linguistic and visual puns, were collectively called *gesaku* (playful fiction) and broadly functioned as social entertainment, a breather from the unreasonable, potentially oppressive reality. In the late nineteenth century, *gesaku* and other related written lineages, such as *kokkeibon* (humorous stories), *kusazōshi* (illustrated booklets), and *yomihon* (historical, often didactic fiction), circulated widely and constituted an important part of urban culture.[57] Literature scholar Kamei Hideo has shown that works originally produced during the Edo period continued to be reprinted on a large scale in the first two decades of the Meiji period.[58] For that reason, Edo *gesaku* writers such as Ryūtei Tanehiko (1783–1842), Takizawa Bakin (1767–1848), and Tamenaga Shunsui (1790–1843) continued to attract Meiji readers and serve as sources of their literary inspiration. According to literary historian Maeda Ai, writings produced as *gesaku* offered essential sites of communal reading experience for literate reciters and illiterate listeners alike in the late nineteenth century.[59] Consumed by a broad range of readers, these fictions nurtured a distinct form of literacy, what Charlotte Eubanks calls a "visual vernacular," that is at once linguistic, sonic, and pictorial, among readers who were primarily the nonelite.[60] There is no doubt that such literacy involved not just the capabilities of reading and understanding but also competences in reproducing style, collocation, rhythm, trope, plot construction, and other literary components. *Gibun* as a writing style carried with it all these cultural memories inscribed in written lineages.[61]

Shōyō was born into the commonality of *gibun*. For him and many of his contemporaries born in the final years of the Tokugawa shogunate, there was nothing exotic about the *gibun* style. He had composed *gibun* and non-*gibun* works alike since the late 1880s, long before the submerged-ideal debate. For instance, the pieces that Shōyō published around the time of the debate, such as "Sokoshirazu no mizuumi" (The bottomless lake) and "Azusamiko" (Shrine maiden), have strong recourse to the style of *gibun*, filled with allegories, caricatures, and satire that poke fun of the contemporary writing scene.[62] The production of those essays was possible because Shōyō's literacy, like that of many of his contemporaries, was cultivated by consistent exposure to and immersion in a range of older written genealogies.[63] That literacy turned into a source of the problem in late nineteenth-century Japan. As Indra Levy discusses, this was the time when different writing styles coexisted, sometimes in competition with one another.[64] The constellation of written language itself was shifting, and as such, a consensus on how to write prose, fictional or nonfictional, was yet to be reached. Nevertheless, one thing was clear: When a new mode of critical reading had to be unprecedented and rigorous enough to advance Japan's civilizational status, the style of *gibun* as a mode of expression did not match those expectations. In short, it was all too familiar and frivolous, and for this reason considered unfit for the practice of critical reading to be exercised by Meiji intellectuals.

Shōyō himself shared that sentiment. Recall that he considered *hihyō* a practice developed in the West and replanted in Japan in the recent past.[65] For him, *hihyō*'s language needed to approximate that of Anglophone writers such as George Lillie Craik and Samuel Austin Allibone, whom he labeled "bosses" of *hihyō*.[66] Shōyō's contemporary Takata Sanae also understood *hihyō* as a distinctly Western method of commentary that had little in common with the traditions of critical reading long exercised in Japan.[67] *Hihyō* was yet to be established, and had to be conceived as anything but what had previously circulated in the Japanese literary world. Shōyō and his contemporaries, well versed in *gesaku* and related genres, consistently marked those genealogies of written language as distant, even excluded, from the realm of *hihyō*.

On the conceptual level, Shōyō made a conscious effort to institute writing practices appropriate for Meiji Japan by differentiating existing linguistic conventions from modes of writing yet to come. His *Shōsetsu shinzui* was one such attempt that he took to systematize the realm of fiction writing, and he did so by drawing negatively on what he had been familiar with. As John Mertz explains, established genres of fiction such as *gesaku* "bore the stigma of association with a progressively outdated image of the lower classes" even though those "outdated" writings still circulated broadly in the early Meiji period.[68] Because of their ubiquity, those genres and their stylistic features served as reference points for "improvement," against which things "new and better" could be envisioned. To break with the stigma attached to fiction, *Shōsetsu shinzui* rhetorically downplays existing writing conventions of *gesaku* and in contrast constructs *shōsetsu*, now casually understood as the novel, as a form of fiction that would suit a new Japan.[69] The ways in which Shōyō approaches fiction, or *shōsetsu*, parallels his conception of nonfictional criticism, or *hihyō*, in that both *shōsetsu* and *hihyō* are postulated as modes of writing yet to be realized. Not that Shōyō was entirely opposed to all earlier writing traditions; as noted, he produced essays in the *gibun* style at the same time as he was brooding over the submerged-ideal as a methodology for *hihyō*. Yet exactly because he *was* capable of handling *gibun* effortlessly, he needed to work to set himself apart from it. Fiction or nonfiction, the distance he imagined between familiar linguistic conventions and alternative modes of writing had to be carefully observed in anticipation of the latter's arrival.

To Fail, or Not to Fail

Despite all his effort to define and respect the distance between written lineages and forthcoming modes, Shōyō brought the familiar writing style of *gibun* into play as *hihyō* in the disjointed, elongated exchange with Ōgai. The appearance of *gibun* in the debate was an unexpected, potentially impermissible move, not only because Shōyō's essays were written as an extension of *hihyō*, but also because they were introduced in a space designated for *hihyō*. *Gibun*, with its signature use of allegories, wordplays, and satire, clearly marked stylistic differences from previous discourses exchanged during the debate. What made the insertion of *gibun* in the debate even more unsettling was that it occurred in the medium dedicated to critical practices, that is, Shōyō's teacherly platform *Waseda bungaku*. When the debate seemed to have reached a deadlock, perhaps he needed something different, something distracting to break the static situation of the ongoing discussion. As a result, however, the pages of the journal designed to offer the cutting edge of literary studies came to be saturated with rhetorical conventions that had been labeled as obsolete by contemporary writers. The mobilization of *gibun* was effective: It marked a violent, unambiguous rupture in the debate's atmosphere and silenced Ōgai. Still, in the peculiar intellectual climate of the late nineteenth century when Shōyō and Ōgai exchanged blows, *gibun* and *hihyō* should not have coincided with one another, or more specifically, *gibun* was not supposed to exist in the realm of *hihyō*. Shōyō's use of *gibun* and its playful nature, in other words, only undermined the premise of *hihyō* as a rigorous critical language and even invalidated Meiji intellectuals' collective efforts to create one, including Shōyō's own.

The out of place-ness of *gibun* in the debate manifests already in the ways in which Shōyō sets up his work. The first essay that Shōyō produced in the *gibun* style in response to Ōgai is titled "Waseda Bungakugayatsu Jibun Hyōron-mura no engi," literally "The origin of the Village of Jibun Hyōron in the Valley of Waseda Bungaku." The term *"jibun hyōron,"* or "evaluations of contemporary writings," is the title of the *hihyō* section in *Waseda bungaku*, which is an academic literary journal for which Shōyō serves as a core editorial member. The essay's title thus references Shōyō's professional platform, albeit in allegorized fashion ("village" and "valley," for instance), to explain his "origin"—where he comes from when confronted by his opponent. On the content level, the essay rewrites the confrontation between two Meiji intellectuals as a battle about to break out during Japan's medieval period.[70] In the allegorical world, the village (that is, the *hihyō* section of the journal) is depicted as a gathering space for pacifistic farmers who wish to cultivate the land of aesthetic writing.[71] The narrative loosely tracks one particular pacifist, "Shepherd Shōyō" (小羊), whose punning name sounds like Shōyō's but with Chinese characters literally meaning "small sheep." The peaceful, idyllic landscape of the village is suddenly disturbed when the army of "Mighty General Ōgai," who considers the village "a nest of heretics" that must be punished, approaches.[72] General Ōgai's force is armed with a variety of "weapons": Chinese characters, German words, imported "explosives called satire and contempt," and so forth.[73] Facing this unexpected attack, Shepherd Shōyō tries to combat the enemy force with an assembly of village members: Chibifude no Matsu (Sentry Worn-Out Writing Brush), Jōken Nyūdō (Lay Priest Common Sense), Gazokusecchūnosuke (Assistant Warrior Elegant-Vernacular Eclectic Style), and Eigo-Zokugo Kyōdai (the brothers of English and Vernacular).[74] At a glance, it is evident that Shōyō's *gibun* writings are drastically different in form, rhetoric, and tone, from his earlier responses to Ōgai.

However absurdly the shift of style took place in the Shōyō-Ōgai interaction, Shōyō's *gibun* decisively changed the course of the debate.

As noted, his *gibun* essays construct a parallel textual world in which they are refashioned as peace-loving shepherd and cold-blooded general in the medieval age. A series of Shōyō's writings, now reworked in a playful style, generate mixed effects, as the high tension of the medieval battlefield is balanced against a comical, rhythmical narrative. Such rhetorical effects also rebound upon Shōyō and Ōgai in the 1890s, highlighting, mocking, alleviating, and ultimately dispersing the intensity of their current exchange. In a jumble of words used in *gibun*, the typical value judgment—what is valid, and who is logical?—is incapacitated throughout. Both vehement and jocular, Shōyō's *gibun* preempts all possible responses from Ōgai. If Ōgai were to respond with the same degree of rigor as he had been, that would mean he took playful writings seriously and lost his cool over something frivolous, which would turn him into a fool. It would also make him appear to have no taste or sense of humor. Before an allegorical world recreated in the old-fashioned style of playful writing, Ōgai has no other option than to drop his claims against the submerged-ideal theory. Useful to understanding the effects of Shōyō's *gibun* is Bakhtin's notion of "creative ambivalent carnival laughter, in which mockery and triumph, praise and abuse are inseparably fused."[75] When matters that are usually polar opposites are no longer separable in the playfully constructed world, no decision can be made with absolute confidence, and ambivalence prevails. Ōgai was caught in such ambivalence. Shōyō's *gibun* and its anarchic use of language thus pointed to serious play; it generated successful effects in shutting down his opponent's move, precisely because it was out of place and laughed away the deadly serious appearance of the battle.

Equally important to its foreclosing of Ōgai's response is the *gibun*'s development of a world that refuses to form a center. As if to put into practice the defocalization of the submerged-ideal method, the allegorical narrative evades providing any singular locus of meaning. The figure of Shepherd Shōyō, for example, is initially presented as a leader of the village. And yet the narrative demonstrates that he is neither a decision maker nor even an active player, but rather something like a messenger who relays information from different sources. The actual battle against General Ōgai's force is fought by the village's army, the primary constituents of which are the medley of styles, such as Gazokusecchūnosuke, and devices, including Chibifude no Matsu, all of them essential for the production of texts. Shepherd Shōyō is by no means their commander, as each of the villagers, all individually personified, speaks and acts freely to combat the enemy. Furthermore, the proposal of a ceasefire does not come from Shepherd Shōyō but from Monju Bosatsu, a bodhisattva of wisdom, who appears in Shepherd Shōyō's dream. The bodhisattva tells the shepherd: "Stop the verbal war. It is full of sour grapes. . . . This is just a nuisance."[76] Thus scolded by the saint, Shepherd Shōyō, now fully awake, sends a note to General Ōgai, announcing the end of the war. One additional twist embedded in the ceasefire exhortation is that the war, initially waged in the name of "Bibun Tennō" (Emperor Aesthetic Writing) and hence evoking the Shinto religion in the context of Meiji Japan, is interrupted by Buddhist wisdom.[77] Monju Bosatsu's presence is vital, as it directs the reader's attention away from the imperial center. And yet Monju Bosatsu too is deprived of stability by appearing only in a dreamscape. In this way, the introduction of the Buddhist saint in the allegory defers positing any single moment as decisive. Just as the submerged-ideal method seeks to identify no fixed point of meaning within a work under examination, so too the world of Shōyō's *gibun* avoids focalizing a singular locus of importance. His *gibun* thus ends up enacting the reading methodology proposed and defended throughout the debate. Said differently, the *gibun* essays bring to the fore effective use of the submerged-ideal for critical engagement with existing discourse.

As the world of *gibun* continues to unfold, what initially triggered the debate gradually recedes into the background. As a result, the primary question of the debate—whether or not the submerged-ideal could function properly as a methodology of *hihyō*—fades away. The allegorical narrative displaces its own origin, relativizing the initial reason it had to come into being, and in so doing, brings a closure to the chaotic battle between the general and the shepherd. Arising from the allegorical world, Shepherd Shōyō's proposal for a ceasefire reaches beyond its immediate receiver General Ōgai and serves to declare a pause in the debate between the real-life Meiji writers. Remaining on the textual surface of the debate is a plethora of playful words, a composition of polyphonic styles that altogether refuse to make sense of themselves.

In the context that *hihyō* hoped to bear no resemblance to the existing written lineages, the debate that ensued from Shōyō's proposal of the submerged-ideal theory failed to make a significant contribution to the creation of new critical reading practice. Shōyō failed to address Ōgai's urgent question, that is, the viability of the submerged-ideal as an appropriate method of *hihyō*. Moreover, Shōyō brought back an "unfit" style of language that had to be negated because of its conventionality and nonseriousness, and did so in a media space specifically carved out for *hihyō*. Although *gibun* successfully intervened in the static, prolonged debate and dissipated Ōgai's queries, Shōyō's writings drifted farther away from actualizing a new form of critical language suitable for *hihyō*.

Nevertheless, in the movements of deviating from the search for normative standards for the practice of *hihyō*, Shōyō's words revived written lineages and redrew the horizons of critical reading. The surprising resurgence of *gibun* in the space of *hihyō* was not anachronism: By letting those lineages flow into his critical reading experience, Shōyō's position made visible the anarchic outlook of *hihyō* as a new language conjoining with what it needed to suppress, a coexistence that otherwise would never have been brought to the textual surface. The writer might have had no intention to exhibit such a linguistic jumble. Yet however accidental, the juxtaposition of different writing styles disrupts the consensus on logical and historical necessity, discloses the arbitrariness of the distance imagined between the "new" and "old" forms of writing, unfastens the bonds that *hihyō* imposed upon itself, and affords a glimpse into what possible form *hihyō*'s language may be able to assume. In this alternative vision, an anomaly may not be the "outdated" playfulness of *gibun*, but a "new" type of critical language, one that is envisioned to be sober, serious, and rigorous. If, as Bakhtin says, "Carnival is the place for working out, in a concretely sensuous, half-real and half-play-acted form, a *new mode of interrelationship between individuals*, counterposed to the all-powerful sociohierarchical relationships of noncarnival life," Shōyō's *gibun* embodied such a carnivalesque site.[78] This is not simply because his *gibun* acted upon the relationship between two Meiji intellectuals, but also because it flashed a possibility of altering the prescribed relationship between the "new" and "old" styles of writing, between critical language and creative production.

I reemphasize the significance of the insertion of *gibun* in the submerged-ideal debate. That is to say, what was brought back in the debate was a writing style that had long embraced laughter as a way to suspend, or even disturb, orders and ideals. With its playful nature, Shōyō's *gibun* not only resuscitated a vast corpus of traditional usages of written language, but also generated room for self-mockery and self-reflection. We can almost hear *gibun* asking itself, "How dare I thought that a new language for critical reading practice could be constituted without reflecting on the lineages of my own?" In an unexpectedly performative way, the *gibun* offers an answer to Ōgai's inquiry about the "self"; what emerges in their exchange is a "self," a critical reader, that retained memories of critical language and survived as a style. Inadvertently or not, Shōyō's *gibun* writings unravel as if to invalidate the possibility of establishing *hihyō* independently of what preceded it. Such a self-questioning gesture arising from *gibun* slipped into the developmental stage of critical reading practice and broached an alternative trajectory of critical language. At once haunting and felicitous, the appearance of *gibun* marked the most critical, creative moment in this debate.

What Shōyō produced in his confrontation with Ōgai radically broke with the prospects of *hihyō*, as it diminished the distance that *hihyō* had to maintain from existing writing conventions. His writings look nothing like critical reading practices that we, academic readers in the twenty-first century, typically encounter in academic monographs and journals on literature. For that very reason, the appearance of *gibun* in the submerged-ideal debate helps us recuperate different, more open possibilities of relating to written words. These possibilities, once flashed upon the scene of critical reading in late nineteenth-century Japan, remind us of what we might have been excluding from our horizons of critical reading. In the next and final chapter, I discuss another unique case of *hihyō*, in particular how critical language reveals and creatively overcomes its own limits.

CHAPTER 6

The Community of No Referent
The Interrelation-with-Life Debate

> Skilled reading is usually thought to be a matter of discerning what is there, but if the example of my students can be generalized, it is a matter of knowing how to *produce* what can thereafter be said to be there. Interpretation is not the art of construing but the art of constructing. Interpreters do not decode poems; they make them.
>
> —Stanley Fish

Readers interpret the text in front of them and, in so doing, create it.[1] The meaning of a text and, by extension, its very life relies on its readers. If we believe Stanley Fish's claim about the reader–text relationship, or at least take seriously the part readers play in critical reading practice, one case of *hihyō* in late nineteenth-century Japan may offer counterintuitive insights.[2]

The case examined here is the so-called interrelation-with-life debate from the early 1890s, in which young intellectuals Yamaji Aizan and Kitamura Tōkoku fought about the essence of literature: Must literature serve a purpose outside literary writing (Aizan), or is it autonomous and "pure" (Tōkoku)? When Aizan proposed literature's instrumentality, that is, its nature as an intentional, human-driven "project," in relation to the accomplishments of Edo writer Rai San'yō (1780–1832), Tōkoku resisted this view and emphasized literature's absolute independence, its nonrelationality to what occurs in historically confined time and space, introducing the rhetoric of "pure literature" or *junbungaku*. Using journals with which they were affiliated, Tōkoku and Aizan exchanged missives to defend their positions and contradict the opposing views, and yet as with the previous case studies the debate did not unfold smoothly. Although this was a publicly staged dispute in print media involving more than one discussant, Tōkoku's discourse immediately assumed a solipsistic tone; moreover, he did not provide an articulate description of what he advocated as the pure realm of literature, thereby confronting Aizan without explaining what he most needed to explain. As demonstrated in part 1, *hihyō* was conceptualized as an intellectual reading practice whose primary task was to evaluate written discourses and make their value legible to a wider audience; so conceived, *hihyō* was expected to manifest dialogic engagement with others in clear linguistic explanations. In that it did not flesh out the notion of pure literature and its specific value, and did not allow others to grasp the stakes in concrete terms, Tōkoku's *hihyō* clearly failed to serve its purpose.

The interrelation-with-life debate interestingly shows a paradoxical outcome of the failure of *hihyō*: Although Tōkoku's writing did not meet the practice's fundamental premise as communication via verbalism, it nevertheless outshone Aizan's in its effect, giving rise to a kind of "Tōkoku favoritism" both in public and in scholarship and fostering a remarkable and longstanding readerly acceptance of "pure literature." These results are rather surprising, given that Tōkoku and Aizan were not necessarily in an antithetical relationship. To be sure, their visions of literature did not look alike, and yet in the sense that both writers were in search of an alternative form of literature that would not conform to the existing trends of writing, the debate was a team effort. They were personal friends, and each attempted to delineate the contours of literature yet to come in collaboration with the other.[3] Yet in spite of their closeness, both the public and later academics have persistently shown a predilection for Tōkoku. That Tōkoku committed suicide in 1894 soon after the debate dissolved, and that his death was dramatized in his friend Shimazaki Tōson's autofictional accounts, probably factored in the rise of Tōkoku favoritism.[4] Tōson's posthumous, somewhat idealized depiction of Tōkoku also encouraged a biographical interpretation of his writings, reinforcing a view that the writer's suicide was a physical enactment of his ideal of pure literature, namely, literature untainted by all the worldly matters. The orientation toward purity, coupled with biographical facts, have prompted readers to position Tōkoku as a romantic, desperate advocate of literature par excellence, leading to the polarized positioning of him against Aizan. Indeed, Nakano Shigeharu famously identified Aizan as a "dirty positivist" in favor of Tōkoku, and similarly Odagiri Hideo called Aizan a "vulgar utilitarian."[5] Even after revisionist scholarship such as Maeda Ai's study approached the debate from a fresh perspective, not as an irrevocable antagonism between the two writers but in more relational terms, Tōkoku favoritism seems to persist.[6]

CHAPTER 6

What Tōkoku set in motion as pure literature generated a long-lasting impact on the scenes of production and consumption of literature. Even as Tōkoku failed to use language when a verbal explanation of the purity of literature was most desired, the rhetoric of pure literature continues to reach readers beyond the immediate context within which he fought against Aizan: What was called pure literature helped to build a small, sect-like literary community, including the *Bungakukai* group that launched literary journal *Bungakukai* (The world of literature) at the end of the nineteenth century, and ever since, this idea of purity has been one of the driving forces of the literary industry in contemporary Japan. The prestige of the Akutagawa Prize (established in 1935), granted semiannually to writers of pure literature to this day, exemplifies the continuing effect of Tōkoku's rhetoric.[7] I have mentioned in the introduction that few of the discourses and practices surrounding late nineteenth-century *hihyō* survived the test of time. Tōkoku is a unique exception. The afterlife of Tōkoku's term, especially how it continues to elicit readerly engagement, makes the interrelation-with-life debate a particularly interesting point of reference for my contemplation of the potentials of critical reading in the current century.

This chapter examines Tōkoku's rhetorical moves in the debate and speculates about what has so long sustained his *hihyō* language. While existing scholarship on Tōkoku and the debate almost exclusively focuses on the content—the "what" in his writings, that is, the meaning of the purity of literature—I draw attention to the "how" of his writings and track the rhetoric with which the purity of literature is presented. Notably, Tōkoku repeatedly creates a linguistic void—that which cannot be verbalized—to indicate what he promotes as the pure realm of literature. The sign exists ("purity"), but the referent is not illustrated with comprehensible, descriptive qualities. In other words, Tōkoku's rhetoric deemphasizes the conventional sign–referent relationship, and his discussion unfolds as if he did not hope to be understood semantically by a general readership, including his immediate opponent, Aizan. Because Tōkoku says nothing concrete about what constitutes the purity of literature, the possibility of interpreting it with exactitude is preempted. My contention is that precisely because the sign remains unfilled, the referent undescribed, Tōkoku's writings invite readerly participation and help to sustain a literary community surrounding pure literature, whatever it may point to. This effect is fortified in a distinctively linguistic way by Tōkoku's substantial use of the deictics.[8] As the writer frequently mobilizes the first-person pronoun, *I*, he interpellates the addressee, *you*, out of anonymous readers. The intersubjective, "complementary" relationship between the *I* and the *you*, as French linguist Émile Benveniste notes, helps the *I* (here Tōkoku's) enlist readers to identify themselves as the hailed *you*, if they wish.[9] Combined with the recurring use of the imperative, Tōkoku's language calls forth readers' investment in pure literature, a commitment that does not necessarily rely on semantic understanding of what remains unsaid.

I use the term "community" in reference to Fish's deliberation of interpretive communities, but with a modest twist: A readerly community revolving around pure literature does not find common ground in articulate information to be interpreted by readers, but in orientation toward unsaid information. It is this orientation toward the unsaid—what constitutes the purity of literature—that binds readers together. What emerges from this orientation is a community without a referent, a community that maintains the unsaid as it is instead of unraveling what it is. If, as Fish claims, "whatever they [commentators] do, it will only be interpretation in another guise because, like it or not, interpretation is the only game in town," the community sustaining pure literature affords an opportunity to productively expand our understanding of interpretation; what we see in this case is an interpretive force that does not necessarily construct what it interprets but rather hopes to reside in a pathway toward what is posited, thereby preserving it.[10]

I close my exploration of fin de siècle *hihyō* in this book with Tōkoku so that I and you, my readers, can linger in the effect of Tōkoku's inadvertent community building. But let me be clear: Tōkoku's *hihyō* features as a final case study, not because my book endorses his style of critical reading as a model to be emulated, but because the case illuminates the position of readers. Tōkoku's *hihyō* had a peculiar afterlife, continuing to recruit readers' commitment to pure literature, even as the writer himself left the idea unarticulated. This book entertains the possibility of considering that aspect of Tōkoku's *hihyō* to be an open invitation for us, twenty-first-century readers, to begin reflecting on our own relationships with readers, without whom our critical reading practice cannot exist.

The Purity of Literature

In January 1893, Aizan contributed the essay "Rai Noboru o ronzu" (Discussing Rai Noboru [also known as Rai San'yō]) to *Kokumin no tomo*, in which he stipulated the act of writing:

Writing is a project. Writers wield their pen, just like heroes swing their swords. Both of them do what they do, not in order to shoot the air, but to aim at what needs to be achieved. Ten thousand bullets and thousand swords—if they do not benefit the world, they just vanish into the void. Flamboyant phrases and graceful sentences—if they are left in hundreds of volumes in the world, they too come to nothing unless they interrelate with life. Writing should be respected precisely because it is a project. I discuss Rai Noboru, which means I discuss his project.[11]

Attacking "flamboyant phrases and graceful sentences," Aizan prioritizes historical writing as a more important constituent of literature. After this brief introduction, Aizan spends the rest of the essay situating Edo writer San'yō as a prominent historian, whose representative work *Nihon gaishi* (Unofficial history of Japan, 1827) was read with high enthusiasm by young patriots and helped the formation of revolutionary thoughts toward the end of the Edo period.[12]

A little over a month later, Aizan's contemporary and friend Tōkoku published "Jinsei ni aiwataru to wa nan no ii zo" (What does interrelation with life even mean?) in the journal called *Bungakukai*, specializing in literature. In this piece, Tōkoku condemned Aizan for assailing "pure literature" with the "hammer of historical writing." Tōkoku's attack is directed against the ways in which Aizan identifies writing practice with projects that must serve an immediate purpose in human life:

> Literature does not take projects as its purpose. Literature does not need to interrelate with life, nor does it necessarily turn to Kyōzan-esque [Edo writer Santō Kyōzan] fact-based description. Literature does not require becoming like San'yō-esque imperial worship when it attacks its enemy. Finally, literature does not have to shoot an enemy, or hundreds of them, who are visible.[13]

For Tōkoku, literature need not accomplish a purpose in a visible, immediately recognizable form, and "literature's dignity" should not be maimed by "worldly matters such as projects."[14] Thus constructed, how literature should be positioned vis-à-vis purposiveness in life becomes a primary point of contention.[15] Throughout their exchange, Tōkoku repeats, in strong tones but ambiguous content, that pure literature germinates from the realm of the idea, and that this realm is absolutely immovable and untouchable.

THE COMMUNITY OF NO REFERENT 163

Aizan, however, refuses to invest in the notion of pure literature at all. In his rebuttal, he equates artistic, aesthetic literature to "figures of speech," and explains that what he means by "projects" does not simply point to visible, tangible accomplishments in the "materialistic world" but also includes "projects in the spiritual world."[16] While Tōkoku persistently takes issue with thinking about literature in terms of its instrumental value, Aizan objects that Tōkoku and his fellow Christians in the *Bungakukai* group tend to be "pantheistic and mentalistic," always refusing direct engagement with human affairs.[17] In support of Aizan's position, his superior at the Min'yūsha School who founded *Kokumin no tomo*, Tokutomi Sohō, also reproaches Tōkoku for being a "highbrow hermit" harmful to society.[18]

To these attacks coming from the Min'yūsha-based intellectuals, Tōkoku humbly responds by explicating what initially drove him into starting the controversy:

> The focal point of the discussions between Aizan and me (who is independent of the *Bungakukai* group) lies in whether or not literature in the sense of fact-based transcription needs to interrelate with life, or whether or not literature allows the thing called the ideal to be applied to life. I am not a worshiper of the ideal at all. Just because Aizan tends to force literature toward facts all too strongly, I just tried to hit him back once on a whim. On second thought, it is a trivial fight, isn't it?[19]

Tōkoku's personal, regretful tone signals an attempt to come to terms with his opponents. But in making a compromise proposal, Tōkoku also stipulates "literature" in his own terms and underlines the difference between his literature—literature in the purest form—and Aizan's literature, which Tōkoku reduces to a "fact-based" type of writing. In other words, despite the pacifying tone of the reply to the Min'yūsha affiliates, Tōkoku remains consistent in his rhetorical manipulation of what the term "literature" means. The result of this usage is twofold: After singling out purposiveness from what the Min'yūsha School envisions as literature, Tōkoku's rhetoric also identifies such instrumentality as a detrimental element incompatible with the purity of literature.

Of course, there is no a priori necessity that that which is called literature be exempt from purposiveness. At one point Aizan asks Tōkoku to verbalize and elaborate on what makes pure literature pure:

> I here request clarification, What is pure literature? Is it poetry? Or plays? Anyone who had made poetry and plays in the past did so

with purpose, and none had taken their pens without an aim. Perhaps some used their pens to narrate their emotions, or describe natural scenery, or place current events on record, or entertain others, or promote good and punish bad. My request is that you clarify among these things what so-called pure literature points to.... Pure literature, I have trouble understanding its meaning.... If you understand there is no such thing as pure language, you must also see there is no such thing as pure literature.[20]

Literature as a linguistic composition whose medium is already so diverse cannot be pure. Arguing so, Aizan suggests that there is no such thing as "purity" in a strong sense of the term. His inquiry is crucial, as an insufficient reply would destabilize the foundations of Tōkoku's claim. Despite that, neither Aizan nor Tōkoku delves further into it in the debate. As a result, the question is left untouched, and what Tōkoku proposes as literature remains unchallenged. Indeed, the discussion of literature's purposiveness, as well as its independence, itself did not develop any further after Tōkoku's apologetic note. With no clear marker of an ending, the exchange soon ceased.[21]

The Limits of Linguistic Representation

When we review the exchange between Tōkoku and Aizan, it is noticeable that the focal point of the conflict, that is, the pure, uncontaminated realm of literary composition, is not thoroughly scrutinized. The interrelation-with-life debate arose because Tōkoku took issue with Aizan's subjugation of literature to projects. Yet a clear explanation of the ultimate autonomy or "purity" of literature—the very ground upon which Tōkoku built his counterdiscourse—is nowhere to be found. In the end, what pure literature entails, as well as how it is attained in actuality, remain unexplained. Due to this absence, Tōkoku's account ends up missing the mark, collapsing as an ineffective *hihyō* of Aizan's view.

In fact, Tōkoku's writings are full of additional, unexplained voids quite beyond the semantics of the purity of literature. One major example is the position of language in the realm of pure literature. Literature, *bungaku*, or knowledge of letters, depends on linguistic expressions to exist; it must be verbally and thus tangibly externalized to be recognized as such. Pure or not, literature requires materiality to come into being as a corporeal object to be read. Importantly, Tōkoku's writings never bring up the lingual–material factor essential to, but also contradictory to, the realization of (pure) literature, and this despite the way Tōkoku's own writings carry traces of writerly struggles that foregrounds the materiality of language. As a series of essays he produced in the early 1890s shows, what Tōkoku says about pure literature is characterized through "formless" (*mukei*) qualities such as "sublime" (*saburaimu*), "idea" (*sō*), "spirit" (*rei*), and "emptiness" (*kū*). In his writings, those intangible qualities are mobilized to accentuate pure literature's otherworldliness in contrast to the worldly affairs of the physical sphere. If we follow Tōkoku's presentation, however, the core of his theory—the purity of literature—falls straight into that which cannot be represented in language, the inevitably material written medium. His theory thus prohibits his own account from articulating what it postulates: The materiality of language does not reconcile with the immateriality of pure literature.

This lack of verbalism where the possibility of representation—rendering tangibility to what does not have a corporeal shape—is at stake is not limited to Tōkoku. Visual or linguistic, regardless of the modality we have at hand, the conundrum arises whenever mimesis—the recreation of physical likeness—is impossible due to the initial absence of corporeality of what is to be represented. While the problem itself is not unheard of in the genealogies of representation studies, it uniquely manifests in the Tōkoku-Aizan correspondence through the ways in which the former deals with the problem rhetorically in his own writings. Tōkoku handles the question by creating a void, a vacuum into which all that cannot be verbalized is sucked. And then, without accounting for what constitutes the content, namely, the purity of literature, his writings simply index a direction toward it. Put differently, instead of offering the explanatory *what it is*, his rhetoric signals *this is it*. When confronting Aizan, Tōkoku tries to detail the germination process of pure literature. And yet he halts his explanation at the crucial moment, immediately before the realm of pure literature is about to unravel, only to prohibit himself and his readers from proceeding further. Verbalization of the purity of literature becomes disallowed at the moment, such that the essence of the theory of pure literature escapes linguistic capture. At the same time, however, Tōkoku brings us the closest to *what it is*. Even as it is left unsaid, what is about to unfold persists as a void with his rhetorical *this is it*.

Let us track Tōkoku's rhetoric in his counterdiscourse to Aizan, so that we can observe his indexical gesture toward the void. As an exemplary manifestation of pure literature, Tōkoku cites Edo poet Matsuo Bashō's haiku:

> The bright moon,
> Wandering around the pond,
> All night long

Bashō's haiku is followed by an elaborate description in which Tōkoku provides an imaginary reenactment of the path that the poet took in bringing the haiku into being. I quote the passage at length so as to illuminate Tōkoku's rhetorical movement:

> Remember: The individual who stands by the pond is a human composed of flesh. Remember: He is surrounded by all the bonds caused by love, all the attachment, and all the sensual senses. Remember: He has fought against these formless enemies as much as his visible, materialistic power allowed him to. Remember: He has been given many opportunities to get his hands on fame, benefits, and projects. Remember: He had no difficulty in participating in projects that interrelated with life. Nevertheless, he was not able to satisfy himself. He was never able to believe that he won a victory. He could not consider what was regarded as a victory from a shallow viewpoint as a victory. At this point, he stopped shooting the real and started struggling to aim at the emptiness. He did not get satisfaction by standing by one side of the pond and staring at one part of the pond. Slowly, he started strolling. He took one cycle around the pond. Learning that one cycle was not enough to stare at the entire surface of the pond, he went around again. The second cycle was enough to see the entire surface of the pond, and yet, he was unable to look through the bottom of the pond. So, he went on the third time, and the fourth time. In the end, he strolled around all night long. The pond was the real. When he stared at the pond, he did so, unlike a child hitting the water in the dark, by having something reflected on the pond, by throwing something in the pond, and by having something shed light on the pond. "Staring" is the word that can refer to the beginning of how he sees. "Annihilation"—no other words can describe the aftermath of how he sees than this word. He forgot the real. He exited from humans. He was removed from flesh. Forgetting the real, removed from flesh, and exiting from the human realm, where has he gone? Stop

THE COMMUNITY OF NO REFERENT   167

asking the whereabouts of the cuckoo. He has flown away to the heavenly shores and reached the absolute, namely, "Idea."[22]

In his creative rendition of Bashō's experience before the poet reached the point of composing the haiku, Tōkoku offers surprisingly concrete, though imaginative, details of the poet's course of action. What ensues from this elaboration is perhaps more surprising, in that Tōkoku's account suddenly breaks when the poet is "annihilated" and enraptured into the otherworldly realm of the idea. Supposedly, that is where the haiku, the incarnation of pure literature according to Tōkoku's assessment, comes into being. Quite shockingly, however, the moment the explanation arrives at the apex, Tōkoku quits, as if there is nothing more left to be explained. The poet is gone, and that is the end. Those of us anticipating elaboration of what it is that makes literature pure are suspended on the spot with nowhere else to proceed. As we have followed Tōkoku's lead up to this point, the purity of literature, *what it is*, should be right in front of us where the poet vanishes. And yet our escort ceases to move beyond that point, abruptly letting go of his guiding hand. What is more, the guide discourages us from posing a question. *Ask no more*. Without direction, we are brought to a standstill, silenced.

The poet disappears, Tōkoku stops, and readers are suspended, all at once. The essence of Tōkoku's journey and by extension ours—inquiry into the birth of pure literature—is left unsaid. The purity of literature cannot be rendered in linguistic, material form because, as Tōkoku repeats, it does not belong in this world. It is the unsayable. When the realm of pure literature is "sublime," as he describes, the perfect commensuration of word and *what it is* is simply impossible.[23] The experience of "sublime" lies beyond the grasp of existing language. In this state, to think that language can represent *what it is* emerges as naive, even arrogant. *What it is* has to remain a void, which gives rise to a peculiar writerly demeanor: *I dare not represent what it is*. In a sense, Tōkoku is faithful to what he posits as pure literature because he does not articulate *what it is* through the worldly medium that is language. Tōkoku's withdrawal here indicates a point at which language meets its limits. Because of his halt, his accounts do not risk imperfectly hypostatizing what language fails to approximate. When no words can appropriately describe *what it is*, all language can do is to reveal the point of incapacity. If language inevitably falls short, it must recede into the distance so that it can at least point to the unsayable, *this is it*, without filling *what it is* in an insufficient manner.

A similar rhetorical move—*this is it* instead of *what it is*—appears in many of Tōkoku's writings. In a seminal essay, "Enseishika to josei" (The pessimistic poet and a woman, 1892), written about a year before his confrontation with Aizan, Tōkoku discusses a dilemma of a poet: Doomed to defeat in the world of the real, the poet seeks refuge in the world of the idea through romance, and yet romance ends up redirecting the poet toward the world of the real by way of such materialist institutions as marriage. The dilemma eventually drives the poet to exit the world.

> Through romance, he acquires his ideal marrying mate. Through marriage, he becomes ruptured from the world of the idea, only to be restrained in that of the real. Through death, he parts from the world of the real and that of the material.[24]

Death is the only way out. In the end, the pessimistic poet can only escape the double bind at the cost of his life, and this path is inevitable if the poet wishes to commit himself to the ostensible premise of literature's purity.[25] As to what awaits the poet in the pure realm of literature, Tōkoku explains no further. In the figures of Bashō and the pessimistic poet, the writer painstakingly leads us closer to pure literature and points his readers toward *what it is*. His writings do so by recreating the poets' path to pure literature and having his readers track the same route, be it circling around the pond countless times or oscillating between the real and the idea. Suddenly, however, the navigation discontinues, leaving readers alone on the spot. Tōkoku's writings proceed as if to acknowledge that there is no other way of communicating *what it is* in linguistic form, hence offering only *this is it* instead.

While Tōkoku's way of delineating the unsayable resembles the construction of *what* in the negative as in negative theology, I differentiate his rhetorical gesture from negativity. Tōkoku generates a void. It is to the presence of a void that his writerly finger points. When there is nothing to be said about *what it is*, the only utterance possible is *this is it*. No further verbal explanation is appropriate or necessary because it is, as Tōkoku says, "right there" (*kashiko*).[26] The indexical gesture by no means equates the writer's intellectual incompetence. If it were incompetence, Tōkoku must have arrived at it as a result of his struggle to register the void with vocabularies available to him in whatever way possible. What is *right there* is a referential vacuum, and Tōkoku himself mobilizes the term "emptiness" (*kū* or *kyo*) to refer to it. This usage therefore quite literally—and not at all figuratively—shows that what he says about *what it is* is empty, at least in terms of what an existing system of language can appropriately capture. Such emptiness lies *right there*, awaiting his readers. One needs to "shoot the emptiness, of the emptiness, of the emptiness" to reach the pure realm, Tōkoku urges.[27] The iteration has less to do with the making of the void from the negative than with "accession to the *literal*," to borrow Roland Barthes's phrase.[28] The tautology in Tōkoku's writing is the literal, not metaphorical, affirmation of the void, its emptiness, *right there*, that no word can represent. The repeated emptiness thus signals Tōkoku's saying *that it is*, not saying *what it is*.

The ways in which Tōkoku's writings guide readers to the realm of pure literature, only to point to the "emptiness" that is *right there*, come very close to haiku's exclamation as observed by Barthes, who lectured extensively on the workings of haiku. Examining a variety of works and writers, Bashō included, Barthes asserts that "a (good) haiku *sets a bell ringing* → triggering, as the only possible remark: '*That's it!*' . . . Clearly, the *bell* is anti-interpretative: it blocks interpretation."[29] In Barthes's reading, the "that's it" of haiku designates that there is nothing more to say, that there is no other way of saying anything, about the thing that the haiku poet experiences. To be clear, I am not suggesting that Tōkoku's writings are haiku or even similar, in either form or content; rather, my point is that in both cases, language is used to communicate its own limits, that no word can compare *what it is* because this *it* rejects verbalism. In a very literal sense, *what it is* is linguistically unavailable. When the referent is without contents graspable by language, it can be registered only by the deictic terms, *this*, *that*, or *there*. The attempt to describe *what it is* with other parts of speech could only result in a flawed list of modifiers. If linguistic representation can only approximate, and is thereby destined to fail, there is no way for language to adequately represent *what it is*. In Tōkoku's accounts, the limits of verbal representation coincide with the invalidation of "correct" interpretation. *I dare not represent what it is* marks the ultimate unidentifiability of *what it is*.

Community, Still Arises

During the interrelation-with-life debate, Tōkoku brings himself to a halt immediately before the point at which verbal representation is most desired as a counter to Aizan. Where Tōkoku ceases to explain the gist of his theory, readers are left in front of what he posits as the pure realm of literature, unidentifiable and ineffable. At this moment in Tōkoku's account, language no longer affords the representational function. His *hihyō*—written, inevitably linguistic discourse—withdraws itself from a use of language to represent what it needs to say and forecloses the reader's direct access to what it promotes.

Tōkoku's writing does not abandon language completely, of course. Several scholars have suggested that Tōkoku's total body of work, including the ones produced during the debate, exhibits uniquely historical, linguistic traces. Saitō Mareshi, for instance, identifies in Tōkoku's writing the writer's desire for de-Sinification, that is, his struggle to seek more "transparent" expressions of "things before one's eyes and minds" that are not bound by Sinographic rhetorical conventions.[30] Saito's analysis resonates with Noguchi Takehiko's observation of the unorthodoxy of Tōkoku's composition. According to Noguchi, Tōkoku often conjoins different genealogies of writing usually used separately from one another and generates a hybrid of classical Japanese grammatical constructions mixed with Sinographic terminology, which makes his writing digress from the writerly norms of the late nineteenth century.[31] In the same way that these scholars consider Tōkoku's rhetorical maneuvers noteworthy, I too find that his use of words needs scrutiny, but for a different reason: His writings demonstrate a peculiar combination of linguistic components that, bound together, allows room for strong readerly commitment to emerge. It is a kind of commitment that does not hinge upon a semantically shared value, even as it is linguistically solicited.

To revisit the previous discussion, we have seen in Tōkoku's writings the demotion of the representational use of language, coupled with the recourse to the deictic. The *right there* is mobilized to index the realm of pure literature while there is no explanation for *what it is*. Such traits obscure the purity of literature, the very gist of the writer's theory. Yet seen from a different perspective, this sidestepping of representation does not necessarily entail the uninterpretability of pure literature; in fact, it might help to stretch its interpretability. This means that the nonrepresentational *right there* can give rise to a surprisingly reader-oriented effect.

A useful linguistic tool for inquiry into Tōkoku's *right there* is the category of grammatical units with a deictic function, or what Roman Jakobson once called "shifters."[32] Shifters are semantically contentless, and therefore, their referents shift with each utterance; every time shifters are used, their denotations need to be determined individually. Theoretically, there could be as many *right there*s as there are occasions on which someone directs another's attention to something in the vicinity.

THE COMMUNITY OF NO REFERENT 171

Shifters like *right there* can thus become many different things, as the inaccessibility of their content translates into their adaptability. That Tōkoku indexes the purity of literature *right there* and never articulates *what it is* ensures that there can be an inexhaustible number of possible referents, the *what it is*, the thing *right there*. Precisely because the writer leaves open the semantics of pure literature, its interpretation is left to the discretion of whoever intends to reach it. What is *right there* turns into a vessel to be filled by anyone willing to do so. This trait of shifters allows readers to make sense of *what it is* more freely, unbound by predetermined meanings. Out of ultimate unidentifiability comes space for interpretive flexibility.

At the same time, however, shifters revoke their own flexibility. Jakobson identifies the peculiarity of shifters not in their "multiplicity of contextual meanings" or in "egocentrism" as they are generally understood, but in their "compulsory reference to the given message." For the linguist, shifters are distinguished from other linguistic units because they "cannot be defined without a reference to the message."[33] In other words, code (the sign *right there*) must overlap with message (the specific referent of the sign *right there*). The sign *right there* thus draws an existential connection between Tōkoku's utterance and what he, only he, and nobody other than he can point to in front of him at a singular, isolated moment. Because of the contentlessness of the sign *right there*, however, no one has adequate access to what Tōkoku registers. What is *right there* is categorically unreachable, private only to the one saying *"right there."* The ultimate secrecy of the speaker's experience persists.

Shifters are therefore self-contradictory. They can be anything and nothing but; they are always available and absolutely private, flexible and exclusive, empty and full. While Tōkoku himself offers no explanation of his recourse to shifters and the contradiction inherent in the grammatical units, the paradoxical nature of shifters in fact plays a crucial role in facilitating reader commitment to his writings. Shifters liaise between Tōkoku and his reader. In their distinct workings, shifters invite the reader to join his vision and experience the singular *right there* that theoretically belongs to him alone.

For Jakobson, the category of shifters is not limited to indexical markers, such as *right there*, but also includes personal pronouns, *I*, *you*, or *they*, for instance. Personal pronouns are crucial components of speech, at least in many Anglo-European languages: Without them, many languages would not function sensibly, especially in writing. While personal pronouns can be mobilized by anyone, their referents can change with each utterance. When there is an *I*, there may be innumerable people who could be the *I* or replace the *I*. Personal pronouns are shifters for this reason, and in fact, Tōkoku's writings are crowded with personal pronouns. He mobilizes the first-person pronoun *I* unusually often, its abundance in itself yet another peculiarity of his use of language. This *I* is key to understanding the effect of Tōkoku's writings and how they unfold in a way that elicits readerly participation.

Consider the following exemplary passage, in which Tōkoku seeks to rebut Aizan:

> Against the enemy called "immortality," I [*gojin (wa)*] wield my [*gojin (no)*] sword in the same manner that, as Aizan describes, heroes wield theirs. Nevertheless, as if the final judgment was predetermined, I [*gojin (wa)*] stand in front of nature as force only to reveal myself as a vulnerable soldier. . . . I [*gojin (wa)*] can make my [*gojin (no)*] spirit grip again the freedom—the freedom that I [*gojin (no)*] lost as the flesh—as it wishes, in the otherly, spiritual world free of material constraints.³⁴

The dramatic tone aside, Tōkoku's writing assumes a sense of immediacy because of the recurrent references to the self, *I*. On a simple calculation of Tōkoku's *I* (*gojin*) against Aizan's, Tōkoku uses such shifters more than six times as often.³⁵ This dramatic contrast carries grave importance: Because it is a shifter, each utterance of the *I* fixes the referent, Tōkoku, the biological figure, for only an instant, and yet when repeated again and again, thirty times in a 7,500-character essay, the sign *I* ceaselessly conjures and inscribes Tōkoku both as an utterer and referent. The repetition is a constant reminder that readers should be directed to the undeniable, singular existence of Tōkoku.³⁶

In addition to the frequency of the appearance of the *I*, Tōkoku often places the first-person pronoun *I* before "*wa*," a case particle that generally marks a subject and/or a topic of the sentence. This trait is noteworthy because Tōkoku's way of mobilizing the *I* in the subjective case is unprecedented in the history of writing in Japan. The construction of Japanese writing, "X [a subject and/or a topic] *wa* Y [a predicative expression]," as in Tōkoku's "I [*gojin wa*] . . . ," may not seem awkward to twenty-first-century anglophone readers. In late nineteenth-century Japan, however, the composition was quite unusual. The conventional structure of Japanese often did not entail the articulation of the subject case or a topic that correlated with a predicative expression; that is to say, it did not need the clarification of the subject case when other parts of the language easily supplemented the information. During the latter half of the nineteenth century, linguistic conventions—especially those of written form—underwent drastic transformations as Japan actively exposed itself to information written in Anglo-European languages. As a result of Japanese intellectuals' collective efforts to digest varied forms of information in different languages, "a component that looks and functions like a 'subject' of the sentence came into existence," as linguistic historian Yanabu Akira puts it.[37] Tōkoku and some of his contemporaries, such as Sohō, were the earliest to incorporate the newly emerging structure of the case *"wa,"* paired with the first-person pronoun *"gojin,"* to express "I am" and "I do." Using this structure in their writings, Tōkoku and other intellectuals helped to normalize the then-unfamiliar linguistic construction, a form of self-assertion that unambiguously identifies the subject who speaks.[38]

The construction with the *I*, *"gojin wa,"* underlines that it is nobody other than Tōkoku who indexes the unsayable existing *right there* in front of him. Coupled, these two classes communicate a sense of immediacy, as well as the singularity, of the experience of the speaker *I*. Yet what is distinct about Tōkoku's use of language is that while those shifters interlock and anchor one another only to magnify the exclusivity of Tōkoku's pure literature, his writings still convince readers to join him in advocating the very thing inaccessible to them. The question redirects us to the self-contradictory nature of shifters, their concurrent singularity and availability. On this point, Benveniste offers valuable insight when, noting the particularity of the first-person pronoun *I*, he writes:

> Language is possible only because each speaker sets himself up as a *subject* by referring to himself as *I* in his discourse. Because of this, *I* posits another person, the one who, being, as he is, completely exterior to "me," becomes my echo to whom I say *you* and who says *you* to me. . . . [N]either of the terms can be conceived of without the other; they are complementary, although according to an "interior/exterior" opposition, and, at the same time, they are reversible.[39]

As a shifter, the first-person pronoun *I* positions the utterer Tōkoku as an existential being. In so doing, Benveniste reveals, Tōkoku's *I* cannot but hail the reader as *you*. The extensive recourse to the first-person pronoun on Tōkoku's part enables the coemergence of the *I* and the *you*. It also alters the relationship between the writer and the reader into the more inclusive and intersubjective, potentially more inevitable kind.

In praise of Benveniste, Barthes glosses the mutual dependency between those two pronouns in the following way: "there are only locutors; moreover—and this is Benveniste's incessant reminder—there are only *interlocutors*. . . . [T]he linguistics of interlocution, language, and consequently the whole world, is articulated around this form: *I/you*."[40] For present purposes, Barthes's framing of Benveniste's account is useful because Tōkoku's *I* sets in motion the "world" around "*I/you*." When those personal pronouns "exist only insofar as they are *actualized* in the instance of discourse" (emphasis added) as Benveniste explains, each instance of utterance has the potential to build an existential relationship between the *I* and the *you*.[41] Tōkoku's word may not be able to convince every single reader it encounters, and yet it continues to speak as the *I* until it reaches someone who agrees to be the *you*. Tōkoku's *I* is therefore an invitation to any reader, irrespective of temporal and spatial limits, to join him in the experience of what he says is *right there*.

For the reader, accepting the position of the *you* serves as a down payment on participating in Tōkoku's view of pure literature. That being the case, Tōkoku's writing does not simply hail the reader as *you*; it presses them to fall in the position of the *you* by repeating the imperative. Readers are not simply invited, but sometimes ordered, to become the *you*, directly addressed by Tōkoku's *I*. In the passage quoted in the previous section, for instance, where Tōkoku offers his imaginative account of Bashō's poem making, the imperative form of the verb "remember" (*kiokuseyo*) appears five times. As the writing nears its end, the final passage again repeats the imperative and intensifies the tone of locution:

> Lift your head, look, and then seek. Mobilize the lofty, empty idea, and then aim at the truly broad inhabitation, sincerely pleasant land, and genuinely enormous project. Then pursue them. Throw your longing to the limits of the empty air. And from there, grab the vocation that you must offer to humans. Alas, you writer, why would you limit yourself, only to strive to interrelate with life?[42]

Tōkoku's word, originally written as *hihyō* denouncing Aizan's view, ultimately leaves Aizan out and instead makes various requests of the reader. The imperative-ridden passage urges anyone who encounters it to follow the writer's directions, ensuring that the reader is conjured and "*actualized*" as the *you* until its last breath. Moreover, by concluding with this overbearing tenor paired with a rhetorical question, "why would you . . . ," Tōkoku's writing prolongs the effect of the hailing, holding the reader suspended in the position of the *you* and responsible for Tōkoku's address.

The exactitude of the origin of pure literature eludes verbalism, and yet that has little effect on the formation of readership in Tōkoku's case. The writer *I* raises his finger, points toward pure literature, and tells *you*, the interpellated, that *this is it*. Even as *what it is* remains without a referent, the ample usage of the personal pronoun easily, even forcefully, draws the reader closer to the writer and, in so doing, generates a feeling that the *I* and the *you* are in front of the same *right there*. Out of this feeling arises a communion: The *I* entrusts the unsaid to the *you*. There is no way of grasping *what is right there* accurately in language. By the same token, this impossibility means that there is no way of understanding it improperly. It is the contradiction innate to deictic shifters, the simultaneous exclusivity and availability that they entail, that facilitates the elicitation of commitment from the reader. Since shifters "do not assert anything, they are not subject to the condition of truth and escape all denial," as Benveniste would have it.[43] Having become the *you*, the reader, standing by Tōkoku's side, is free to insert themselves into the writer's private vision; they can appropriate the fugitive deictic at will without needing to agree with the writer on the semantics of *what it is*. What emerges is a "world" around Tōkoku and the reader, an intersubjectively rising community that registers, though nonverbally, the purity of literature. A community with no referent—its foundation, membership, and sustenance do not necessarily prioritize hermeneutics of the idea that it embraces.

The persistence of Tōkoku favoritism and pure literature to this day is a manifestation of the effectiveness of his rhetoric. His words can reach not just his contemporary readers but also anyone willing to be hailed. Irrespective of the contextual contingencies that come with every reading experience, his writings urge the reader to be in tune with his *I* and what he points *right there*. *You* are in, as long as *you* agree to respond to the *I*.

Engaging (with) the Reader

In this chapter I have examined the case of the interrelation-with-life debate with a special focus on Tōkoku's writings and contemplated what *hihyō* wrote when there was no language that compared what it had to promote. With language's referential function incapacitated, Tōkoku's word does not represent what it proposes. The only thing it can appropriately say is that it can say no more. What is particularly noteworthy about Tōkoku's rhetorical move is the timing in which it came into being. When *hihyō* emerged as a shared concern of young intellectuals in the 1880s, it was posited as metadiscourse, that is, written discourse that would efficiently evaluate written discourse. Thus conceived, *hihyō* was premised upon the use of language for the purpose of elucidating the value of a given discourse. If this was the zeitgeist surrounding critical reading practice, Tōkoku's writings did not conform to it. Instead of explaining what he valued by way of verbalism, the writer provided an index and left his readers with the value unexplained. The enrollment of readers through explicitly verbalized information, which *hihyō* was expected to offer, did not ensue. Tōkoku's *hihyō*, in other words, did not seek to complete the tasks set for the practice and thereby canceled itself from assuming the prescribed form of critical reading.

As paradoxical as it may sound, however, the self-canceling motion continues to enlist readers' participation in Tōkoku's view of literature and what his language indexes. While sidestepping *hihyō*'s preset goals, Tōkoku's *hihyō* avoids inadequately—"inadequate" at least in the vision that he constructs for the pure realm of literature—rendering substance to what it most prioritizes as the unsayable. More important, even as his writings keep the purity of literature in secrecy, Tōkoku simultaneously escapes falling into total solipsism. The emergence and sustenance of a readerly commitment to Tōkoku's key idea—pure literature—is a result of layers of rhetorical motions that the writer, intentionally or not, ends up making. Precisely because Tōkoku leaves the sign unfilled, the purity of literature can be validated every time the reader, upon encountering Tōkoku's rhetoric, responds to his intersubjective addresses. The temporal and spatial gap between the writer and the reader is susceptible to the potential of collapse, if the latter decides to be in sync with the immediacy of Tōkoku's language.

Oddly enough, the immediacy effect that Tōkoku's *hihyō* generates—the distance crumbling between the writer and the reader—corresponds to the new style of prose fiction (*shōsetsu*) developing around the same period. There were trends in the scene of writing, especially in the production of fictional prose, in late nineteenth-century Japan, in which writers sought and experimented with styles different from conventional ones so as to give rise to an unprecedented type of fiction-reading experience. In the analysis of those trends, postwar intellectual Tsurumi Shunsuke emphasized the magnitude of "language as (physical) gesture" in the formation of the new prosaic writing style in Meiji Japan.⁴⁴ It is well known that Meiji writer Futabatei Shimei closely studied the shorthand-based transcription of professional storyteller San'yūtei Enchō's performance when fashioning the alternative form of prose.⁴⁵ Noting that the transcription of oral performance retains the traces of spoken language, which initially emanated from a living being and operated inseparably from the speaker's bodily motion, Tsurumi holds:

> When the storyteller goes *"this* sort of," "more than *this,*" and "the left shoulder *here,"* these phrases transform into the storyteller's physical gestures and perform on their own amid words. Those crude expressions have little referential function when removed from each context. And yet when employed adroitly in a singular, specific context, they exercise their magical power and let the audience touch the actuality of the feeling of terror peculiar to the scene [emphasis added].⁴⁶

When language gestures, it "acts upon those who are inside the circle directly and individually," and thereby "serves the situation to vitalize it."⁴⁷ The imprints of physical gestures coinciding with spoken language, according to Tsurumi, slipped into the written form of language when Meiji writers were struggling to reinvent writing, and helped to shape a novel style of prose fiction in the late nineteenth century.

Examining the linguistic components of Futabatei's fiction *Ukigumo* (*The Drifting Clouds*, 1887–89), Maeda Ai advances Tsurumi's observation. Futabatei's writing, Maeda argues, has extensive recourse to linguistic gestures such as "varied intonations, tempos, and rhythm." As those gestures generate the "effects of directness and firsthand-ness," they also allow readers to accord with the addresser on the affective level.⁴⁸ The result of such a writing style is twofold. First, it annihilates the barrier between writer and reader; second, it creates a feeling that the "reader can face the writer in isolation and hear, without mediation, the secret story that the writer whispers."⁴⁹ In this way, Maeda's study highlights the link between the formation of alternative writing style for prose fiction and the emergence of the new "solitary reading" practice (which largely supplanted the communal, read-out-loud style of reading exercise). Both Tsurumi and Maeda suggest that in the context of late nineteenth-century Japan, language as gesture facilitated a sense of close companionship between writer and reader, an experience that the reader could become proximate to the writer privately through written language.

CHAPTER 6

What Tōkoku's style of *hihyō* enacts approximates the affective ramifications that the newly rising style of prose fiction brought about, although the parallel was perhaps inadvertent. In the case of Tōkoku's work, *hihyō*, contemporaneously expected to serve as a fair, objective, and distanced judge of a given discourse, ended up securing intimacy between the critic and each individual reader. Such intimacy points to at least two breakages: the collapse of the distance between critic and reader, and the blurring of difference between the capacity of critical language and that of fictional writing. I mention these weakened distinctions not to attack Tōkoku's oeuvre with respect to the ideal realm of *hihyō* but rather to highlight that those moments of intimacy, nurtured in secrecy between the writer critic and the reader, continue to inscribe Tōkoku's writing as *hihyō* and perpetuate its long-lasting effect.

The ways in which Tōkoku's rhetoric unfolds shed light on a path that is worth bearing in mind when we, twenty-first-century readers in literary studies, practice critical reading. This is certainly not to propose that Tōkoku's use of language is superior to others in the workings of critical reading. After all, I still believe that we owe linguistic clarification to our readers. Rather, I place my deliberation of Tōkoku's *hihyō* at the end of this book because it affords an opportunity to reflect on what we do in the name of critical reading and, more specifically, how we engage (with) readers throughout our specialized practice of reading literature. The question of readerly engagement is particularly urgent in our times, when the value of reading can no longer be taken for granted. Tōkoku's writings push us into a direction where we have to open ourselves up to different ways of envisioning our work and, in particular, to consider the sense of intersubjective reading experience that our critical readings may bring into being. If we can be in tune with what Tōkoku registers as *right there*—where the essence of literature germinates—perhaps it may be also possible for us to write and make known our own *right theres*—why we read literature—to our readers. In 1932, Miki Kiyoshi remarked, "Critics are not the ones who criticize, but the ones who are criticized."[50] If we embrace Miki's self-reflection, ultimately, our work as critical readers, which we can become only in our being read, hinges upon readers.

Conclusion
Failing Well

This book had two core aims: first, to offer an early history of *hihyō* in Meiji Japan, and second, to think about how to read in the postcritical age. By tracking the processes through which *hihyō* came into being in late nineteenth-century Japan, I have suggested that the failures of fin de siècle *hihyō* perhaps speak less about the flaws of Meiji practitioners than they do about our implicit assumptions about what critical reading is. Precisely because Meiji intellectuals' *hihyō* practices did not unfold in a way easily understandable to us, their writings counterreveal the bounds of how we do what we do. To bring my account to a close, I want to offer two perspectives, corresponding respectively to the two goals of this project, so that we can reflect on our here and now in relation to *hihyō*.

Afterlives of *Hihyō*

To begin, I want to consider the afterlives of Meiji Japan's *hihyō* and briefly describe what happened to *hihyō* in the twentieth century with two points in mind. First, when it was under construction in fin de siècle Japan, it was accompanied by a sense of uncertainty about what it is to be "critical" in reading practice; of particular relevance, then, is how, when the practice of *hihyō* became more standardized in the twentieth century, the confusion or wavering over the meaning of "critical" continued. Second, concurrent with *hihyō*'s emergence in print media was the formation of a special relationship between *hihyō* and literature, even though the boundaries of literature were also undergoing transformation. For most of the twentieth century, literature occupied a central position to the practice of *hihyō*, and yet the tight connection between the two began to fade toward the end of the century. In light of these two points, several key moments in the trajectories of twentieth-century *hihyō* deserve our attention. The following account is by no means comprehensive; it is intended to provide a point of departure for those interested in mulling over Japanese criticism and its future.

The first moment to highlight is the early twentieth century, between the 1920s and the 1930s. In this period, with the development of the print industry, *hihyō* became further ingrained and systematized in the intellectual sphere, especially the literary sphere. While the Great Kantō Earthquake (1923) destroyed a large part of the print industry in the Tokyo area, it also prompted the *enpon* (one-yen book) boom, starting with a new collection of contemporary Japanese literature launched in 1926 by Tokyo-based publisher Kaizōsha. By the time the *enpon* boom waned in the early 1930s, the mass production and sales of cheap books had become common practice. As Edward Mack demonstrates, this period saw "literary value"—value as conceptualized against commercial value—was widely contested among writers and intellectuals.[1] In addition, it was in this period that the intellectual, journalistic, and cultural field of speech through print media was irrevocably stabilized in Japan.[2] According to Ōsawa Satoshi, the establishment of the field of speech, including literature, was accompanied by reinforcement of the institution of *hihyō*, in particular the reification of now-common genres and structures of *hihyō*, such as roundtable discussion (*zadankai*) and personality *hihyō* (*jinbutsu hihyō*).[3] In short, in the 1920s and 30s, heated discussions about literary value coincided with further cultivation of *hihyō* in the growing space of print media. These two threads went hand in hand, informing and reinforcing each other.

The same period also witnessed the height of the proletarian literary movement, best represented by writer Kobayashi Takiji (1903–33), and of Marxism-influenced *hihyō*, exemplified by such figures as Hirabayashi Hatsunosuke (1892–1931) and Aono Suekichi (1890–1961). As Heather Bowen-Struyk and Norma Field observe, in the proletarian movement, which was a dominant force in the early twentieth century, political problems were literary problems, and also the reverse.[4] *Hihyō* in this period thus functioned more or less as discourse that spoke of politics and literature as inseparable, in which the political was at once the literary.

That Kobayashi Hideo, a leading twentieth-century *hihyō* practitioner, made his debut in 1929 with "Samazamanaru ishō" (Multiple designs) is noteworthy in two ways. First, while Kobayashi continued his career in *hihyō* for many decades, his initial rise as a young, dilettantish *hihyō* practitioner at this historical moment confirms aforementioned Ōsawa's point about the stabilization of the print media environment at the time. That is to say, in order for a professional *hihyō* practitioner like Kobayashi to appear and practice his work as an expert, the durability of the industry that could sustain *hihyō* needed to precede. Second, Kobayashi's debut essay, written when Marxist *hihyō* was at its height, in a sense predicted the downfall of that strand of *hihyō* in the following decade. Though at times an influential force, Kobayashi did not espouse Marxist thought as a definitive ideology, instead identifying it as one of the imported and available "designs."[5] While Kobayashi's claim was clearly digressive from the zeitgeist, Marxist *hihyō* quickly lost its privilege in the 1930s, as if to validate its nondefinitive quality seen by Kobayashi. These historical factors facilitated the rise of Kobayashi as a *hihyō* professional and subsequent valorization of his style of *hihyō* that looked highly self-reflective, setting the tone for critical practice to follow.

The decline of Marxist *hihyō* paralleled the expansion of the Japanese empire in the late 1930s. The notorious Chian iji hō (Peace Preservation Law) of 1925, which aimed at aggressive thought control, led to the police torturing and murdering Kobayashi Takiji in 1933; not until 1945 would leftist *hihyō* regain traction in the intellectual sphere. In this period of oppression, many left-leaning intellectuals were expelled from academia (for example, Miki Kiyoshi was dismissed from the professoriate in 1930 for his scholarly investment in Marxism), and some found an alternative career path in journalism as professional, freelance *hihyō* practitioners. This segment of *hihyō*'s history contributed to the somewhat fluid relationship between academism and journalism in twentieth-century Japan, as well as the uniquely privileged position of practitioners of *hihyō*.

Post-1945 *hihyō* began with reflections on Japan's recent past of warfare and literature's relationship to it. Literature must have been responsible for atrocities of such scale and duration; something must have gone wrong in the scene of literary production and critical reading in the 1930s, especially in the proletarian literary movement, to allow militarism to flourish; those who participate in the literary scene must reposition themselves vis-à-vis the past, present, and future; literature should (or should not) be separated from political ideology; and its association with humanism too needs to be reconfigured. Multiple intellectual figures, most of them leftists in the 1920s and 1930s, addressed these points through roundtable discussions, exchanges of opinion, and debates; a good example is the "Seiji to bungaku" (politics and literature) debate (1946–47), in which such intellectuals as Hirano Ken (1907–78), Ara Masahito (1913–79), Honda Shūgo (1908–2001), and Nakano Shigeharu (1902–79) engaged in convoluted discussions about literature's war responsibility.

These post-1945 discussions, especially the politics and literature debate, offer useful insight for thinking about *hihyō*'s relationship to literature, as throughout them *hihyō* was reinscribed as a powerful intellectual device in and for Japan's postwar present. Recent scholarship on the politics and literature debate by Atsuko Ueda and others has shown that the debaters unanimously "believed in the absolute power of literature.... Despite the fact that the contours of literature were in flux and that these writers differed greatly in their views of the 'literary,' they never questioned the fundamental power they ascribed to it."[6] Even as the nature of the "literary" and, by implication, what the "critical" position in the "literary" scene meant varied from discussant to discussant, the participants considered literature's authority to be a given. This has important implications for *hihyō*'s status. If literature is absolute, then *hihyō* that engages with literature must also have a special, unshakable standing. The position of those who practice *hihyō*, by extension, is not in question, and from this very position, *hihyō* practitioners maintain the "contours of literature" upon which they rely. Ueda observes that Hirano began to produce new literary histories from his postwar present (1959–71) specifically by taking the 1920s and 1930s—the rise and fall of the proletarian literary movement—as the "origin of their postwar literary movement."[7] In other words, Hirano could attempt to rewrite literary history because he was a *hihyō* practitioner, standing in a privileged position. His revisionist gesture attests to the unwavering authority of literature—and by extension *hihyō*—in intellectual circles at that time. *Hihyō* was thus revitalized as an institution in the late 1940s specifically in connection to the proletarian literary movement. The earlier, mutually reinforcing relationship between literature and *hihyō* was then reiterated.

The Marxist overtones that marked *hihyō* in the 1950s and 60s receded, at least from the surface, around the 1970s, along with the end of the so-called "season of politics" (*seiji no kisetsu*). The disintegration of the student protest movements (for example, the Anpo struggle, the anti-Vietnam War movement, the protests against the construction of a new airport in Sanrizuka, Narita) revealed that Marxism no longer held the intellectual authority it used to. Nakamasa Masaki explains the fall of Marxism from the frontline of intellectualism in the 1970s that Marxism's premised bourgeois-proletariat distinction fell out of touch with the reality of the emerging mass consumption society, in which everyone, including wage workers, became consumers.[8] The years that followed also witnessed the arrival of *gendai shisō* (contemporary thought) in the 1970s and the *nyū akademizumu* (new academism) in the 1980s. These changes altered the boundaries of *hihyō* considerably; simply put, over the course of the 1970s and 80s, *hihyō* stopped having an exclusive connection to literature and began to fuse with *shisō* (thought) and *riron* (theory) to form more dispersed relationships with a diverse range of topics beyond literature. A brief sketch of this gradual decline of the *hihyō*–literature exclusivity is in order.

First, the 1970s *gendai shisō* boom significantly expanded the scope of intellectualism. Several new periodicals launched in the late 1960s and into the 1970s translated and introduced trends of contemporary Euro-Anglo-American thought—semiotics, structuralism, deconstruction, psychoanalysis, and so forth—to a Japanese audience; examples include the quarterly *Paideia* (1968-73), the monthly *Gendai shisō* (Contemporary thought, established in 1973), and the monthly *Episutēmē* (Episteme, 1975-79).[9] The contents of these journals, generally called *gendai shisō*, encouraged promiscuous reading of a wide variety of trends in intellectual and philosophical thought. The so-called linguistic turn in literary scholarship in the 1970s and 1980s, that is, a turn prompted by the incorporation of new reading methodologies, such as semiotics and structuralism, took place against a backdrop of the *gendai shisō* boom.[10]

What the *gendai shisō* boom had initiated in the seventies was amplified by the publication of economist Asada Akira's *Kōzō to chikara: Kigōron o koete* (Structure and power: Beyond semiotics, 1983) and the *nyū akademizumu* boom that followed in the 1980s.[11] In that book, Asada offered a broad overview of *gendai shisō*, including detailed explanations of structuralism and poststructuralism and their limits, as well as of the positions of leading intellectual figures such as Jacques Lacan, Gilles Deleuze, and Félix Guattari. Most of the chapters included first

CONCLUSION

appeared in the journal *Gendai shisō*. Asada's discussions are abstruse, and yet *Kōzō to chikara* became a bestseller in the 1980s, selling far beyond the academic market. Presumably, that Asada was only twenty-six years old when he published the book helped to create an appearance of youthful new energy galvanizing the intellectual sphere. Together with Asada, such figures as religion scholar Nakazawa Shin'ichi and economic anthropologist Kurimoto Shin'ichirō were featured by media journalism as forces in *nyū akademizumu* in the 1980s. Despite the moniker, *nyū akademizumu* was not confined to academia; it was an unprecedented form of intellectual performance that was academism, journalism, and entertainment all at once. "New academics" like Nakazawa and Kurimoto frequently appeared in popular magazines and TV shows as smart, privileged, but entertaining commentators. Many of their "academic" works were interdisciplinary and boundary crossing in nature and thus escaped the limits of any single field of knowledge.[12]

The journal medium such as *Gendai shisō* clearly facilitated the transition from the *gendai shisō* boom to *Kōzō to chikara*, and on to the *nyū akademizumu* boom. Reflecting on the increasing popularity of *gendai shisō* among young Japanese intellectuals from the 1970s onward, Nakamasa argues that *gendai shisō* "replaced" Marxism when the latter no longer matched the changing reality of production and consumption in society.[13] Sasaki Atsushi similarly contends that the "Japanese youth who wanted to think" (*shisō-shitai wakamono*) lost their playground after the end of the season of politics, but found the perfect outlet for their desires in new configurations of intellectualism on an entirely different plane from political radicalism.[14] What Nakamasa calls the "replacement" was possible because, according to Sasaki, such intellectual fads as *gendai shisō* and *nyū akademizumu* served as receptors for the young generation's intellectual libido that could no longer be satisfied by direct political activism. Asada's famous phrase in the introduction to *Kōzō to chikara*, "be apathetic while getting high, be high while getting apathetic" ("*shirake tsutsu nori, nori tsutsu shirakeru*"), adequately captured the new demeanor of intellectualism fervently welcomed by Japanese youth who was seeking alternative models of knowledge beyond leftist, activist ideologies.[15]

These trends of intellectualism significantly enlarged the ambit of *hihyō*. Both *gendai shisō* and *nyū akademizumu* entailed endeavors of critical reading, and yet the practice of reading manifest in these newer trends marked a crucial disconnect from the *hihyō* conceived before the 1970s. The position of literature is key to this change. Ōsawa Satoshi, in his analysis of the disconnect, argues that while during a large part of the Shōwa period (1926–89), literature was enshrined as an absolute center in the practice of *hihyō*, that configuration had ceased to function by the middle of the 1970s, as the scope of *hihyō* became much broader than critical reading of fundamentally literary texts.[16] The special relationship between *hihyō* and literature had existed since the late nineteenth century, and the connection was still in place in post-1945 Japan when *hihyō* practitioners like Hirano were active. But this was no longer the case in the seventies. It is suggestive that Asada's *Kōzō to chikara* (published in September 1983) came out just several months after the death of Kobayashi Hideo (March 1983). The demise of Kobayashi, whose prolific writing practices, while extremely multidisciplinary, still embodied the centrality of literature in *hihyō*, literature as a ground for *hihyō*'s self-reflective undertakings, immediately followed by the rising of Asada, a standard-bearer of *nyū akademizumu*, marked a break in the modes of intellectualism and general assumptions about critical practice. The purview of *hihyō* changed drastically in the seventies and eighties in relation to shifting configurations of intellectualism, and as a result, *hihyō*'s once-foundational connection to literature faded into the background.[17]

Another important moment begins with the publication of the journal *Hihyō kūkan* (Critical space) in the early 1990s, established by Karatani Kōjin, Asada, and others (predominantly male intellectuals) with strong affiliations to *gendai shisō* and *nyū akademizumu*. As the title indicates, the journal offered a "critical space" to introduce contemporary Euro-Anglo-American intellectual discourses to Japanese audience, just as had *Gendai shisō* and its ilk a generation before. *Hihyō kūkan* stands in a peculiar position in the history of twentieth-century *hihyō*. In its attempts to create dialogue between Euro-Anglo-America and Japan, the journal endorsed the slippage between *hihyō* and *riron* (theory). At the same time, while it inherited from *gendai shisō* and *nyū akademizumu*, which had contributed to the degradation of the *hihyō*-literature exclusivity, it remained persistently attached to literature as an essential site of *hihyō*.

A glance at the 1991 inaugural issue may prompt a feeling of incongruity after the present book's tracking of the history of modern *hihyō* because what appears in *Hihyō kūkan* does not obviously align with the central premise of Meiji *hihyō*, that is, evaluative discourse illuminating the value of another discourse. The front cover, for instance, shows such titles as "The Rhetoric of Temporality" (Paul de Man, 1983), "The Politics of Theory: Ideological Positions in the Postmodernism

Debate" (Fredric Jameson, 1988), and *The Sublime Object of Ideology* (Slavoj Žižek, 1989), all in Japanese translation. Many of those authors' works circulate generally as *gendai shisō* in Japan and "theory" (*riron*) in the United States. In the editorial postscript Karatani remarks in passing that all contributed essays are written and/or presented in "theoretical Japanese" (*rirontekina Nihongo*).[18] Such rhetoric postulates that the "critical" language used in this journal is the "theoretical" one. The journal thus naturalizes an association of *hihyō*, *gendai shisō*, and *riron* with no clear explanation of how to bridge them, though when we reflect on the trajectories of *hihyō* since the Meiji period such an association is not a given.

That being the case, the first issue also makes an interesting move because it revives the crucial standing of literature in "critical" space. For example, two leading scholars of literature, Komori Yōichi and Noguchi Takehiko, who engaged with the linguistic turn in their scholarship during the *gendai shisō* and *nyū akademizumu* booms, contributed scholarly writing: Noguchi's "Kindai Nihon bungaku to 'hihyō' no hakken" (Modern Japanese literature and the discovery of "*hihyō*," pp. 6–26) and Komori's "Kindai hihyō no shuppatsu" (The overture of modern *hihyō*, pp. 69–84). Noguchi also joined a roundtable discussion with the journal's editorial members to consider the emergence of *hihyō* in the late nineteenth century, the transcript published as "Meiji hihyō no shomondai, 1868–1910: Kokumin kokka no keisei to 'bungaku' to iu seido" (Problems of Meiji *hihyō*, 1868–1910: The formation of the nation-state and an institution called "literature," pp. 27–68).[19] Thus two essays and one roundtable discussion, all addressing the rise of *hihyō* in the Meiji period in relation to literature, make up the first three major entries in the issue. To this, we may also add Karatani's essay, "*Nihon kindai bungaku no kigen*, saikō" ("Rethinking *Origins of Modern Japanese Literature*," pp. 85–99), which immediately follows. In short, the first one hundred pages of the first issue of this "critical" space is dedicated to "literary" discussions, while the piece by de Man and other "theoretical" works come later. In the wake of *gendai shisō* and *nyū akademizumu*, which were premised on new, boundary-crossing constellations of knowledge, the centrality of literature in the organization of *Hihyō kūkan* appears backward-looking, as if seeking to recuperate *hihyō*'s predilection for literature.

Hihyō kūkan presents these proper names—de Man, Jameson, Žižek, Karatani, Asada, Komori, and Noguchi—and terms—*hihyō*, *gendai shisō*, *riron*, and literature—next to each other. On the one hand, the contiguity makes it appear that "literature" no longer assumes an absolute position in the "critical" space, confirming that the connection between *hihyō* and literature had been weakened. On the other hand, the organization of this issue also suggests that what allows the contiguity of these names and terms remains a "literary" concern. *Hihyō kūkan*, at least when launched in the early 1990s, seems to waver between the newer semantic economy of *hihyō* (as *shisō* and *riron*) and *hihyō*'s foundational connection to literature, without being able to integrate the two. There is, in other words, a rift within *Hihyō kūkan*, one that Karatani and other editorial members did not fix or perhaps even recognize. To conclude this discussion, then, I want to contemplate this rift, or to be more precise, how the coexistence of different manifestations of *hihyō* that *Hihyō kūkan* embodied in the early 1990s might be situated in the history of *hihyō*.

In the twenty-first century, a new group of intellectuals, some of them heirs to the affiliates of *Hihyō kūkan*, began to assess the *hihyō* practiced in the 1970s onward. One of them, Azuma Hiroki, in a 2016 essay, scans Karatani's works since the 1970s and suggests that Karatani's late twentieth-century intellectual endeavors show symptoms of "illness" (*yamai*)[20]:

> For Karatani, *hihyō* was nothing other than the experience of illness, that is, the experience of confusion between existence [*jitsuzon*] and politics [*seiji*], literature [*bungaku*] and politics [*seiji*], and the particular [*tokushu*] and the general [*ippan*]. . . . The essence of an illness called *hihyō* lies in the experience of confusion. Is it a text analysis? "Theory"? Ethics? Ontology? Politics? Or literature? In principle, not just readers but also writers themselves cannot determine what it is.[21]

According to Azuma, at the core of Karatani's illness was *hihyō*'s unidentifiability, which accelerated in the post-1945 context when Japan could not freely explore speech under the occupation. If we believe Azuma's claim, then the rift manifested in *Hihyō kūkan*'s first issue may be yet another symptom of its chief editor's illness, as "writers themselves cannot determine what it [*hihyō*] is." Azuma argues that instead of pursuing why the ultimately unidentifiable practice of *hihyō* was accepted and circulated so widely in postwar Japan's readerly community (and, I would add, instead of confronting the rift in *Hihyō kūkan*), Karatani was "cured" of his illness and stopped being bogged down in *hihyō*'s unidentifiability as he had at the height of his career.[22] The "cure" here points to the obliteration of the "disconnect between language and reality"—that postwar intellectuals did not, and could not, match their word to their reality through their practice—which the defeat and occupation imposed upon Japan.[23] Karatani was "cured," Azuma thinks, because his post-Fukushima intellectualism began to prioritize immediate deeds and political activism, which finally allowed the sick thinker to believe in a perfect approximation of word and reality.[24]

Importantly, for Azuma, Karatani's recovery from the illness, here understood as his newly acquired belief in the enactment of word into reality, does not indicate the progress of *hihyō*, but signals the regression or even repression of its genealogies. Azuma claims that *hihyō*'s identity was in its very unidentifiability, and yet, as Karatani's trajectory exemplifies, such unidentifiability no longer constitutes a dominant force in the contemporary scene of *hihyō*. Thus Azuma laments, "To avoid the inward tendencies of academia without completely becoming journalism, such dual-natured language—what Mikhail Bakhtin would likely call polyphony—was once referred to as *criticism* [*hihyō*] in Japan.... In fact, however, the term *criticism* is no longer used in such a fashion."[25] The recent dissolution of its constitutive unidentifiability leads to Azuma's contention that we twenty-first-century readers need to restore the state of illness, linger in *hihyō*'s unidentifiability, and ask "what people have done in the name of *hihyō*," in order to imagine how we do what we do as *hihyō* in the future.[26] The journal *Genron* (Speech) founded in 2015 is Azuma's attempt to create another "critical" space for reinstating the ambivalent, polyphonic nature of *hihyō*, what it used to be.

Azuma's proposal to embrace *hihyō*'s unidentifiability resonates with my concerns for what was said about and done as *hihyō* in fin de siècle Japan. While there is a contextual difference between Azuma's postwar focus and mine, the experience of what Azuma describes as the "confusion" of *hihyō* was not a new phenomenon in the postwar intellectual sphere. To entertain possible future designs for *hihyō*, a Japanese invention of critical reading, it is necessary to reflect on the moments of confusion inscribed since its inception. My hope is that this book joins the contemporary endeavor to better comprehend *hihyō* and contributes to the reconception of this reading practice.

Reading Otherwise

The second focal point in this book is what Meiji *hihyō*'s generative failures show us, as we think about how to read in the discipline of literature in the twenty-first-century North American academia. Because the cases of *hihyō* from late nineteenth-century Japan intervened in the genealogies of critical reading in creative ways, I have suggested, they afford us room to explore how we may reconfigure our own critical reading practice.

Consider particularly how such critical reading might be compared to, for instance, suspicion or paranoia. I have said in the introduction that a reading method in the postcritical age cannot be posited concretely in a formulaic way because if our reading activity follows a template, one lucid and strong enough for practitioners to deploy consistently, we inevitably abandon the premise of reading anew. For that reason, instead of prescribing what should be done, I draw anecdotally on my teaching experiences to give the second point of my book some tangibility.[27] After all, a classroom is a space full of surprise utterances and encounters, and furthermore, what happens in class is always personal and collective. As such, this setting provides unusually fertile opportunities for reflection on what reading a text *does* rather than on what that text *means*.

I once assigned proletarian writer Hayama Yoshiki's (1894–1945) short story "Letter Found in a Cement-Barrel" (1926). In it, a middle-aged male laborer at a cement factory picks up a small, sealed box in one of the cement-barrels. Inside the box is a letter from a young female factory worker, which discloses that her lover (another laborer at a cement factory) fell into the rock crusher by accident, where he was pulverized and transfigured into cement powder. The sender of the letter begs whoever receives the letter to tell her the whereabouts of her cement lover. Despite this poignant request, the ending suggests that the receiver, depicted as someone overwhelmed by his own life constraints, takes no action. While "Letter Found in a Cement-Barrel" was immediately recognized in contemporary proletarian literary circles, its literary life did not last long. Ivan Morris, the translator of this piece, explains that "the plot is obviously contrived to convey a message," and that "much of what he [Hayama] wrote, like the story translated here, is likely to strike the reader as a downright parody on 'proletarian' literature."[28] And indeed, the story does not seem to be read beyond the scope of the proletarian literary movement in 1920s Japan; I myself selected the piece to explore that world in class.

One of my students had a surprising reading experience of this story. She said in class that she finally found language to describe the relationship that she, as a wage worker at a coffee shop, had with the coffee drinks she served minute by minute, each cup of which somehow cost more than her hourly earnings. Reading Hayama's piece, this student

CONCLUSION

reached a fresh understanding of the world and her position in it. In this world, her time-stamped labor was transfigured into the dark-colored luxury liquid, which has more monetary value than her one-hour labor but was consumed in a much shorter time. The transfiguration of labor into coffee, and its swift consumption, appeared magical—but she also felt that the magic was inescapable. The student "failed" to see the cookie-cutter construction of Hayama's story and contextualize this piece in the broader history of early twentieth-century Japanese literary movements. Yet she also discovered a sincere connection with the description of labor in the story, through which she began to reorient herself to this strange, magically capitalist world and question its viability. In the world that she newly configured based on her reading experience, the butt of the "parody" was not the story's recourse to the typical, message-driven plot but the highbrow academic position that could only focus on its flaws. The translator did not imagine, understandably enough, how the proletarian predicament in Hayama's story could touch a struggling college student in twenty-first-century America. Yet when the student "failed" to register the translator's points, she, perhaps accidently, allowed "Letter Found in a Cement-Barrel" to extend itself over time, across space, in a way that helped her redraw her relationship with the world.

In another class, I asked my students to watch Ōshima Nagisa's 1983 film *Merry Christmas Mr. Lawrence*. The story takes place in a prisoner of war camp in Japan-occupied Java in 1942, in which various forms of male-male relationships—violence, dominance, friendship, and reverence—manifest. I selected this piece thinking that it would ignite productive discussion about representations of homosociality, homoeroticism, and race in cinema. By accident, however, I assigned a version without English subtitles. While most of the dialogue is in English, ten minutes or so at the beginning—the establishing sequences of the film—are predominantly in Japanese. By the time I realized my mistake it was too late to upload the correct version or change the assignment. I went to class, wondering how I could wring some useful discussion out of my error. As expected, many students did not follow what was happening at the beginning of the story—for example, why one of the "Japanese" soldiers is beaten, and in particular that this soldier is in fact an ethnic Korean supposedly mobilized in the Japanese army under colonial rule. Clearly I "failed" and ruined their viewing experience, I thought. Yet unexpected comments followed. First, most of the students ended up watching the film at a normal speed, not at 1.5× or faster speed, as they confessed they had usually done, because of the need to gather nonverbal clues to the story; more important, they actually enjoyed doing so. One said that watching a film at a regular speed felt like a privilege, as if she had reclaimed her freedom from self-imposed temporal constraints. Second, watching this film without subtitles made many students feel incapacitated, not just linguistically but also existentially. One said that he felt as if he had taken a glimpse into a world without him, one that would not beg for his interpretation or even his presence. The experience of being estranged in a foreign language as a twenty-first-century viewer unwittingly imitated, despite its qualitative difference, the experience of being stranded in a foreign landscape as a prisoner of war. While trying to process the film, another student added, the linguistic disqualification overlaps with military impotence, pushing him into a space where (hetero)normativity no longer holds. After class discussion, some students sent me notes, saying that they felt lifted from normative restrictions in their lives and more receptive to different ways of engaging with what is in front of them in the world, be it time, language, or gender.

These anecdotes bring to light refreshing readerly experiences of linguistic and visual texts, experiences that do not necessarily rely on suspicion or paranoia. These students did not pull "what it means" from the text at hand. Instead, their reading experiences afforded the formation of a new relationship between the text, the reader, and the world in which the reader encountered the text. The text pushed the students and altered the ways in which they related to the world, as well as the ways in which the world emerged to them. At the same time, the students also resituated the text in the world. The coming together of such a relationship gestates one possibility we might entertain as we think about how to read—and why reading matters. For, beyond skepticism and historicism, the discipline of literature and by extension the humanities excel at making relationships through reading.

A last anecdote: my own reading and relationship making. For this book, I collected rare materials, sat in front of a microfilm reader for days, and consulted with dictionaries of Chinese characters, in the same way that many other scholars specializing in the nineteenth century have done before me. I fondly remember the crisp texture of the paper forms needed to gain entry to the Meiji Shinbun Zasshi Bunko; the "click" when I inserted a microfilm into the machine usually placed in the least popular room at the library; the many pages that I flipped to identify the radical of an unfamiliar ideogram; and not least the musty, almost surreal smell of the Mori Ōgai Bunko. My body vividly remembers those moments. Ultimately, those physically inscribed moments have continually facilitated my attunement and my unconditional yielding to the reading of language and its magical capacities. I was and still am enchanted by the world unfolding in front of me, the world that for some reason—this is my unsayable—Meiji's *hihyō* brings closer to me.

I had a felicitous, chance encounter with Karl Popper's autobiography as I prepared my manuscript, where I found the following:

> What characterizes creative thinking, apart from the intensity of the interest in the problem, seems to me often the ability to break through the limits of the range—or to vary the range—from which a less creative thinker selects his trials. This ability, which clearly is a critical ability, may be described as *critical imagination*.[29]

As Popper reminds us, we need not be specialists who only read creativity that someone else shared in their writings. We can graft our creative imagination onto our critical reading practice. We can allow room for the interplay between being critical and being creative to arise in our own practice. We can, in other words, read anew. When we do so, we may have a more intimate glimpse into a vision that Ōnishi Hajime entertained in 1888, in which critic and creator become one and the same.

Acknowledgments

I like the acknowledgment sections of scholarly monographs. I read for them, sometimes with stronger enthusiasm than I do for the middle body of books. A unique genre as it is, acknowledgements are always placed in the margins, that is, constitutive spaces without which the content cannot be presented. All of the people I mention here read in me something that I did not realize that I had had until they made me, and I wish to say, with sincerest gratitude, they bequeathed me margins that have reshaped my journey as a reader. I am eternally grateful that they made me understand real fireworks happen in the margins.

I am indebted to the intellectual communities at Princeton University, the University of Kentucky, the University of Virginia, and the University of Massachusetts. Atsuko Ueda taught me how to embrace the chaos of texts, and Eduardo Cadava illustrated ways to play with language's madness. Both of them initiated me into the intoxication of reading. My world collapsed many times as I saw them read, the experiences of which helped me lose and reorient myself as a reader. The teachers and advisors I met as a graduate student, Doris Bargen, Patrick Caddeau, Richard Calichman, Steven Chung, Komori Yōichi, Federico Marcon, Stephen Miller, Richard Okada, Keiko Ono, and Amanda Seaman, kindly shared their expertise with me as I grew into a more attentive reader. Liang Luo, Douglas Slaymaker, and Akiko Takenaka have read many incarnations of my writing and offered me their insights. My colleagues, Molly Blasing, Valerio Caldesi Valeri, Martin Chan, Liliana Drucker, Yoko Horikawa, Masamichi Inoue, Sheila Jelen, Wei Jiang, Taylor Kincaid, Emily Mokros, Jeffrey Peters, Joannah Peterson, Karen Petrone, Tomomi Sato, Jeorg Sauer, Yuanyuan Su, Keiko Tanaka, Koji Tanno, and Sharon Yam, prepared an environment in which I could believe my work was valued. All were essential to the making of this book, and I do not take their attention and encouragement for granted.

Those who have held my hand as I walked through and beyond graduate school, Erin Brightwell, Yanie Fecu, Kaoru Hayashi, Otilia Milutin,

ACKNOWLEDGMENTS

Takashi Miura, Yuko Mizue, Megan Sarno, Megan Steffan, and Ron Wilson, constantly reminded me that communal reading was a fun, life-changing activity, especially when there were disagreements. In the early stages of my career, William Bridges, Erin Huang, Reginald Jackson, Shion Kono, Astrid Lac, and Franz Prichard showed me what I could pursue moving forward as an academic. The passion for books and book lovers that Sharon Domier, Yasuko Makino, and Setsuko Noguchi had was contagious, thoroughly infiltrating my work. Conversations with students and other staff members at these institutions always invigorated me, carrying me through the hardest times.

With heartfelt appreciation, I thank Ayako Kano for modeling what I understand as reparative reading. Her careful look at the earlier version of my monograph helped me remember why critical reading matters and rejuvenated my project.

It has been a genuine pleasure to work with Alexis Shimon as I began to conceive a possibility of rendering material shape to this book. Their words, rather magically, always directed me to the right spot. Their colleagues at Cornell University Press, including Katlyn Bond, patiently walked me through as I prepared the final version of my manuscript, of which I am very appreciative. I am humbled by the generosity of anonymous reviewers of my manuscript, who helped me identify and rearticulate the strength of this project. I also wish to extend my gratitude to Christopher Lehrich and Brad Allard for thoroughly examining my writing and ensuring its readability.

Research funds from the Japan Foundation, Princeton University, and the University of Kentucky enabled multiple trips to archives and on-site research. I am thankful to the National Diet Library, the Meiji Shinbun Zasshi Bunko and the Ōgai Bunko at the University of Tokyo, the National Institute for Japanese Language and Linguistics, and Nippon Hyōronsha for allowing me to use their collections and data.

Earlier versions of chapter 4 appeared in the *Journal of Japanese Studies*, and chapter 6 in *Japan Forum*. I appreciate that these journals granted me permission to reprint part of my previous publications.

My final thank you remark goes to my family. The arrival of Sasha and Eissa in this world transformed me into what I imagine to be a Yokomitsu Riichi-esque "fourth-person" reader. Surreal as it sounds, becoming a fourth person has been one of the most fantastic readerly experiences I have had. Support from the Goldings, the Gotos, the Takaokas, and the Tessiers has been strongly felt as I navigated academia.

Naru deserves a special mention for her abilities to turn everything into festivity, which brightened my mood countless times.

My greatest thanks go to Eric, an amazing reader of my mind, whose presence prepared me for all sorts of cathexes. Every word I have written was possible because of him. This book thus does not quite belong to me, but to Eric, the enormous, most important margin of my life.

NOTES

Introduction: That Which Is Casually Called Criticism

1. "Jitchi yūeki hakurankai no zu," in *Gōtō: Dai Nihon kokumin sen'yō jitchi yūeki taizen*, ed. Tamura Mie (Yūekidō, 1886).
2. Yayoshi Mitsunaga, *Mikan shiryō ni yoru Nihon shuppan bunka* (Yumani Shobō, 1990), 288–91.
3. Peter Kornicki states that woodblock printing succumbed to new print technologies around 1890. According to Edward Mack, multiple actors such as the Meiji government and publishing companies ended up collectively, though not necessarily collaboratively, contributing to the spreading of new print technologies during the late nineteenth century. Peter Kornicki, *The Book in Japan: A Cultural History from the Beginnings to the Nineteenth Century* (Brill, 1998), 6 and 165; and Edward Mack, *Manufacturing Modern Japanese Literature: Publishing, Prizes, and the Ascription of Literary Value* (Duke University Press, 2010), 23–30.
4. Kōno Kensuke, *Shomotsu no kindai: Media no bungakushi* (Chikuma Shobō, 1992), 22.
5. Tsubouchi Shōyō, "Hihyō no hyōjun," *Chūō gakujutsu zasshi* 58 (September 15, 1887): 1.
6. This is not to say that "criticism" has been and is singular in English. John Guillory provides a convoluted, institutional, professionalization history of criticism in relation to literary study in the Anglo-American context. The history of criticism Guillory offers in fact shows many overlaps with that of *hihyō*, including the practice's semantic instability and its affiliation with literature. See John Guillory, *Professing Criticism: Essays on the Organization of Literary Study* (University of Chicago Press, 2022); see especially the preface and chapter 2.
7. Kobayashi Hideo, "Samazamanaru ishō," *Kaizō* (September 1929): 103.
8. In addition to Kobayashi, I consider figures like Yoshimoto Takaaki (1924–2012) and Karatani Kōjin (1941–) as practitioners of this type of *hihyō*.
9. We can think of, for instance, Miki Kiyoshi (1897–1945), a liberal intellectual who was active through the interwar period until his ill-fated death in prison in 1945, as an exemplary figure of the former category, a maven for humanities knowledge. As a representative of the latter, dilettante figure, Nagai Daisuke, a fictional character in Natsume Sōseki's novel, *Sorekara* (*And Then*, 1909), is a good fit.
10. The *hihyō*–literature dynamics surfaced on many occasions in the discourses and practices of late nineteenth-century *hihyō*, and this book will address manifestations of those dynamics throughout. Chapter 2 will

feature discussions on *hihyō*'s specialized relationship to literature. Four case studies in part 2 will analyze varied ways in which *hihyō* behaved and engaged with the topic of literature. The conclusion will also revisit the *hihyō*–literature relationship.

11. Tokutomi Sohō, "Genkon no Nihon wa tekiyō no jidai nari hihyō no jidai nari," *Kokumin no tomo* 20 (April 1888): 9–12.

12. I thank Joannah Peterson for directing me to the importance of these genealogies.

13. Chinese literature scholar Saitō Mareshi uses the term *kanbunmyaku* (漢文脈, the Literary Sinitic context) to refer to the Sinosphere. This language cosmopolis encompasses many areas of Asia, including Japan and Korea, that inherited and relied on the Chinese characters and literary conventions to develop cultural sensibilities. Saitō Mareshi, *Kanbunmyaku to kindai Nihon: Mō hitotsu no kotoba no sekai* (Nihon Hōsō Shuppan Kyōkai, 2007). I have also referred to the English translation of this book. Saitō Mareshi, *Kanbunmyaku: The Literary Sinitic Context and the Birth of Modern Japanese Language and Literature*, ed. Ross King and Christina Laffin, trans. Sean Bussell et al (Brill, 2021).

14. Emmanuel Lozerand, "The Rise of Criticism (1886–1889): Sohō, Hanpō, Ōnishi, Ōgai," *Cipango: French Journal of Japanese Studies* 2 (2013): 90.

15. The course was taught by American instructor William A. Houghton in 1881. Yanagida Izumi, *Shōsetsu shinzui kenkyū* (Shunjūsha, 1966), 10–12.

16. The amorphousness held true for many other systems of the new Japan. Such notions as polity, education, or language, to name a few, lacked clearly defined structures in the first two decades of the Meiji period.

17. Lisa le Feuvre, *Failure* (Whitechapel Gallery and the MIT Press, 2010), 12.

18. Jack Halberstam, *The Queer Art of Failure* (Duke University Press, 2011), 2–3.

19. Halberstam, *Queer Art of Failure*, 2–3.

20. My deliberation on failure is indebted to Jing Tsu's scholarship on the positioning of "failure" in the modern Chinese psyche, as it helped me articulate the specificities—inadvertency and nonnegativity—of what I see in Meiji *hihyō*'s failing moments. Tsu's work focuses on the failing party's awareness of its own failure, which, according to Tsu, Chinese intellectuals actively instrumentalized in order to ground the country's identity formation around the turn of the twentieth century. Tsu argues that "Failure becomes the embedded consciousness of an identity in search of the 'Chinese'" (17), and as such, defeatist, self-chastising sentiments such as "[h]umiliation, despite its dishonorable beginnings, have inaugurated a productive condition for national and cultural identity in China in the twentieth century" (223). While Tsu's observation is compelling, her model of failure does not appear to challenge the commonly accepted idea of failure itself because failure in her account evokes such negative feelings as frustration, sadness, and anxiety. Even as she claims that those feelings were "productive," in that they substantiated the condition for national identity, the failure in this model remains in a dark, miserable realm. In contrast, I consider fin de siècle Japanese criticism's failure an inadvertent, unrecognized outcome, and in so doing attempt to sever failure from a set of negative feelings often associated with it. I thank Liang Luo for directing me to Tsu's

work. Jing Tsu, *Failure, Nationalism, and Literature: The Making of Modern Chinese Identity, 1895-1937* (Stanford University Press, 2005).

21. I am aware that saying this may sound idealistic about humanists' work in contemporary academia. The searches for reading methodologies are tightly connected to the "publish or perish" pressure that many contemporary academics feel. Discussions on reading methodologies are in part driven by the search for newness: In order to put our names in ink, we are constantly in need of something new, be it material about which no one has written, a new interpretation of well-known material, or a new perspective on how to read. That being the case, I also separate the last of these from the others: If the goal is to get published and tenured, then thinking of a new way of engaging with material at hand, inevitably a more difficult type of newness to conceive compared to the other two, does not quite serve the purpose—or at least, it is not the most efficient, fastest path to achieve the goal. I consider that the urge to seek newer modes of reading, therefore, cannot simply be reduced to practical reasons.

22. Halberstam, *Queer Art of Failure*, 2-3.

23. Joseph North, *Literary Criticism: A Concise Political History* (Harvard University Press, 2017), 1.

24. North, *Literary Criticism*, 117.

25. Karatani Kōjin, "Henshū kōki," in *Hihyō kūkan* 2, no. 12 (1997): 234.

26. Karatani's use of Marxist terminologies here insinuates his condescension toward scholars who only pay attention to the "base," that their scholarship is menial work and does not require intellectual labor.

27. Guillory, *Professing Criticism*, 69-71.

28. Halberstam, *Queer Art of Failure*, 12

29. In addition to the works included in my discussion, I have referred to scholarship by Heather Love, Merve Emre, and Dora Zhang to contextualize the state of the method debates in which contemporary literary studies have been involved. Heather Love, "Close Reading and Thin Description," *Public Culture* 25, no. 3 (2013): 411-12; Heather Love, "The Temptations: Donna Haraway, Feminist Objectivity, and the Problem of Critique," in *Critique and Postcritique*, eds. Elizabeth S. Anker and Rita Felski (Duke University Press, 2017), 50-72; Merve Emre, *Paraliterary: The Making of Bad Readers in Postwar America* (University of Chicago Press, 2017), 218-19; and Dora Zhang, *Strange Likeness: Description and the Modernist Novel* (University of Chicago Press, 2020), chapter 1.

30. Susan Sontag, *Against Interpretation and Other Essays* (Picador, 2001), 5. Originally written in 1964.

31. Fredric Jameson, *The Political Unconscious: Narrative as a Socially Symbolic Act* (Cornell University Press, 1981), 9.

32. Jameson, *Political Unconscious*, 60.

33. Paul Ricoeur, *Freud and Philosophy: An Essay on Interpretation*, trans. Denis Savage (Yale University Press, 1970), 32-34.

34. Stephen Best and Sharon Marcus, "Surface Reading: An Introduction," *Representations* 108, no. 1 (Fall 2009): 1.

35. Bruno Latour, "Why Has Critique Run Out of Steam? From Matters of Fact to Matters of Concern," *Critical Inquiry* 30, no. 2 (Winter 2004): 227 and 225, respectively.

36. Latour, "Why Has Critique Run Out of Steam?," 225.

37. Silvan Tomkins, *Affect, Imagery, Consciousness* (Springer, 2008), 519. Also quoted in Eve Kosofsky Sedgwick, "Paranoid Reading and Reparative Reading, Or, You're So Paranoid, You Probably Think This Essay is About You," in *Touching Feeling: Affect, Pedagogy, Performativity* (Duke University Press, 2003), 134.

38. Jameson, *Political Unconscious*, 17.

39. Latour, "Why Has Critique Run Out of Steam?," 243.

40. North, *Literary Criticism*, 117.

41. Sontag, "Against Interpretation," 14. Italics in original.

42. Best and Marcus, "Surface Reading," 1.

43. Franco Moretti, *Distant Reading* (Verso, 2013), 43–62. It needs to be noted that although proposing a "distance" from close reading to explore alternative approaches to world literature, Moretti reintroduces national literatures and its language- or area-based specialists as quintessential forces in literary studies. The "world" in his model therefore does not challenge, but relies on, the existing institutions of knowledge that attend to cultural specificities and national literatures.

44. Michelle Boulous Walker, *Slow Philosophy: Reading Against the Institution* (Bloomsbury, 2017), 33.

45. Boulous Walker, *Slow Philosophy*, 32.

46. For Felski's work on readers' affective reactions, see especially Rita Felski, *Uses of Literature* (Blackwell, 2008); and Rita Felski, *Hooked: Art and Attachment* (University of Chicago Press, 2020).

47. Rita Felski, *The Limits of Critique* (University of Chicago Press, 2015), 186–87.

48. Rita Felski, "Response," *PMLA* 132, no. 2 (March 2017): 384–91.

49. Diana Fuss's remark on this point is worth noting: While identifying the "fuzziness of postcritique," she provides a compelling justification by pointing out the futurity inscribed in the notion of postcritique. Fuss states in a footnote to her review of Felski's *The Limits of Critique*, "Felski's book is stronger on what postcritique is not than on what it is. But the fuzziness of postcritique, and the few pages devoted to it, can be explained by the nature of the concept, which Felski defines as a 'placeholder for emerging ideas and barely glimpsed possibilities' (173). New ways of reading remain for her largely in the future and will only emerge when we stop assuming that critique is the only or best way to read. One example, however, of what a sustained postcritique reading might look like can be found in Felski's previous book, *Uses of Literature*, especially the chapter 'Enchantment' (51–76)." Diana Fuss, "But What About Love?" *PMLA* 132, no. 2 (March 2017): 355. Fuss's review appeared in the March 2017 issue of *PMLA*, which dedicated a special forum to Felski's proposal for postcritique and included multiple scholars' reviews of her book. In her more recent work, Felski draws on actor-network theory and provides more tangible views of what postcritical reading practice might look like in scholarship and in the classroom setting. Felski, *Hooked*, chapter 4.

50. While Felski states "aesthetic experience can happen only in the first person: no one can listen or read or look for you; no one else can have *your*

response," this does not mean that our aesthetic experience is completely unmediated. As Felski goes on to explain, what allows our response is always mediated and touched by what surrounds us, be it a social context, a friend, a course syllabus, or a book review. Felski's point is that when *"[a]esthetic experience is mediated; aesthetic experience can feel intensely immediate,"* we need not pit mediation against immediacy but instead seek language that "blends response with relations, the personal with the transpersonal," so that we may "acknowledge the force of aesthetic immediacy while tracing mediations." Felski, *Hooked*, 15 and 145. Italics in original.

51. Latour, "Why Has Critique Run Out of Steam?," 246.

52. Ōsawa Satoshi, *Hihyō media ron: Senzenki Nihon no rondan to bundan* (Iwanami Shoten, 2015), 277.

53. Ōsawa, *Hihyō media ron*, 10.

1. The Age of *Hihyō*

1. Epigraph from Immanuel Kant, *Critique of Pure Reason* (1871), trans. and ed. Paul Guyer and Allen Wood (Cambridge University Press, 1998), 100–101.

2. Sohō, "Genkon no Nihon wa tekiyō no jidai nari hihyō no jidai nari," 11. The prefatory note to this entry discusses the background and trajectory of Sohō's speech.

3. Tokutomi Sohō, "Tekiyō no jidai, hihyō no jidai," *Rikugō zasshi* 89 (May 15, 1888): 167–74; and Tokutomi Sohō, "Tekiyō no jidai, hihyō no jidai," *Rikugō zasshi* 90 (June 15, 1888): 219–23.

4. Sohō, "Genkon no Nihon wa tekiyō no jidai nari hihyō no jidai nari," 10–12.

5. Sohō, "Genkon no Nihon wa tekiyō no jidai nari hihyō no jidai nari," 12.

6. While I place emphasis on journals in my discussion for their medium specificity, it is not that daily papers did not constitute the public sphere or the space of critical public discourse. As Komori Yōichi demonstrates, papers such as *Tokyo nichinichi shinbun* (Tokyo daily newspaper) and *Yūbin hōchi shinbun* (Postal dispatch newspaper) played a crucial role in the diffusion and contestations of political opinions during the Freedom and People's Rights Movement. Komori Yōichi, *Nihongo no kindai* (Iwanami Shoten, 2000), 44–56.

7. Jürgen Habermas, *The Structural Transformation of the Public Sphere: An Inquiry into a Category of Bourgeois Society*, trans. Thomas Burger and Frederick Lawrence (MIT Press, 1991), 27–31. As per Habermas, the public sphere is considered a site that mediates the private realm (basic socioeconomic activities and family) and the public authority (state and court) to facilitate the formation of public opinions.

8. Kyu Hyun Kim, *The Age of Visions and Arguments: Parliamentarianism and the National Public Sphere in Early Meiji Japan* (Harvard University Press, 2007), part 1.

9. Both in the context of late nineteenth-century Japan and in eighteenth-century Europe that Habermas analyzes, the "public" did not equal all-inclusive or open to everyone, as who could participate in the public sphere were conditioned by such factors as gender and class.

10. In the case of 1880s Japan, while the freedom of speech and the press was one of the major concerns of young intellectuals, and even guaranteed in the Constitution of the Empire of Japan (promulgated in 1889 and came into force in 1890), it was often overridden by the state control, the exemplary attempts of which include the 1875 Defamation Law (Zanbōritsu), the 1875 Press Regulations (Shinbunshi Jōrei) and its tightening in 1883 and 1887, and the Publication Regulations (Shuppan Jōrei) that developed alongside the Press Regulations. The Meiji government regulated speech in fear of overthrows. Jay Rubin, *Injurious to Public Morals: Writers and the Meiji State* (University of Washington Press, 1984), chapter 2.

11. Habermas, *Structural Transformation of the Public Sphere*, 51–67. Habermas presents that in eighteenth-century Anglo-Europe, criticism (as in critical public opinions that would influence the decisions of the state authority) developed step by step, from the intimate, private sphere, the literary public sphere, into the public sphere in the political realm. Habermas is clear that what he describes is one model, not a universal scenario, and as such I do not consider what took place in Japan as a deviation.

12. Lydia Liu, *Translingual Practice: Literature, National Cultures, and Translated Modernity—China, 1900–1937* (Stanford University Press, 1995), 32.

13. The original lectures were delivered at Nishi's private school and transcribed by one of his disciples, Nagami Yutaka.

14. Contemporary scholar Yamamoto Takamitsu estimates that Nishi referred to English dictionaries such as *A Dictionary of the English Language* compiled by Noah Webster, presumably the 1864 edition, to prepare for his lectures. Yamamoto Takamitsu, Hyakugaku renkan o yomu (Sanseidō, 2016), 134–38, 228–29, 505–6.

15. Nishi Amane, *Hyakugaku renkan*, in *Nishi Amane zenshū*, vol. 1, ed. Ōkubo Toshiaki (Nihon Hyōronsha, 1945), 11. Regarding this Greek term, "Ενκυκλιος παιδεια," Yamamoto examines slight differences in transcription between Nagami's initial transcription (Ενκυκλιος παιδεια [enkyklios paideia]), the edited version of Nagami's transcription (Εγκυλοςπαιδεια [egkylospaideia]), Nishi's memo (Εγκυκλοςπαιδεια [egkyklospaideia]), and what typically appears in a Greek dictionary (Εγκυκλιος παιδεια [egkyklios paideia]), and observes that these differences indicate traces of interaction Nishi had with Nagami as they prepared the manuscript. Yamamoto, *Hyakugaku renkan o yomu*, 34–40. I thank Valerio Caldesi Valeri for helping me provide romanization of these variants.

16. Nishi, *Hyakugaku renkan*, 18.

17. The original term is *bunshō*. Nishi oftentimes uses the terms *bunshō* (writing), *moji* (letters), *bunshōgaku* (the learning of writing), *bun* (letters, sentences), *bungaku* (literature, knowledge) interchangeably. For consistency and clarity, I use "writing" as a primary translation of *bunshō*.

18. Nishi uses "literature" in English and lists another term *bunshōgaku* (the learning of writing) as the title of the section. This shows that a similar type of linguistic and conceptual negotiation was happening with "literature" as well. Nishi, *Hyakugaku renkan*, 83–84.

19. This sentence is written in the main text but presented in a smaller font.

20. Nishi, *Hyakugaku renkan*, 92–93.
21. Liu, *Translingual Practice*, 25–27.
22. Many of the Sinographic terms presented in the dictionary were coinages. As such, it is necessary to remember that the appearance of "equivalence" is a retroactively generated one. This includes the term *tetsugaku* (as in *Tetsugaku jii*), as a translation of "philosophy."
23. Inoue Tetsujirō, Ariga Nagao, Kōdera Shinsaku, and Wadagaki Kenzō, eds., *Tetsugaku jii* (Tokyo Daigaku Sangakubu, 1881), 21.
24. Shōyō, "Hihyō no hyōjun," 1.
25. Shōyō and Takata attended the University of Tokyo together in the early 1880s. Their friendship continued after graduation, and both of them contributed to the cultivation of Tokyo Senmon Gakkō and taught there.
26. Takata Sanae, "*Tōsei shosei katagi* no hihyō," *Chūō gakujutsu zasshi* 21 (February 1, 1886): 28.
27. Takata Sanae, "Hihyō no hitsuyō," *Yomiuri shinbun* (May 4, 1887), 1.
28. Takata, "Hihyō no hitsuyō," 1.
29. Shōyō, "Hihyō no hyōjun," 7–8.
30. Sohō, "Genkon no Nihon wa tekiyō no jidai nari hihyō no jidai nari," 10.
31. Kimura Naoe, "'Hihyō' no tanjō," *Hikaku bungaku* 45 (2002): 9.
32. Kimura, "'Hihyō' no tanjō," 9.
33. The "Ronpyō" section (the only piece included in this section is Inoue Tetsujirō's "*Tokyo keizai zasshi ni kotau*"), *Tōyō gakugei zasshi* 6 (March 1882): 110–15. The "Hihyō" section (Inoue Tetsujirō's "Kan-shi Gendō o yomite"), *Tōyō gakugei zasshi* 7 (April 1882): 139–41.
34. "Honshi kairyō no shushi o nobu," *Chūō gakujutsu zasshi* 20 (December 25, 1885): 1.
35. "Honshi kairyō no shushi o nobu," 4.
36. *Jogaku zasshi* (The women's magazine), which will be discussed in chapter 3, set up an independent *hihyō* section in June 1886. This medium also nurtured an active readership community; the readers' column of the journal was often filled with voices from female readers, visualized the reader-journal bond, and welcomed feedback, including *hihyō* of the journal itself, from readers.
37. In doing so, Takata also signals that his own work embodies "Western *hihyō*" and is thus apart from the privileged conventions of reading in the realm of "Oriental literature."
38. "*Shuppan geppyō* no hatsuda," *Shuppan geppyō* 1 (1887): 1.
39. "*Shuppan geppyō* no hatsuda," 2.
40. Yayoshi, *Mikan shiryō ni yoru Nihon shuppan bunka*, 288–91.
41. "*Shuppan geppyō* no hatsuda," 3.
42. "*Shuppan geppyō* no hatsuda," 3.
43. The original rhetoric of "mixture of good and bad" is *gyokuseki konkō*, literally a mixture of (precious) gems and (trifling) stones. The same rhetoric is frequently used to refer to the field of publications at the time. See, for example, "*Shuppan geppyō* no hatsuda," 5; and Takata, "Hihyō no hitsuyō," 1.
44. Yatabe Ryōkichi, "*Shuppan geppyō* hatsuda ni tsuki shokan o nobu," *Shuppan geppyō* 1 (1887): 36. Other than Yatabe, such intellectuals as Nakamura

Masanao and Konakamura Kiyonori also published their congratulatory remarks to *Shuppan geppyō*, also mentioning the importance of "selection" in the practice of *hihyō*.

45. "Shakoku," *Kokumin no tomo* 8 (September 1887). The announcement appeared on the back page of the front cover, with no page number assigned.

46. These are self-reported numbers taken from *Kokumin no tomo*'s "Shakoku" (announcement) sections that usually appeared on the back of the cover title page. The journal sold a total of 80,549 copies in 1887; 275,753 in 1888; and 446,727 in 1889. Yayoshi, *Mikan shiryō ni yoru Nihon shuppan bunka*, 59-60.

47. Lozerand, "The Rise of Criticism (1886-1889)," 74. I must add that *Kokumin no tomo* was a "public sphere," only insofar as a male readership was concerned.

48. "Shakoku," *Kokumin no tomo* 9 (October 1887). This announcement too appeared on the back page of the front cover, and hence no page number assigned.

49. "*Shuppan geppyō* no hatsuda," 5.

50. Komori Yōichi, "Kindai hihyō no shuppatsu," *Hihyō kūkan* 1 (April 1991): 73-74.

51. Walter Ong, *Orality and Literacy: The Technologizing of the Word* (Methuen, 1982), 124. I thank Ron Wilson for mentioning Ong's account of "lists" in one of our conversations about Sei Shōnagon's *Pillow Book*.

52. Suzuki Sadami demonstrates the conceptual history of *bungaku* or "literature." Suzuki Sadami, *Nihon no "bungaku" gainen* (Sakuhinsha, 1998).

53. Saeki Junko's study examines the notion of *bi* or "beauty" and its implications in late nineteenth-century Japan. Saeki Junko, "'Bi' e no akogare," *Nihon no bigaku* 21 (July 1994): 178-90.

54. Saeki also investigates the implications of the term *shizen* or "nature" in Meiji Japan. Saeki Junko, "'Shizen' to 'Shinjitsu,'" *Nihon no bigaku* 19 (December 1992): 142-59.

55. Lozerand, "Rise of Criticism," 73.

56. Tokutomi Sohō, *Shōrai no Nihon* (Keizai zasshi sha, 1886), 3.

57. "*Shuppan geppyō* no hyō," *Kokumin no tomo* 8 (September 15, 1887): 42.

58. "*Shuppan geppyō* no kōyō," *Kokumin no tomo* 11 (November 4, 1887): 31.

59. Kōdokusha no hitori, "*Shuppan geppyō* e no jogen o kou," *Kokumin no tomo* 12 (November 18, 1887): 30.

60. "*Shuppan geppyō* no hatsuda," 3.

61. Kōdokusha no hitori, "*Shuppan geppyō* e no jogen o kou," 30.

62. The *hihyō* about Īda's piece appeared in the "Hihyō" section of *Kokumin no tomo*. "Kinkan zassho," *Kokumin no tomo* 17 (March 2, 1888): 33-34.

63. Īda Ō, "*Kokumin no tomo* no hihyō o yomu," *Shuppan geppyō* 9 (April 30, 1888): 154.

64. Īda, "*Kokumin no tomo* no hihyō o yomu," 152-54.

65. Noguchi Takehiko, "Kindai Nihon bungaku to 'hihyō' no hakken," *Hihyō kūkan* 1 (1991): 7.

66. Ningetsu refers to Mori Ōgai's "Meiji nijūni-nen hihyōka no shigan," *Shigarami zōshi* 4 (January 25, 1890): 1-27.

67. Ishibashi Ningetsu, "Chikagoro no sanki," *Kokumin no tomo* 73 (February 13, 1890): 28.
68. Paul de Man, "Criticism and Crisis," in *Blindness and Insight: Essays in the Rhetoric of Contemporary Criticism* (University of Minnesota Press, 1983), 8.
69. de Man, "Criticism and Crisis," 8.

2. Critical Reading, Creative Production

1. Yanagida Izumi and Suzuki Sadami, for instance, sketch the historical development of the concept of *bungaku*. Kamei Hideo and Atsuko Ueda offer accounts of how the Meiji aestheticization of prose fiction was linked to cultural production on a broader, global scale. Tomiko Yoda and Indra Levy demonstrate how the idea of femininity played a crucial part in the modernization and nationalization of literature in Japan. Maeda Ai, Ri Takanori, and Seth Jacobowitz direct our attention to the environmental—both technological and infrastructural—factors that to a significant extent affected the formation of literature as a modern cultural practice. Yanagida Izumi, *Meiji shoki no bungaku shisō*, in vols. 4 and 6 of *Meiji bungaku kenkyū* (Shunjūsha, 1965); Suzuki Sadami, *Nihon no "bungaku" gainen* (Sakuhinsha, 1998); Kamei Hideo, *"Shōsetsu"-ron: Shōsetsu shinzui to kindai* (Iwanami Shoten, 1999); Atsuko Ueda, *Concealment of Politics, Politics of Concealment: The Production of "Literature" in Meiji Japan* (Stanford University Press, 2007); Tomiko Yoda, *Gender and National Literature: Heian Texts in the Constructions of Japanese Modernity* (Duke University Press, 2004); Indra Levy, *Sirens of the Western Shore: The Westernesque Femme Fatale, Translation, and Vernacular Style in Modern Japanese Literature* (Columbia University Press, 2006); Maeda Ai, *Maeda Ai chosakushū: Kindai dokusha no seiritsu*, vol. 2 (Chikuma Shobō, 1989); Ri Takanori, *Hyōshō kūkan no kindai: Meiji "Nihon" no media hensei* (Shin'yōsha, 1996); and Seth Jacobowitz, *Writing Technology in Meiji Japan: A Media History of Modern Japanese Literature and Visual Culture* (Harvard University Asia Center, 2015).

2. The synonymous relationship between *hihyō* and *bungei hihyō* dissolved toward the end of the twentieth century. I will bring back this topic in the concluding chapter.

3. I thank Richard Okada for his inspiration regarding literature's relationship to other fields: Richard Okada, "Areas, Disciplines, and Ethnicity," in *Learning Places: The Afterlives of Area Studies*, ed. Masao Miyoshi and Harry Harootunian (Duke University Press, 2002), 202–3.

4. Topic-specific journals were not uncommon. Other than literature, a variety of themes made independent topics. *Kyōiku jiron* (Education review), established in 1885 by Kaihatsusha, an organization that promoted education, is one example. The medical journal *Eisei shinshi* (New journal of hygiene), launched by Ōgai in 1889, is another. The emergence of journals specializing in literature was in tandem with the contemporary movement in the scene of print business.

5. "Meiji nendai no bungaku o ronji awasete hihyō no hitsuyōnaru yuen o toku," *Meiji nippō*, August 4, 1883. This piece appeared in three different entries,

with the first entry on August 1, the second on August 2, and the last on August 4, 1883. I thank Setsuko Noguchi for helping me acquire this material.

6. Shōyō, "Hihyō no hyōjun," 1–2.

7. Takata, "*Tosei shosei katagi* no hihyō," 28–29.

8. Mori Ōgai, "*Shigarami zōshi* no honryō o ronzu," *Shigarami zōshi* 1 (October 25, 1889): 1–2.

9. Ōgai, "*Shigarami zōshi* no honryō o ronzu," 2.

10. Ōgai, "*Shigarami zōshi* no honryō o ronzu," 3.

11. Ōgai, "*Shigarami zōshi* no honryō o ronzu," 3.

12. Tokyo Senmon Gakkō established the department of literature in 1890. Tsubouchi Shōyō was one of the first faculty members of the department as a Shakespearean scholar and also a main contributor to *Waseda bungaku*. Chapter 5 will further discuss this journal. Chapter 6 will mention *Bungakukai* in relation to Kitamura Tōkoku.

13. Sohō's seminal works, such as *Shin Nihon no seinen* (The youth in new Japan, 1887) and *Shōrai no Nihon* (The future Japan, 1886), repetitively exhibit the idea of "old Japan" progressing into "new Japan" by way of continuous efforts.

14. Sohō, "Seijijō no bungyō," *Kokumin no tomo* 21 (May 4, 1888): 1.

15. Sohō, "Seijijō no bungyō," 1.

16. Sohō, "Seijijō no bungyō," 1.

17. Sohō, "Seijijō no bungyō," 2.

18. Ōnishi's contribution to this journal makes sense as he and Sohō were close friends. They exchanged personal missives. Itō Takashi et al., eds., *Tokutomi Sohō kankei monjo*, Kindai Nihon shiryō sensho, 7-1 (Yamakawa Shuppansha, 1982), 58–69.

19. Ōnishi Hajime, "Hihyōron." *Kokumin no tomo* 21 (May 1888): 27.

20. In the thirteenth issue of *Kokumin no tomo* (December 27, 1887), all five *hihyō* pieces in the section were written by Takahashi. The publications that he evaluated vary from fictional works to a guide to foreign exchange, to an abbreviated translation of Henry Buckle's work on civilization.

21. Takahashi Gorō, "*Kokumin no tomo* naru Saidō-koji no 'Hihyōron' o yomu," *Rikugō zasshi* 90 (June 15, 1888): 224.

22. Takahashi disagrees with many of Ōnishi's claims: He does not sense a stagnancy in the current scene of writing, or an absence of genuine *hihyō* practitioners in contemporary Japan (225). He also contradicts Ōnishi's vision of dividing *hihyō* from creative practice, naming multiple figures, such as Alexander Pope and his French contemporary Nicolas Boileau-Despréaux, both renowned for their poetic work and critical writing. Takahashi, "*Kokumin no tomo* naru Saidō-koji no 'Hihyōron' o yomu," 225, and 230–31, respectively.

23. Takahashi, "*Kokumin no tomo* naru Saidō-koji no 'Hihyōron' o yomu," 226.

24. Takahashi, "*Kokumin no tomo* naru Saidō-koji no 'Hihyōron' o yomu," 226.

25. Takahashi, "*Kokumin no tomo* naru Saidō-koji no 'Hihyōron' o yomu," 226.

26. Takahashi, "*Kokumin no tomo* naru Saidō-koji no 'Hihyōron' o yomu," 227.

27. Takahashi, "*Kokumin no tomo* naru Saidō-koji no 'Hihyōron' o yomu," 227.

28. Ōnishi, "Hihyōron," 27–28.

29. Ōnishi, "Hihyōron," 28.

30. Ōnishi, "Hihyōron," 27.
31. Ōnishi, "Hihyōron," 28.
32. Ōnishi, "Hihyōron," 30.
33. For Ōnishi's connection to Arnold, see Satō Zen'ya, "Ōnishi Hajime no hihyōkan to sono gensen (ge)," *Rikkyō Daigaku kenkyū hōkoku: Jinbun kagaku* 38 (1979): 23-58. For the Ōnishi-Kant relationship, see Watanabe Kazuyasu, "Ōnishi Hajime: Criticism and Aesthetics," in *A History of Modern Japanese Aesthetics*, trans. and ed. Michael Marra (University of Hawai'i Press, 2001), 95-105.
34. Ōnishi Hajime, "Hōkon shisōkai no yōmu," *Rikugō zasshi* 100 (April 15, 1889): 15-23. The journal also presents the title of Ōnishi's essay in English: "Philosophical Needs of the Present Age."
35. Tokutomi Sohō was also familiar with Arnold's *Essays in Criticism* (1865), and drew on it when he declared the "age of *hihyō*" in his 1888 essay, "Genkon no Nihon wa tekiyō no jidai nari hihyō no jidai nari," in *Kokumin no tomo* (discussed in chapter 1). It is likely that Ōnishi introduced Arnold to Sohō: In a letter dated February 23, 1888, Ōnishi indicated where Sohō could find a copy of Arnold's work. Itō et al., *Tokutomi Sohō kankei monjo*, 59-60.
36. Kant, *Critique of Pure Reason*, 100-101.
37. Matthew Arnold, "The Function of Criticism at the Present Time" (1865), in *Matthew Arnold's Essays in Criticism*, ed. Sister Thomas Marion Hoctor, S. S. J. (University of Chicago Press, 1968), 18.
38. Ōnishi, "Hihyōron," 28.
39. Ōnishi, "Hihyōron," 25.
40. Ōnishi, "Hihyōron," 25-26.
41. Ōnishi, "Hihyōron," 25.
42. Takahashi, "*Kokumin no tomo* naru Saidō-koji no 'Hihyōron' o yomu," 230-31.
43. Ōnishi, "Hihyōron," 26.
44. Ōnishi, "Hihyōron," 26.
45. Ōnishi, "Hihyōron," 26.
46. Ōnishi, "Hihyōron," 26.
47. Komori, "Kindai hihyō no shuppatsu," 76-77.
48. Arnold, "Function of Criticism at the Present Time," 30.
49. Moments of creativity are also inscribed in Arnold's own work. Mark Taylor indicates that Arnold's criticism is highly creative, composing and inventing texts by "arranging, comparing, and evaluating masses of written material to produce a coherent and meaningful object." Mark Taylor, "The Lower Criticism," *Representations* 150, no. 1 (Spring 2020): 43. Mary Poovey's work also demonstrates that what Arnold posits as "critical vision" has a strongly imaginative, creative quality. Mary Poovey, "The Model System of Contemporary Literary Criticism," *Critical Inquiry* 27, no. 3 (Spring 2001): 425.

3. On Dividing: The "Literature and Nature" Debate

1. Epigraph from Peggy Kamuf, *The Division of Literature: Or the University in Deconstruction* (University of Chicago Press, 1997), 39.
2. Mori Rintarō [Ōgai], "Shōsetsuron," *Yomiuri shinbun* (January 3, 1889).

3. Ōgai, "Shōsetsuron."

4. Thomas LaMarre refers to this doctor-writer as "Mori" and tracks the intersections of science and literature manifest in a diverse range of his writings. Using his last name is one of LaMarre's strategies to remain in a middle region where science and literature cannot be schematically severed from one another. Thomas LaMarre, "Bacterial Cultures and Linguistic Colonies: Mori Rintarō's Experiments with History, Science, and Language," *Positions: East Asia Cultures Critique* 6, no.3 (1998): 597–635.

5. *Jogaku zasshi* also functioned as the bulletin of Meiji Jogakkō (Meiji women's school), a Christian-led women's school that advocated the improvement of women's social status through education between 1885 and 1909. As Iwamoto was deeply involved in the establishment and administration of Meiji Jogakkō, *Jogaku zasshi* was naturally his primary platform.

6. Iwamoto Yoshiharu, "*Kokumin no tomo* dai yonjūhachi gō: Bungaku to shizen," *Jogaku zasshi* 159 (April 27, 1889): 10.

7. Explaining the institutionalization process of fine arts in late nineteenth-century Japan goes beyond the scope of this book. I am indebted to Satō Dōshin's historical and theoretical analyses of the production of arts in Meiji Japan. Satō Dōshin, *Meiji kokka to kindai bijutsu: Bi no seijigaku* (Yoshikawa Kōbunkan, 1999).

8. Tokutomi Sohō, "Genron no fujiyū to bungaku no hattatsu," *Kokumin no tomo* 48 (April 22, 1889): 1.

9. Ishibashi Ningetsu, "*Jiji shinpō* to *Jogaku zasshi* ni tadasu," *Kokumin no tomo* 48 (April 22, 1889): 33.

10. Mori Rintarō [Ōgai], "'Bungaku to shizen' o yomu," *Kokumin no tomo* 50 (May 11, 1889): 18. Kobori Keiichirō has examined how Ōgai's essay owed a debt to the German writer Rudolf von Gottschall's *Poetik*. While it is important to know what readings informed Ōgai's conceptualization of literature, such efforts often posit "the West" as something whole and intact, and position anything "non-Western" as a latecomer or (insufficient) appropriator, not questioning the hierarchy between the West and the Rest, and thus delimiting our approaches. Kobori Keiichirō, *Wakaki hi no Mori Ōgai* (Tokyo Daigaku Shuppansha, 1969), 389–407.

11. Ōgai, "'Bungaku to shizen' o yomu," 21.

12. Ōgai, "'Bungaku to shizen' o yomu," 22.

13. Ōgai, "'Bungaku to shizen' o yomu," 22.

14. Iwamoto Yoshiharu, "*Kokumin no tomo* dai gojū gō ni okeru 'Bungaku to shizen' o yomu, o kindokusu," *Jogaku zasshi* 162 (May 18, 1889): 15.

15. Iwamoto, "*Kokumin no tomo* dai gojū gō ni okeru 'Bungaku to shizen' o yomu, o kindokusu," 15.

16. Iwamoto, "*Kokumin no tomo* dai gojū gō ni okeru 'Bungaku to shizen' o yomu, o kindokusu," 16.

17. Mori Rintarō [Ōgai], "Futatabi shizen sūhaisha ni tadasu," *Kokumin no tomo* 52 (June 1, 1889): 33.

18. Iwamoto Yoshiharu, "Shizen sūhaisha no kotae," *Jogaku zasshi* 165 (June 8, 1889): 30; the quotation appears in English. See Ralph W. Emerson, "Nature," in *Ralph Waldo Emerson: Essays and Lectures* (Literary Classics of the United States, 1983), 19.

19. Iwamoto, "*Kokumin no tomo* dai gojū gō ni okeru 'Bungaku to shizen' o yomu, o kindokusu," 17.
20. I have in mind, for example, Togawa Shinsuke's scholarship. Togawa Shinsuke, *"Dorama," "Takai"*: *Meiji nijūnendai no bungaku jōkyō* (Chikuma Shobō, 1987), 145-69.
21. Karatani Kōjin, *Origins of Modern Japanese Literature*, ed. Brett de Bary (Duke University Press, 1993), 11-44.
22. Inoue Teruko, "*Jogaku zasshi* no shippitsusha kōsei: Meiji nijūnendai jānarizumu kōzō kaimei no tame no shiron," *Shuppan kenkyū* 2 (1971): 98.
23. Iwamoto's disadvantage was not simply a generational one. Sohō was born in Higo, which was geographically close to Hizen, and thus unlike Iwamoto, who was born in Izushi, far from all of the winning domains of southern Japan, Sohō had tangible exposure to the political atmosphere that shaped the ideology of the Restoration.
24. Pierre Bourdieu, "The Field of Cultural Production, or: The Economic World Reversed," in *The Field of Cultural Production: Essays on Art and Literature*, ed. Randal Johnson (Columbia University Press, 1993).
25. Bourdieu, "The Field of Cultural Production," 30. I recognize that Iwamoto and other *Jogaku zasshi* administrators were not the only people who sought to construct "positions" through the medium. Social historian Okada Akiko's study has detailed the processes through which the journal's readers and contributors, many of them young, "awakened" women, used the medium in their favor to establish themselves in society. Okada's phrasing—"sleeping together, dreaming different dreams" or *dōshōimu*, by which she describes the varied ways that *Jogaku zasshi* allowed itself to be used by different groups of people—is compelling. Okada Akiko, Jogaku zasshi *to ōka: Kirisutokyō chishikijin to jogakusei no media kūkan* (Shinwasha, 2013), 100-143.
26. The 1881 political turmoil included the dismissal of leading politician Ōkuma Shigenobu, a major counterforce to the Meiji oligarchs; the disintegration of the Freedom and People's Rights Movement; and the issuing of the imperial edict for the Imperial Diet in 1890.
27. Sohō's mentioning of "restrictions of free speech" in "Genron no fujiyū to bungaku no hattatsu" was linked to the press and speech control implemented by the Meiji state, which was anxious about the first election and opening of the Diet.
28. Iwamoto contributed to this issue an episode in which his students at Meiji Jogakkō sang six lyrics to celebrate the new constitution on February 11, 1889. Iwamoto Yoshiharu, "Kenpō happu o shukushitaru uta," *Jogaku zasshi* 149 (February 16, 1889): 12-13.
29. "Kenpō," *Jogaku zasshi* 149 (February 16, 1889): 25-26.
30. "Kenpō," 26.
31. "Ā senzai no ittoki," *Kokumin no tomo* 41 (February 12, 1889): 1-8. Most likely, Sohō wrote this.
32. Iwamoto Yoshiharu, "Kan'in no kūki, fujunketsu no kūki," *Jogaku zasshi* 150 (February 23, 1889): 4.
33. "Ichikawa Danjūrō," *Jiji shinpō* (March 30, 1889); and Iwamoto Yoshiharu, "Ichikawa Danjūrō to *Eisei shinshi*," *Jogaku zasshi* 156 (April 6, 1889): 15-16.

34. According to Yagi Mizuho, the term *"kusaretamago"* transcended the boundaries of Saganoya's individual work, and came to be used more broadly as a metaphor for the debauched morality of people involved in women's education. Yagi Mizuho, *"Jogaku zasshi* o shiza to shita Meiji nijūninen no bungaku ronsō: Joshikyōikukai no moraru fuhai o meguru dōjidaigensetsu tono kōsaku," *Kindai bungaku shiron* 35 (December 1997): 1–12.

35. Okada, *Jogaku zasshi to ōka*, 152–58.

36. *Yomiuri shinbun*'s negative campaign began in 1889 with such articles as "Jogakkō no akuhyō" (Bad rumors about women's school, published June 8, 1889) and "Jogakkō to joseito" (Women's school and female students, published June 9, 1889). The backlash continued into the following year, as more negative articles—including, for example, "Jogakusei no hinkō" (Morals of female students, published February 18, 1890) and Inakaya Bon'yari's reader contribution piece "Jogakusei ni tsuite" (On female students, published February 23, 1890)—appeared in *Yomiuri shinbun*. Literature scholar Kuroda Shuntarō argues that *Yomiuri shinbun* conducted their negative campaign against women's education in the format of *tsuzukimono* (serialized reports), which made the presented information appear factual and trustworthy. Despite their unreliability, scandalous narratives packaged as *tsuzukimono* made readers discover "facts" that might have never existed. Kuroda Shuntarō, "*Yomiuri shinbun* ni okeru 'shinbun shōsetsu' no hensei katei: Meiji nijūnen zengo, Shōyō no shikō to ishi no yukue," *Geibun kenkyū* 93 (December 2007): 10–16.

37. "Jogaku no kyōkō," *Kokumin no tomo* 54 (June 22, 1889): 12–16. Most likely, Sohō wrote this.

38. Okada, *Jogaku zasshi to ōka*, 158.

39. Mori Rintarō [Ōgai], "Baishō no rigai," *Eisei shinshi* 1 (March 25, 1889): 18.

40. Harold Bloom, *A Map of Misreading* (Oxford University Press, 1980); chapters 1 and 4 are particularly useful to my reading of Ōgai's misreading. I thank Ron Wilson for pointing out the proximity between Bloom and this chapter's main argument.

41. Yanabu Akira, *Hon'yakugo seiritsu jijō* (Iwanami Shoten, 1982), 127–48. Other than "nature" (*shizen*), Yanabu examines such terms as "society" (*shakai*), "individual" (*kojin*), and "beauty" (*bi*).

42. Iwamoto, "Bungaku to shizen," 11.

43. Iwamoto's reference to Emerson appears in Iwamoto, "Shizen sūhaisha no kotae," 30. All the other references appear in Iwamoto, "*Kokumin no tomo* dai gojū gō ni okeru 'Bungaku to shizen' o yomu, o kindokusu," 15–16. When Ōgai contradicted Iwamoto's theory, such qualities as the ethical and the religious were also pushed out of the range of aesthetic literature.

44. Ōgai, "'Bungaku to shizen' o yomu," 19.

45. Ōgai, "'Bungaku to shizen' o yomu," 19–22.

46. Ōgai, "'Bungaku to shizen' o yomu," 21–22.

47. Émile Zola, "The Experimental Novel," in *The Experimental Novel and Other Essays*, trans. Belle M. Sherman (Cassell Publishing, 1893), 18.

48. Zola, "Experimental Novel," 3–7.

49. Zola, "Experimental Novel," 9.
50. Émile Zola, "Description," in *The Experimental Novel and Other Essays*, trans. Belle M. Sherman (Cassell Publishing, 1893), 232-33. "Description" is one of the sequel essays to "The Experimental Novel."
51. Zola, "Description," 232.
52. Ōgai and Pavlov via Futabatei come very close to each other in terms of how they associate art with the immaterial (idea), science with the material (form). Pavlov via Futabatei writes that while sciences begin by dealing with visible existence in order to reach ideas, "art transforms ideas into objects" and "transforms things with nonreal spirits (*kyorei*) into those with concrete existence (*jitsuzai*)." Mikhail Pavlov, "Gakujutsu to bijutsu no sabetsu," trans. Futabatei Shimei, *Kokumin no tomo* 19 (April 6, 1888): appendix 7-11.
53. Amano Ikuo, *Daigaku no tanjō* (Chūō Kōron Shinsha, 2009), chapters 2 and 3.
54. Joseph Murphy, *Metaphorical Circuit: Negotiations Between Literature and Science in 20th Century Japan* (Cornell University Press, 2003), 4-5.
55. Murphy, *Metaphorical Circuit*, 11.
56. Murphy, *Metaphorical Circuit*, 15.
57. Ōgai was not alone in contradicting Iwamoto on the topic of literature. While Ōgai attacked Iwamoto conspicuously, some *Jogaku zasshi* affiliates such as Kitamura Tōkoku began to distance themselves from Iwamoto for his ethics-ridden view on literature. Chapter 6 addresses the disconnect between Iwamoto and Tōkoku.
58. Julia Thomas, *Reconfiguring Modernity: Concepts of Nature in Japanese Political Ideology* (University of California Press, 2002), 3.
59. Thomas briefly mentions the Ōgai-Iwamoto confrontation in chapter 7 and highlights different registers that the term *"shizen"* had in the late nineteenth century. Thomas, *Reconfiguring Modernity*, 171.
60. Ōgai, "'Bungaku to shizen' o yomu," 18.
61. Ōgai, "'Bungaku to shizen' o yomu," 19.
62. Ōgai, "'Bungaku to shizen' o yomu," 19.
63. Ōgai, "'Bungaku to shizen' o yomu," 21.
64. Ōgai, "'Bungaku to shizen' o yomu," 21.
65. Ōgai, "'Bungaku to shizen' o yomu," 22.
66. LaMarre, "Bacterial Cultures and Linguistic Colonies," 622.
67. Nishi, *Hyakugaku renkan*, 11.
68. Yamamoto, Hyakugaku renkan *o yomu*, 441.

4. Knowing the Dancer from the Dance: The "Dancing Girl" Debate

1. Epigraph from William Butler Yeats, "Among School Children," in *The Collected Poems of W. B. Yeats* (Macmillan Company, 1933), 251.
2. The earlier version of this chapter appeared as a journal article: Miyabi Goto, "'Maihime' and the Space of Criticism in Meiji Japan," *Journal of Japanese Studies* 46, no. 2 (2020): 345-68. I thank the Society for Japanese Studies for granting me permission to reuse the content of this article.
3. Mori Ōgai, "Maihime," *Kokumin no tomo* 69 (January 3, 1890): 1-17.

4. Komori Yōichi, *Buntai toshite no monogatari* (Chikuma Shobō, 1988); Komori Yōichi, *Kōzō toshite no katari* (Shin'yōsha, 1988); and Masao Miyoshi, *Accomplices of Silence: The Modern Japanese Novel* (University of Michigan Center for Japanese Studies, 1996).

5. Christopher Hill, "Mori Ōgai's Resentful Narrator: Trauma and the National Subject in 'The Dancing Girl,'" *Positions: East Asia Cultures Critique* 10, no. 2 (2002): 365–97; and Tomiko Yoda, "First-Person Narration and Citizen-Subject: The Modernity of Ōgai's 'The Dancing Girl,'" *Journal of Asian Studies* 65, no. 2 (2006): 277–306.

6. Usui Yoshimi, *Kindai bungaku ronsō jō* (Chikuma Shobō, 1956).

7. Chiba Shinrō's book is perhaps the only major piece of scholarship that exclusively focuses on Ningetsu: Chiba Shinrō, *Ishibashi Ningetsu kenkyū: Hyōden to kōshō* (Yagi Shoten, 2006). The dearth of English-language scholarship on Ningetsu reflects the scholarly tendency to focus more on fiction than on *hihyō*, or more broadly on nonfictional works, in the field of Japanese literary studies in the English-speaking world. With its focus on *hihyō*, this book has been partially conceived as my response to such a tendency.

8. Saitō, *Kanbunmyaku to kindai Nihon*, 150–58.

9. On field formation see part 1 of Bourdieu's *The Field of Cultural Production*.

10. Paul de Man, "Semiology and Rhetoric," in *Allegories of Reading: Figural Language in Rousseau, Nietzsche, Rilke, and Proust* (Yale University Press, 1979), 3–19.

11. Iwamoto Yoshiharu, for instance, took issue with the moral aspect of protagonist Ōta's behavior: Iwamoto Yoshiharu, "*Kokumin no tomo* shinnen furoku," *Jogaku zasshi* 195 (January 11, 1890): 7. Takuten Jōsen (aka Noguchi Neisai) categorized the story in the genre of *ninjōbon* (books of romantic emotions), which was marked as "Edo-esque, premodern" during the second decade of the Meiji period: Takuten Jōsen, "Maihime o yomite," *Shigarami zōshi* 4 (January 25, 1890): 51. Several other commentaries appeared in *Shigarami zōshi*'s January 25 issue, including Yamaguchi Toratarō's "Maihime saihyō," *Shigarami zōshi* 4 (January 25, 1890): 46–50. These varied readings offer a glimpse of contemporary expectations for a piece of writing categorized as literature.

12. Ishibashi Ningetsu, "Maihime," *Kokumin no tomo* 72 (February 3, 1890), 38–39.

13. Ningetsu, "Maihime," 38.

14. The first point takes up about one-third of the essay (thirty-two lines). Ningetsu devotes much less space to each of the remaining points (five to fifteen lines apiece), which indicates what his primary concern was.

15. For example, Isogai Hideo writes that because Ningetsu was "emotionally moved," "he became even more intolerant of Ōta's abandonment of Elise, which conveys Ningetsu's youthful romanticism." Isogai Hideo, *Mori Ōgai: Meiji nijūnendai o chūshin ni* (Meiji Shoin, 1979), 179. Ochi Haruo detects "an extremely romantic orientation hidden inside Ningetsu": Ochi Haruo, *Kindai bungaku seiritsuki no kenkyū* (Iwanami Shoten, 1984), 335–56.

16. Ningetsu speaks of the relation between beauty and poetry in such writings as "Shijin to gairaibutsu" (Poets and external objects, 1889) and "Sōjitsuron" (The theory of idea and real,1890), but the discussion of the procedure for creating beauty in literature was absent from the debate. Saeki Junko

has examined how the gesture of discussing beauty was necessitated among Meiji intellectuals, given that beauty was made an indicator of a society's degree of civilization. Saeki, "Bi eno akogare," 178-90.

17. Mori Ōgai, "Kidori Hannojō ni atauru sho," *Shigarami zōshi* 7 (April 25, 1890): 20-27.
18. Ishibashi Ningetsu, "Maihime saihyō," *Kōko shinbun*, April 27, 1890.
19. Ningetsu, "Maihime saihyō."
20. Ōgai, "Kidori Hannojō ni atauru sho," 25-26.
21. Ningetsu's second evaluation, "Maihime saihyō," was published in two parts in *Kōko shinbun* on April 27 and 29, 1890.
22. Mori Ōgai, "Futatabi, Kidori Hannojō ni atauru sho," *Kokumin shinbun* (The nation's paper), April 28, 1890.
23. Ningetsu's third evaluation, "Maihime sanhyō," appeared in *Kōko shinbun* on May 6, 1890.
24. Ōgai, "Shigarami zōshi no honryō o ronzu," 1-2. *Shigarami zōshi* was Ōgai's bully pulpit from which to promote his theory of literature. In some issues, more than half of the contributions were by Ōgai under different pen names.
25. Ishibashi Ningetsu, "Bungaku hyōron shigarami zōshi," *Kokumin no tomo* 67 (November 2, 1889): 36-37. Ningetsu's affiliation with the Min'yūsha School, which ran *Kokumin no tomo* and *Kokumin shinbun*, began in the late 1880s. Between 1888 and 1893, he published more than two hundred essays, about half of which appeared in publications administered by Min'yūsha.
26. Ishibashi Ningetsu, *Tsuyuko hime* (Shun'yōdō, 1889).
27. Ningetsu had more than thirty pen names. Ishibashi Sadakichi, "Kaisetsu," in *Ishibashi Ningetsu hyōronshū* (Iwanami Shoten, 1939), 224.
28. Contemporary readers immediately recognized the correspondence between Kidori and Aizawa as between Ningetsu and Ōgai; indeed, the agreement to identify fictional characters with their authorial creators was already in place in the intellectual reader-writer community, constituting an integral part in the establishment of literature as a field.
29. Ōgai, "Kidori Hannojō ni atauru sho," 26-27.
30. Ōgai, "Kidori Hannojō ni atauru sho," 20.
31. Ōgai, "Maihime," 16.
32. Ōgai, "Maihime," 17.
33. Ōgai, "Kidori Hannojō ni atauru sho," 26.
34. Ōgai, "Kidori Hannojō ni atauru sho," 26.
35. Ningetsu, "Maihime," 38.
36. Aizawa's alternative endings were not examined further in the debate, and their possibilities were suspended, never to be brought back for scrutiny. Aizawa's narrative thus remains as a tissue of unrealized possibilities.
37. Kimura Naoe, *Seinen no tanjō: Meijiki ni okeru seijiteki jissen no tenkan* (Shin'yōsha, 1998), chapters 1 and 3.
38. Tokutomi Sohō, "Meiji nijūsan nen," *Kokumin no tomo* 69 (January 3, 1890): 1.
39. Sohō, "Meiji nijūsan nen," 5.
40. Sohō, "Meiji nijūsan nen," 3.

41. Kimura, *Seinen no tanjō*, 214.
42. Sohō, "Meiji nijūsan nen," 2–3.
43. Kimura, *Seinen no tanjō*, 212–13.
44. Tokutomi Sohō, *Shin Nihon no seinen* (Shūeisha, 1887), 10.
45. Ningetsu wrote this essay in response to the condemnations by Ōgai and Yamaguchi Toratarō, who had harshly attacked Ningetsu for one-sidedly applying "Aristotle's theory of causality" to his reading of novels. Although the correspondence among Ningetsu, Ōgai, and Yamaguchi did not develop further, this altercation could be considered in close relation to the "Dancing Girl" debate. Ōgai, "*Shigarami zōshi* no honryō o ronzu," 3; and Yamaguchi, "Maihime saihyō," 48.
46. Ishibashi Ningetsu, "Zaika ron, sono ichi," *Kōko shinbun*, April 1, 1890.
47. Ishibashi Ningetsu, "Zaika ron, sono ni," *Kōko shinbun*, April 2, 1890.
48. Ishibashi Ningetsu, "Zaika ron, sono san," *Kōko shinbun*, April 3, 1890.
49. Ōgai, "Kidori Hannojō ni atauru sho," 20.
50. For example, see Hasegawa Izumi, *Kindai bungaku ronsō jiten* (Shibundō, 1962), 39.

5. Against Interpretation: The Submerged-Ideal Debate

1. Epigraph from Sontag, *Against Interpretation*, 8.
2. Tsubouchi Shōyō, "Shēkusupiya kyakuhon hyōchū," *Waseda bungaku* 1 (October 20, 1891): 3.
3. Rita Felski, *The Limits of Critique* (University of Chicago Press, 2015), 32–33.
4. Sakai Takeshi's study exemplifies the "why" approach; the entire book is dedicated to the search for reasons, that is to say, "meanings" that are postulated behind authors and texts. Sakai's approach clearly inherits the positivist methodologies that his predecessors demonstrated in their persistent search for authorial intentions. Togawa Shinsuke's work is another example that tries to determine what the debaters "meant" on their behalf. Such a scholarly approach is premised upon the belief that meanings are fixed and locatable. Sakai Takeshi, *Botsurisō ronsō to sono eikyō* (Bukkyō Daigaku Shibunkaku Shuppan, 2016); and Togawa Shinsuke, *"Dorama," "takai": Meiji nijūnendai no bungaku jōkyō* (Chikuma Shobō, 1987), 154–69.
5. Tanizawa Eiichi, for instance, draws conjectures about the root of the antagonism between Shōyō and Ōgai. Kamei Shino too posits Shōyō's "interiority" and Ōgai's "mentality" to explain why they acted as they did during the debate. Tanizawa Eiichi, *Meijiki no bungei hyōron* (Yagi Shoten, 1971), 21–39; and Kamei Shino, "'Bibun Tennō' to 'Kannon': Tsubouchi Shōyō tai Mori Ōgai 'Botsurisō ronsō' ni tsuite," *Hokkaidō daigaku bungakubu kiyō* 47, no. 1 (October 1998): 29–111.
6. Usui Yoshimi, Isogai Hideo, and Ishida Tadahiko downplay the impact of Shōyō's *gibun*, whereas Kamei Shino rejects this passive reading, arguing for the significance of the *gibun* in the debate. Usui Yoshimi, *Kindai bungaku ronsō*

jō (Chikuma Shobō, 1956), 23; Isogai Hideo, *Mori Ōgai: Meiji nijūnendai o chūshin ni* (Meiji Shoin, 1979), 165; Ishida Tadahiko, *Tsubouchi Shōyō kenkyū* (Kyūshū Daigaku Shuppankai, 1988), 286; and Kamei, "'Bibun Tennō' to 'Kannon,'" 88.

7. Mikhail Bakhtin, *Problems of Dostoevsky's Poetics*, ed. and trans. Caryl Emerson (University of Minnesota Press, 1984), 127 and 164. Originally published in 1929.

8. Shōyō, "Shēkusupiya kyakuhon hyōchū," 3–5. I have referred to Ayako Kano and Joseph Murphy's partial translation of Shōyō's text that appeared in Karatani Kōjin's work. Karatani, *Origins of Modern Japanese Literature*, 146.

9. Shōyō, "Shēkusupiya kyakuhon hyōchū," 10. Shōyō mobilized the rhetoric of the submerged-ideal again in the reflective statement in the "Jibun hyōron" (evaluations of contemporary writings) section of *Waseda bungaku* (Waseda literature). Shōyō explains that this section aims to describe "facts" and "real happenings" in the contemporary scene of writing without being judgmental, specifically in order to avoid enforcing narrow explanations of matters and phenomena. This is because, according to Shōyō, judgments should be kept inside readers' minds. Tsubouchi Shōyō, "Ware ni arazu shite nanji ni ari," *Waseda bungaku* 3 (November 15, 1891): 1–3. During the debate, this section served as Shōyō's main platform.

10. Iwamoto Yoshiharu, "Shiekusupia no risō," *Jogaku zasshi* 290 (November 7, 1891): 5–7.

11. Terayama Seisen, "Tsubouchi Shōyōshi no botsurisō ben o yomu," *Jōnan hyōron* 1 (March 21, 1892): 9. Shōyō later spoke of Seisen's complete misunderstanding of the submerged-ideal theory, stating that Seisen's interpretation constituted a true opposition to Hartmann/Ōgai, in that Seisen believed in the complete absence of the ideal. This claim shows how Shōyō's submerged-ideal was not identical to the ideal's nonexistence. Tsubouchi Shōyō, "Jōnan Hyōron jōshu to Shōyōshi to no pārē," *Waseda bungaku* 13 (April 15, 1892): 7–16.

12. Terayama, "Tsubouchi Shōyōshi no botsurisō ben o yomu," 4.

13. According to Shōyō's recollection, he coined this term "in the spring of 1891." Tsubouchi Shōyō, "Botsurisō no yurai," *Waseda bungaku* 13 (April 15, 1892): 176.

14. Tsubouchi Shōyō, "Azusamiko," *Yomiuri shinbun*, June 17, 1891. "Azusamiko" was serialized in *Yomiuri shinbun* from May 15 through June 17, 1891. The essay sets up a pensive narrator "I" (*onore*) who goes to see a shrine maiden for consultation. While describing the process of consultation, Shōyō's essay caricatures Meiji Japan's leading writers and coteries such as Mori Ōgai, Uchida Fuchian, the Ken'yūsha School (Friends of inkstone society), and Shōyō himself.

15. Tsubouchi Shōyō, "Bunkai meisho sokoshirazu no mizuumi," in *Yomiuri shinbun 4866 gō furoku* (Nisshūsha, 1891), 1–17.

16. Shōyō, "Bunkai meisho sokoshirazu no mizuumi," 1–17.

17. Karl Robert Eduard von Hartmann (1842–1906). During the debate, Ōgai mentions Hartmann's *Muishiki no tetsugaku*, which is his translation of *Philosophy of the Unconscious* (1869), as his source of inspiration.

18. Mori Ōgai, "Sanbō ronbun: Sono shichi, *Waseda bungaku* no botsurisō," *Shigarami zōshi* 27 (December 25, 1891): 4. "Uyū" is a set phrase in classical Chinese that functions as a rhetorical question "how could there be (there could not)," meaning "nothing" or "nonexistence."

19. Ōgai, "Sanbō ronbun: Sono shichi, *Waseda bungaku* no botsurisō," 5.

20. Mori Ōgai, "Gendai shoka no shōsetsuron o yomu," *Shigarami zōshi* 2 (November 25, 1889): 9–10. The association Ōgai laid out between Shōyō and Zola is one of the earliest examples of Shōyō being labeled as the origin of mimetic realism in Japan, although this "origin" narrative was challenged by such scholars as Kamei Hideo and Atsuko Ueda: Kamei, *"Shōsetsu" ron*; and Ueda, *Concealment of Politics, Politics of Concealment*.

21. Shōyō, "Azusamiko."

22. Shōyō states that there is no hierarchy among these three, and that the difference between these categories is simply qualitative: Tsubouchi Shōyō, "Shinsaku jūniban no uchi kihatsu yonban gappyō," *Yomiuri shinbun*, December 7–15, 1890. This essay was serialized over several days, and the division of three schools appeared in two entries of December 7 and December 8. All entries were later combined into one piece, renamed "Shōsetsu sanpa" (Three schools of the novel).

23. Mori Ōgai, "Sanbō ronbun: Sono ichi, Shōyōshi no 'Shinsaku jūnibanchū kihatsu shiban gappyō,' 'Baika shishū' hyō oyobi 'Azusamiko,'" *Shigarami zōshi* 24 (September 25, 1891): 4–5.

24. Ōgai, "Sanbō ronbun: Sono ichi, Shōyōshi no 'Shinsaku jūnibanchū kihatsu shiban gappyō,' 'Baika shishū' hyō oyobi 'Azusamiko,'" 4. Ōgai's remark is part of a passage in which he touches remotely on why he chooses Hartmann, though he still does not offer a clear rationale: "When I came across Toyama Masakazu's essay on paintings, it clashed with the idea I had entertained. I could not stop feeling itchy, and I had to draft my rebuttal against Toyama. Thus, I have taken paintings up for discussion by using Hartmann's aesthetic criteria, but I have not done the same with novels. The time has come to pursue that." Ōgai refers to Toyama Masakazu's speech "Nihon kaiga no mirai" (The future of Japanese paintings), presented in April 1890 and later published as *Nihon kaiga no mirai*, (Shūeisha, 1890); Ōgai's response to Toyama, "Toyama Masakazu shi no garon o bakusu," *Shigarami zōshi* 8 (May 25, 1890): 14–50.

25. Scholars such as Kanda Takao and Sakai Takeshi have speculated on why Ōgai selected Hartmann, but unfortunately Ōgai never articulated his reasoning. Kanda Takao, "Mori Ōgai to E. V. Harutoman," in *Hikaku bungaku hikaku bunka*, ed. Shimada Kinji Kyōju Kanreki Kinenkai (Kōbundō, 1961); and Sakai Takeshi, "Ōgai ga Harutoman o eranda wake," *Bukkyō Daigaku bungakubu ronshū* 90 (March 2006): 1–10.

26. Ōgai, "Sanbō ronbun: Sono ichi, Shōyōshi no 'Shinsaku jūnibanchū kihatsu shiban gappyō,' 'Baika shishū' hyō oyobi 'Azusamiko,'" 6.

27. The mission statement of *Waseda bungaku* says that the journal aims at "lecturing and commenting" on various topics related to literature, including literary history, literati, trends of the time, and so forth: "*Waseda bungaku* hakkō no shui," *Waseda bungaku* 1 (October 20, 1891): 1–2.

28. Shōyō's direct responses include:

- "Uyū sensei ni shasu," *Waseda bungaku* 7 (January 15, 1892): 16-17.
- "Botsurisō no gogi o benzu," *Waseda bungaku* 8 (January 30, 1892): 1-5.
- "Uyū sensei ni kotau, sono ichi, sono ni," *Waseda bungaku* 9 (February 15, 1892): 1-12.
- "Shōyōshi ga hiru no yume," *Waseda bungaku* 9 (February 15, 1892): 12-22.
- "Uyū sensei ni kotau, sono san," *Waseda bungaku* 10 (February 29, 1892): 1-17.
- "Sono i wa tagaeri," *Waseda bungaku* 10 (February 29, 1892): 17-20.

29. Shōyō, "Uyū sensei ni kotau, sono san," 2-3.
30. Shōyō, "Uyū sensei ni shasu," 16-17.
31. Mori Ōgai, "Sanbō ronbun: Sono shichi furoku, sono gen o torazu," *Shigarami zōshi* 27 (December 25, 1891): 9-10; and Mori Ōgai, "Sanbō ronbun: Sono jūichi, *Waseda bungaku* no bokkyaku-risō," *Shigarami zōshi* 30 (March 25, 1892): 1. My English translations of Ōgai's neologisms are speculative approximations; I make no claim to fully understand what Ōgai's terms pointed to.
32. Shōyō was well aware of the semantic rupture between their terminologies. He eventually designated Ōgai's discourse as one that was solely rooted in "imagination," "speculation," and "drastic misunderstanding." Tsubouchi Shōyō, "Nyūdō Jōken ga gunhyōgi," *Waseda bungaku* 14 (April 30, 1892): 25.
33. Shōyō, "Uyū sensei ni kotau, sono san," 16.
34. Mori Ōgai, "Sanbō ronbun: Sono jūni, Shōyōshi to Uyū sensei to," *Shigarami zōshi* 30 (March 25, 1892): 34.
35. Ōgai, "Sanbō ronbun: Sono jūni, Shōyōshi to Uyū sensei to," 33. The equation of the submerged-ideal to Zola's naturalism can be found in Mori Ōgai, "Sanbō ronbun: Sono kyū, Emiru Zora ga botsurisō," *Shigarami zōshi* 28 (January 25, 1892): 24.
36. Shōyō's *gibun*-style responses, quickly and prolifically presented, include:

- "Waseda Bungaku-gayatsu Jibun Hyōron-mura no engi," *Waseda bungaku* 12 (March 30, 1892): 17-19.
- "Yosete higashi yori nishi yori semaru," *Waseda bungaku* 12 (March 30, 1892): 20-23.
- "Jintō ni uma o tatete tekishōgun ni monomōsu," *Waseda bungaku* 13 (April 15, 1892): 1-7.
- "Jōnan Hyōron jōshu to Shōyōshi tono pārē," *Waseda bungaku* 13 (April 15, 1892): 7-16.
- "Gazokusecchūnosuke ga gunbai," *Waseda bungaku* 14 (April 30, 1892): 1-22.
- "Nyūdō Jōken ga gunhyōgi," *Waseda bungaku* 14 (April 30, 1892): 22-26.
- "Monju Bosatsu no gōiken," *Waseda bungaku* 14 (April 30, 1892): 26-28.
- "Shōyōshi ga yabumi," *Waseda bungaku* 14 (April 30, 1892): 28-29.

37. Shōyō, "Gazokusecchūnosuke ga gunbai," 13.

38. Shōyō, "Nyūdō Jōken ga gunhyōgi," 26.
39. Mori Ōgai, "Sanbō ronbun: Sono jūsan, *Waseda Bungaku* no kō-botsurisō," *Shigarami zōshi* 33 (June 25, 1892): 1.
40. Shōyō, "Shēkusupiya kyakuhon hyōchū," 3.
41. Shōyō, "Shēkusupiya kyakuhon hyōchū," 3.
42. Karatani, *Origins of Modern Japanese Literature*, 147.
43. Shōyō, "Shēkusupiya kyakuhon hyōchū," 7.
44. The phrase the "infinite, bottomless absolute" appears in Shōyō, "Botsurisō no gogi o benzu," 2.
45. Roman Jakobson, "Two Aspects of Language and Two Types of Aphasic Disturbances," in *On Language*, ed. Linda Waugh and Monique Monville-Burston (Harvard University Press, 1990), 115-33. Originally published in 1956.
46. Jakobson, "Two Aspects of Language and Two Types of Aphasic Disturbances," 131-32.
47. Jakobson, "Two Aspects of Language and Two Types of Aphasic Disturbances," 130.
48. Jakobson, "Two Aspects of Language and Two Types of Aphasic Disturbances," 132.
49. Shōyō, "Hihyō no hyōjun," 7-8, and 2.
50. Karatani, *Origins of Modern Japanese Literature*, 150-51.
51. For instance, Isogai Hideo acknowledges Ōgai's debating strategies to be "faultfinding." Isogai Hideo, *Mori Ōgai: Meiji nijūnendai o chūshin ni*, 165. Tanizawa Eiichi designates Ōgai as a "slanderer." Tanizawa Eiichi, *Bungōtachi no ōgenka: Ōgai, Shōyō, Chogyū* (Chikuma Shobō, 2012), 67.
52. Ōgai, "Sanbō ronbun: Sono ichi, Shōyōshi no 'Shinsaku jūnibanchū kihatsu shiban gappyō,' 'Baika shishū' hyō oyobi 'Azusamiko,'" 14.
53. Ōgai, "Sanbō ronbun: Sono jūichi, *Waseda bungaku* no bokkyaku-risō," 10.
54. Ōgai, "Sanbō ronbun: Sono jūichi, *Waseda bungaku* no bokkyaku-risō," 12.
55. Ōgai, "Sanbō ronbun: Sono jūichi, *Waseda bungaku* no bokkyaku-risō," 19.
56. Ōgai, "Sanbō ronbun: Sono jūni, Shōyōshi to Uyū sensei to," 34.
57. Maeda Ai, "Tenpō kaikaku ni okeru sakusha to shoshi," in *Kindai dokusha no seiritsu* (Yūseidō Shuppan, 1973), 1-33.
58. Kamei, *"Shōsetsu" ron*, 88.
59. Oral recitation and reading aloud in public were common well into the second decade of the Meiji period. Maeda Ai, "Ondoku kara mokudoku e," in *Kindai dokusha no seiritsu* (Yūseidō Shuppan, 1973), 132-39.
60. Eubanks examines the intricate relationship between the visual and the linguistic in early modern Japan's cultural production. Charlotte Eubanks, "Visual Vernacular: Rebus, Reading, and Urban Culture in Early Modern Japan," *Word & Image* 28, no. 1 (May 2012): 57-59.
61. *Gesaku* (戯作) and *gibun* (戯文) share the same Chinese character that stands for "play" and "joke."
62. "Azusamiko," for instance, is set up in a self-canceling manner, destabilizing its own credibility. Before its serialization started in *Yomiuri shinbun*,

"Azusamiko" was advertised as follows: "Is this a novel? Nay. Thesis? Nay. Essay? Nay. Parable? Nay." "Shakoku: 'Azusamiko,' Tsubouchi Shōyō saku," *Yomiuri shinbun*, May 15, 1891.

63. Tsubouchi Shōyō, "Watashi no terakoya jidai," in *Shōyō senshū*, vol. 12 (Daiichi Shobō, 1977–78), 8, 17–18.

64. For a study of the trajectory of writing styles in the final decades of the nineteenth century, see Indra Levy, *Sirens of the Western Shore: The Westernesque Femme Fatale, Translation, and Vernacular Style in Modern Japanese Literature* (Columbia University Press, 2006), especially chapter 1.

65. Shōyō, "Hihyō no hyōjun," 1.

66. Tsubouchi Shōyō, *Tōsei shosei katagi* (Banseidō, 1886), n.p. This phrase appears in the first sentence of the introductory note. It is notable that Shōyō rendered an additional phonetic reading, "*ana-sagashi*" (fault finding), to the Chinese compound term *hihyō*, so that both readings, "*ana-sagashi*" and "*hihyō*," appeared side by side.

67. Takata, "*Tōsei shosei katagi* no hihyō," 28–40.

68. John Pierre Mertz, *Novel Japan: Spaces of Nationhood in Early Meiji Narrative, 1870–88* (University of Michigan Center for Japanese Studies, 2003), 58.

69. Ueda, *Concealment of Politics*, 28–57.

70. In one *gibun* essay, Shōyō discloses that his *gibun* world's background is borrowed from *Taiheiki* (*A Chronicle of the Great Peace*), a late fourteenth-century semi-historical war tale. Shōyō, "Jōnan Hyōron jōshu to Shōyōshi tono pārē," 8.

71. Shōyō, "Waseda Bungaku-gayatsu Jibun Hyōron-mura no engi," 18.

72. Shōyō, "Waseda Bungaku-gayatsu Jibun Hyōron-mura no engi," 19.

73. Shōyō, "Yosete higashi yori nishi yori semaru," 20–21.

74. Shōyō, "Yosete higashi yori nishi yori semaru," 20–22.

75. Bakhtin, *Problems of Dostoevsky's Poetics*, 164.

76. Shōyō, "Monju Bosatsu no gōiken," 27–28.

77. The introduction of a Buddhist saint is noteworthy, given the intense nationalization of Shintoism in the late nineteenth century going along with the deification of the Meiji emperor. The appearance of Monju Bosatsu relativizes the authority of Emperor Bibun in *gibun*, which satirically and allegorically nods to the contemporary political arena.

78. Bakhtin, *Problems of Dostoevsky's Poetics*, 123.

6. The Community of No Referent: The Interrelation-with-life Debate

1. Epigraph from Stanley Fish, *Is There a Text in This Class?: The Authority of Interpretive Communities* (Harvard University Press, 1980), 327.

2. Part of this chapter was previously published as a journal article: Miyabi Goto, "Constitutive Aporia of Literature: The Case of Kitamura Tōkoku's Theory of Literature," *Japan Forum* 33, no. 4 (2019): 731–55. Copyright © 2019 BAJS. Reprinted by permission of Informa UK Limited, trading as Taylor & Francis Group, www.tandfonline.com.

3. For the discursive forces with which Tōkoku and Aizan were negotiating in the late nineteenth century, see Goto, "Constitutive Aporia of Literature," 734–40.

4. Shimazaki Tōson's *Haru* (Spring, 1908) and *Sakura no mi no jukusuru toki* (When the cherries ripen, 1919) present the character, Aoki, modeled after Tōkoku.

5. Nakano Shigeharu, "Akutagawa shi no koto nado," in *Nakano Shigeharu zenshū*, vol. 9, ed. Matsushita Yutaka (Chikuma Shobō, 1959), 103-4. Nakano's essay was originally published in *Bungei kōron* in 1928. Odagiri Hideo, "Sannin no seinen sakka: Kitamura Tōkoku, Ishikawa Takuboku, Kobayashi Takiji," in *Kitamura Tōkoku ron* (Yagi Shoten, 1970), 186.

6. Maeda Ai, "Kinsei kara kindai e," in *Nihon bungaku*, vol. 9 (Sanseidō, 1969), 14-15.

7. The Akutagawa Prize and the Naoki Prize were established in 1935 by Kikuchi Kan, the former for "pure literature" and the latter for "popular literature." While the distinction between the two persists in the twenty-first century, the measurability of the two qualities, "pure" and "popular," and the differences between them were already ambiguous and highly contested from the prizes' inauguration: Edward Mack, *Manufacturing Modern Japanese Literature: Publishing, Prizes, and the Ascription of Literary Value* (Duke University Press, 2010), chapter 5.

8. Dora Zhang's analysis of modernist use of indexicals inspired me to delve into Tōkoku's use of language. Zhang, *Strange Likeness*, chapter 5.

9. Émile Benveniste, "Subjectivity in Language," in *Problems in General Linguistics*, trans. Mary Elizabeth Meek (University of Miami Press, 1971), 225.

10. Fish, *Is There a Text in This Class?*, 355.

11. Yamaji Aizan, "Rai Noboru o ronzu," *Kokumin no tomo* 178 (1893): 39.

12. Christopher Hill demonstrates how the concept of history underwent a drastic shift in the first two decades of the Meiji period, and how young intellectuals like Aizan began to conceptualize themselves anew as historical beings who relay the past to the future in order to construct a new Japan. Christopher Hill, "How to Write a Second Restoration: The Political Novel and Meiji Historiography," *Journal of Japanese Studies* 33, no. 2 (2007): 337-56.

13. Kitamura Tōkoku, "Jinsei ni aiwataru to wa nan no ii zo," *Bungakukai* 2 (1893): 3.

14. Tōkoku, "Jinsei ni aiwataru to wa nan no ii zo," 2-3. Note that Tōkoku replaced Aizan's term "writing" (*bunshō*) with "literature" (*bungaku*) in his rebuttal. As discussed in part 1, in the same way that the nature of *hihyō* was contested, there were multiple, competing ideas of what "literature" could be in late nineteenth-century Japan. The switch between "writing" and "literature" in Tōkoku's account demonstrates the shifting relationship between these words and their referents. For further information on these terms, see Suzuki, *Nihon no "bungaku" gainen*, 50-80.

15. Aizan and Tōkoku debated through publications in their affiliated journal platforms. Even while fighting publicly, in private they were close friends and interacted frequently. The performative aspect of the debate is important when we consider the position taking of each debater and the fields that they attempted to cultivate in Meiji Japan's new social order.

16. Yamaji Aizan, "Meiji bungakushi, dai ni," *Kokumin shinbun*, March 5, 1893.

17. Kitamura Tōkoku, "Nihon bungakushi kotsu," *Hyōron* 1 (1893): 11; and Yamaji Aizan, "Yuishinteki, hanshinteki keikō ni tsuite," *Kokumin Shinbun*, April 19, 1893.

18. Tokutomi Sohō, "Shakai ni okeru shisō no sanchōryū," *Kokumin no tomo* 188 (1893): 6.

19. Kitamura Tōkoku, "Jinsei no igi," *Bungakukai* 5 (1893): 5.

20. Yamaji Aizan, "Junbungaku," *Kokumin shinbun*, May 3, 1893.

21. For more detailed information on the debate, see Satō Zen'ya, *Kitamura Tōkoku to jinsei sōshō ronsō* (NHK Bukkusu, 1998).

22. Tōkoku, "Jinsei ni aiwataru to wa nan no ii zo," 6–7.

23. Tōkoku, "Jinsei ni aiwataru to wa nan no ii zo," 7.

24. Kitamura Tōkoku, "Enseishika to josei" (sequel), *Jogaku zasshi* 305 (February 20, 1892): 7. This essay was published in two entries: Kitamura Tōkoku, "Enseishika to josei" *Jogaku zasshi* 303 (February 6, 1892): 4–8; and Kitamura Tōkoku, "Enseishika to josei" (sequel), *Jogaku zasshi* 305 (February 20, 1892): 6–8.

25. Two years after "Enseishika to josei," Tōkoku exited the world by terminating his life, as if he had enacted the poet's dilemma. Such scholars as Nakano and Odagiri consider Tōkoku's suicide his desperate attempt to retain the purity of literature at the cost of his life, or his obedience to the promise of a pure literature that could never be sustained in the world of the real. It is noteworthy that Tōkoku committed suicide in May 1894, immediately before the outbreak of the Sino-Japanese War. This timing further enhanced the effect of the scholarly narrative that prioritized Tōkoku's rejection of the real world.

26. Tōkoku, "Jinsei ni aiwataru to wa nan no ii zo," 24.

27. Tōkoku, "Jinsei ni aiwataru to wa nan no ii zo," 3–4.

28. Roland Barthes, *The Preparation of the Novel: Lecture Courses and Seminars at the Collège de France (1978–1979 and 1979–1980)*, trans. Kate Briggs (Columbia University Press, 2010), 81.

29. Barthes, *Preparation of the Novel*, 78.

30. Saitō Mareshi carefully differentiates de-Sinification (*datsu-kanbunmyaku*) from anti-Sinification (*han-kanbunmyaku*), links these two orientations with contemporary discourses on literature in late nineteenth-century Japan, and associates Tōkoku's view of literature with the former and Japanese naturalist writers' position with the latter. The early 1890s when Tōkoku was most active was a chaotic, transitional period for writing practices in Japan, as the question of how to systematize written language prompted heated discussions among intellectuals. Sinographic writing, Japanese phonetic writing, and countless variations coexisted in mutual negotiation. Tōkoku's writing, Saitō argues, testifies to a moment at which the written Japanese language began to distance itself from codified Sinographic conventions. Saitō, *Kanbunmyaku to kindai Nihon*, 206–9.

31. Noguchi, "Kindai Nihon bungaku to 'hihyō' no hakken," 7–8.

32. Roman Jakobson, "Shifters, Verbal Categories, and the Russian Verb," in *Russian and Slavic Grammar: Studies 1931–1981*, ed. Linda R. Waugh and Morris Halle (De Gruyter, 1984).

33. Jakobson, "Shifters, Verbal Categories, and the Russian Verb," 42–43.

34. Tōkoku, "Jinsei ni aiwataru to wa nan no ii zo," 5.

35. Aizan has nine usages of the *I* (*gojin*) in his "Rai Noboru o ronzu" (roughly 14,000 characters), versus Tōkoku's thirty in "Jinsei ni aiwataru to wa nan no ii zo" (about 7,500). I limit my counts of the first-person pronoun to the term, "*gojin*," excluding other first-person pronouns such as "*ware*" and "*yo*," for the sake of clarity.

36. Paul Ricoeur refers to this phenomenon as "inscription." Ricoeur writes that shifters inscribe the "absolute" (singular individuals) onto a "system of objective coordinates," examples of which include the institution of family registration and the calendrical time. He thus intends to reconcile the paradoxical duality of pronouns—singular and universal—by understanding it as a process of inscription. Paul Ricoeur, *Oneself as Another*, trans. Kathleen Blamey (University of Chicago Press, 1992), 53–54.

37. Yanabu attributes the language's structural change happening at the time to the processes of translating legal language from Indo-European precursors that unambiguously held subjects such as *Volkenregt* (international law) and kaiser (emperor) in sentences. Yanabu's examples include the language used in the Constitution of the Empire of Japan issued in 1889, adapted from German, and Nishi Amane's *Bankoku kōhō* (Public law of all nations, 1867), reconstructed from Dutch. Yanabu Akira, *Kindai Nihongo no shisō: Hon'yaku buntai seiritsu jijō* (Hōsei Daigaku Shuppankyoku, 2004), 2–18, 239.

38. For instance, Sohō's seminal work *Shōrai no Nihon* (The future of Japan, 1886) shows innumerable uses of "*gojin*," marking the strong presence of the utterer, Sohō, himself.

39. Benveniste, "Subjectivity in Language," 225.

40. Roland Barthes, "Why I Love Benveniste," in *The Rustle of Language*, trans. Richard Howard (University of California Press, 1989), 166. Asserting language's precedence to the subject, Barthes's account carries language's essentiality to extremes. My focus in the chapter is not on Barthes's view of language's primacy but on his observation on the world construction based on personal pronouns.

41. Émile Benveniste, "The Nature of Pronouns," in *Problems in General Linguistics*, trans. Mary Elizabeth Meek (University of Miami Press, 1971), 220.

42. Tōkoku, "Jinsei ni aiwataru to wa nan no ii zo," 8.

43. Benveniste, "Nature of Pronouns," 220.

44. Tsurumi acknowledges his debt to Richard P. Blackmur's work, though he inserts a disclaimer that his use of the term "language as gesture" is narrower than Blackmur's. My understanding of Tsurumi's disclaimer is that when Tsurumi discusses "language as gesture" it points specifically to language's evocation of the physical, corporeal presence of the writer/speaker. Tsurumi Shunsuke, "Enchō ni okeru miburi to shōchō," *Bungaku* 26, no. 7 (1958): 12; and Richard P. Blackmur, *Language as Gesture: Essays in Poetry* (Harcourt, Brace, 1952).

45. Futabatei Shimei, "Yo ga genbun itchi no yurai," in *Futabatei Shimei zenshū*, vol. 5 (Iwanami Shoten, 1965), 170–72. The essay originally appeared in the literary journal *Bunshō sekai* in 1906.

46. Tsurumi, "Enchō ni okeru miburi to shōchō," 4.

47. Tsurumi, "Enchō ni okeru miburi to shōchō," 5–6.
48. Maeda, "Ondoku kara mokudoku e," 160.
49. Maeda, "Ondoku kara mokudoku e," 165.
50. Miki Kiyoshi, "Hihyō no seiri to byōri," *Kaizō* (December 1932): 14.

Conclusion: Failing Well

1. Mack, *Manufacturing Modern Japanese Literature*, chapter 4.
2. Ōsawa, *Hihyō media ron*, 39.
3. In *Hihyō media ron*, Ōsawa dedicates five chapters to different genres of *hihyō*, including roundtable discussion (chapter 3) and personality *hihyō* (chapter 4), to describe the ways in which these genres were instituted in the years surrounding 1930.
4. In their edited volume Bowen-Struyk and Field highlight that the disputes surrounding proletarian literature from the 1920s onward demonstrate the conflicts between the necessity and the inability to sever the literary from the political: *For Dignity, Justice, and Revolution: An Anthology of Japanese Proletarian Literature* (University of Chicago Press, 2016).
5. Marxism's momentum is revealed by the fact that Miyamoto Kenji (1908–2007), a core member of the Japanese Communist Party from 1931 to the postwar period, entered an essay prize competition hosted by progressive Kaizōsha in 1929 and won the first prize with his "Haiboku no bungaku" (Literature of defeat), on writer Akutagawa Ryūnosuke (1892–1927) and his suicide. Kobayashi's "Samazamanaru ishō" came second to Miyamoto's, verifying the prevalence of the nondefinitive "design" (Miyamoto's Marxist hihyō) placed above Kobayashi's discourse that exposes the nondefinitive nature of the "design."
6. Atsuko Ueda, Michael Bourdaghs, Richi Sakakibara, and Hirokazu Toeda, eds., *The Politics and Literature Debate in Postwar Japanese Criticism, 1945–52* (Lexington Books, 2017), xiii.
7. Ueda et al., *Politics and Literature Debate*, xxiv. The editors further argue that these new literary histories ended up underlining a "seemingly continuous 'Japan' from the prewar to the postwar present" while concealing the "hybridity that invariably resulted from Japan's colonial rule."
8. Nakamasa Masaki, *Shūchū kōgi! Nihon no gendai shisō: Posutomodan to wa nan datta no ka* (Nihon Hōsō Shuppan Kyōkai, 2006), chapter 3.
9. The term *paideia* refers to the "system of education and training in classical Greek and Hellenistic (Greco-Roman) cultures that included such subjects as gymnastics, grammar, rhetoric, music, mathematics, geography, natural history, and philosophy." Britannica, s.v. "Paideia," accessed December 31, 2023, www.britannica.com/topic/paideia.
10. Literary scholars associated with the linguistic turn include, for instance, Kamei Hideo, Komori Yōichi, and Noguchi Takehiko.
11. Although his highest degree was in economics, Asada did not produce "academic" works in that discipline, which is striking, given his prolific publications in the fields of *gendai shisō* and *nyū akademizumu*.

12. The *nyū akademizumu* boom was further bolstered by such journals as *Herumesu* (Hermes, 1984–97). As the titular Greek god of travel suggests, the journal promoted mobile, boundary-crossing, interdisciplinary forms of intellectualism.

13. Nakamasa, *Shūchū kōgi!*, 23.

14. Sasaki Atsushi, *Nippon no shisō* (Kōdansha, 2009), 34–38.

15. Asada Akira, *Kōzō to chikara: Kigōron o koete* (Keisō Shobō, 1983), 6.

16. Ōsawa Satoshi, "Hihyō to media: 'Shi' ni setsuzokusuru tame no rejume," in *Gendai Nihon no hihyō 1975–2001*, ed. Azuma Hiroki, Ichikawa Makoto, Ōsawa Satoshi, and Fukushima Ryōta (Kōdansha, 2017), 21–22.

17. Satō Izumi attributes this change in the scope of *hihyō* in the 1980s to the linguistic turn. Satō Izumi, "Hachijū-nendai posuto modanizumu saidoku: Baburu to hihyō," in *Shiseiji noseishinshi: "Kikigaki" to teikō no bungaku* (Seidosha, 2023), 93.

18. Karatani Kōjin, "Henshū kōki," in *Hihyō kūkan* 1 (1991): 258.

19. Asada Akira, Karatani Kōjin, Noguchi Takehiko, Hasumi Shigehiko, and Miura Masashi, "Kyōdō tōgi: Meiji hihyō no shomondai, 1868-1910," *Hihyō kūkan* 1 (1991): 27–68.

20. Clearly Azuma borrowed the term illness (*yamai*) from one of Karatani's major works, *Imi to iu yamai* (An illness called meaning, 1975).

21. Azuma Hiroki, "Hihyō to iu yamai," *Genron* no. 4 (November 2016): 41–42.

22. Azuma, "Hihyō to iu yamai," 43.

23. Azuma, "Hihyō to iu yamai," 35–37.

24. Azuma uses as his example Karatani's active participation in the street protests after the 3/11 Fukushima disaster. Azuma, "Hihyō to iu yamai," 35–36. For further context, see Karatani's interview with *Shūkan dokushojin* (Weekly readers paper): Karatani Kōjin, "Han-genpatsu demo ga Nihon o kaeru," *Shūkan dokushojin*, June 17, 2011, republished on Karatani's website: www.kojinkaratani.com/jp/essay/post-64.html.

25. Azuma Hiroki, "Sōkan ni atatte," *Genron* no. 1 (December 2015): 28–29; English translation by Christopher Lowy, "On Our Inaugural Issue," *Genron* no. 1 (December 2015): E02.

26. Azuma, "Hihyō to iu yamai," 31.

27. I thank Ayako Kano for prompting me to include these anecdotes to enliven my claim about generative failures.

28. See Morris's introduction to his translation of Hayama Yoshiki, "Letter Found in a Cement-Barrel," trans. Ivan Morris, in *Modern Japanese Stories: An Anthology*, ed. Ivan Morris (Tuttle Publishing, 1962), 204–5.

29. Karl Popper, *Unended Quest: An Intellectual Autobiography* (Open Court Publishing, 1976), 47.

Bibliography

"Ā senzai no ittoki." *Kokumin no tomo* 41 (February 12, 1889): 1–8.
Amano Ikuo. *Daigaku no tanjō*. Chūō Kōron Shinsha, 2009.
Arnold, Matthew. "The Function of Criticism at the Present Time." In *Matthew Arnold's Essays in Criticism*, edited by Sister Thomas Marion Hoctor, S.S.J. University of Chicago Press, 1968. First published 1865.
Asada Akira. *Kōzō to chikara: Kigōron o koete*. Keisō Shobō, 1983.
Asada Akira, Karatani Kōjin, Noguchi Takehiko, Hasumi Shigehiko, and Miura Masashi. "Kyōdō tōgi: Meiji hihyō no shomondai, 1868–1910." *Hihyō kūkan* 1 (1991): 27–68.
Azuma Hiroki. "Hihyō to iu yamai." *Genron* no. 4 (November 2016): 30–48.
Azuma Hiroki. "On Our Inaugural Issue," translated by Christopher Lowy. *Genron* no. 1, (2015): E02–E06.
Azuma Hiroki. "Sōkan ni atatte." *Genron* no. 1 (December 2015): 28–34.
Barthes, Roland. *The Preparation of the Novel: Lecture Courses and Seminars at the Collège de France (1978–1979 and 1979–1980)*, translated by Kate Briggs. Columbia University Press, 2010.
Barthes, Roland. "Why I Love Benveniste." In *The Rustle of Language*, translated by Richard Howard. University of California Press, 1989. First published 1974 in *La Quinzaine littéraire*.
Bakhtin, Mikhail. *Problems of Dostoevsky's Poetics*, edited and translated by Caryl Emerson. University of Minnesota Press, 1984. First published 1929.
Benveniste, Émile. "The Nature of Pronouns." In *Problems in General Linguistics*, translated by Mary Elizabeth Meek. Coral Gables: University of Miami Press, 1971. First published in 1956 in *Journal de psychologie*.
Benveniste, Émile. "Subjectivity in Language." In *Problems in General Linguistics*, translated by Mary Elizabeth Meek. University of Miami Press, 1971. First published in 1958 in *Journal de psychologie*.
Best, Stephen, and Sharon Marcus. "Surface Reading: An Introduction." *Representations* 108, no. 1 (Fall 2009): 1–21.
Blackmur, Richard P. *Language as Gesture: Essays in Poetry*. Harcourt, Brace, 1952.
Bloom, Harold. *A Map of Misreading*. Oxford University Press, 1980. First published 1975.
Boulous Walker, Michelle. *Slow Philosophy: Reading Against the Institution*. Bloomsbury, 2017.
Bourdieu, Pierre. *The Field of Cultural Production: Essays on Art and Literature*, edited by Randal Johnson. Columbia University Press, 1993.
Bowen-Struyk, Heather, and Norma Field. *For Dignity, Justice, and Revolution: An Anthology of Japanese Proletarian Literature*. University of Chicago Press, 2016.

Chiba Shinrō. *Ishibashi Ningetsu kenkyū: hyōden to kōshō*. Yagi Shoten, 2006.
de Man, Paul. "Criticism and Crisis." In *Blindness and Insight: Essays in the Rhetoric of Contemporary Criticism*. University of Minnesota Press, 1983.
de Man, Paul. "Semiology and Rhetoric." In *Allegories of Reading: Figural Language in Rousseau, Nietzsche, Rilke, and Proust*. Yale University Press, 1979.
Emerson, Ralph W. "Nature." In *Ralph Waldo Emerson: Essays and Lectures*. Literary Classics of the United States, 1983.
Emre, Merve. *Paraliterary: The Making of Bad Readers in Postwar America*. University of Chicago Press, 2017.
Eubanks, Charlotte. "Visual Vernacular: Rebus, Reading, and Urban Culture in Early Modern Japan." *Word & Image* 28, no. 1 (May 2012): 57–70.
Felski, Rita. *Hooked: Art and Attachment*. University of Chicago Press, 2020.
Felski, Rita. *The Limits of Critique*. University of Chicago Press, 2015.
Felski, Rita. "Response." *PMLA* 132, no. 2 (March 2017): 384–91.
Felski, Rita. *Uses of Literature*. Blackwell, 2008.
Fish, Stanley. *Is There a Text in This Class?: The Authority of Interpretive Communities*. Harvard University Press, 1980.
Fuss, Diana. "But What about Love?" *PMLA* 132, no. 2 (March 2017): 352–55.
Futabatei Shimei. "Yo ga genbun itchi no yurai." In *Futabatei Shimei zenshū*. Vol. 5. Iwanami Shoten, 1965. First published 1906 in *Bunshō sekai*.
Goto, Miyabi. "Constitutive Aporia of Literature: The Case of Kitamura Tōkoku's Theory of Literature." *Japan Forum* 33, no. 4 (2019): 731–55.
Goto, Miyabi. "'Maihime' and the Space of Criticism in Meiji Japan." *The Journal of Japanese Studies* 46, no. 2 (2020): 345–68.
Guillory, John. *Professing Criticism: Essays on the Organization of Literary Study*. University of Chicago Press, 2022.
Habermas, Jürgen. *The Structural Transformation of the Public Sphere: An Inquiry into a Category of Bourgeois Society*, translated by Thomas Burger and Frederick Lawrence. MIT Press, 1991.
Halberstam, Jack. *The Queer Art of Failure*. Duke University Press, 2011.
Hasegawa Izumi. *Kindai bungaku ronsō jiten*. Shibundō, 1962.
Hayama Yoshiki. "Letter Found in a Cement-Barrel," translated by Ivan Morris. In *Modern Japanese Stories: An Anthology*, edited by Ivan Morris. Tuttle Publishing, 1962.
Hill, Christopher. "How to Write a Second Restoration: The Political Novel and Meiji Historiography." *Journal of Japanese Studies* 33, no. 2 (2007): 337–56.
Hill, Christopher. "Mori Ōgai's Resentful Narrator: Trauma and the National Subject in 'The Dancing Girl.'" *Positions: East Asia Cultures Critique* 10, no. 2 (2002): 365–97.
"Honshi kairyō no shushi o nobu." *Chūō gakujutsu zasshi* 20 (December 25, 1885): 1–4.
"Ichikawa Danjūrō." *Jiji shinpō*, March 30, 1889.
Īda Ō. "*Kokumin no tomo* no hihyō o yomu." *Shuppan geppyō* 9 (April 30, 1888): 151–54.
Inakaya Bon'yari. "Jogakusei ni tsuite." *Yomiuri shinbun*, February 23, 1890.
Inoue Teruko. "*Jogaku zasshi* no shippitsusha kōsei: Meiji nijūnendai jānarizumu kōzō kaimei no tame no shiron." *Shuppan kenkyū* 2 (1971): 96–137.

Inoue Tetsujirō, Ariga Nagao, Kōdera Shinsaku, and Wadagaki Kenzō, eds. *Tetsugaku jii*. Tokyo Daigaku Sangakubu, 1881.
Inoue Tetsujirō. "Tokyo keizai zasshi ni kotau." *Tōyō gakugei zasshi* 6 (March 1882): 110–15.
Inoue Tetsujirō. "Kan-shi Gendō o yomite." *Tōyō gakugei zasshi* 7 (March 1882): 139–41.
Ishibashi Ningetsu. "Bungaku hyōron shigarami zōshi." *Kokumin no tomo* 67 (November 2, 1889): 36–37.
Ishibashi Ningetsu. "Chikagoro no sanki." *Kokumin no tomo* 73 (February 13, 1890): 27–28.
Ishibashi Ningetsu. "Jiji shinpō to Jogaku zasshi ni tadasu." *Kokumin no tomo* 48 (April 22, 1889): 33.
Ishibashi Ningetsu. "Maihime." *Kokumin no tomo* 72 (February 3, 1890): 38–39.
Ishibashi Ningetsu. "Maihime saihyō." *Kōko shinbun*, April 27 and 29, 1890.
Ishibashi Ningetsu. "Maihime sanhyō." *Kōko shinbun*, May 6, 1890.
Ishibashi Ningetsu. "Shijin to gairaibutsu." *Kokumin no tomo* 62 (September 12, 1889): 24–26.
Ishibashi Ningetsu. "Sōjitsuron." *Kōko shinbun*, March 20–30, 1890.
Ishibashi Ningetsu. *Tsuyuko hime*. Shun'yōdō, 1889.
Ishibashi Ningetsu. "Zaika ron." *Kōko shinbun*, April 1–April 3, 1890.
Ishibashi Sadakichi. "Kaisetsu." In *Ishibashi Ningetsu hyōronshū*. Iwanami Shoten, 1939.
Ishida Tadahiko. *Tsubouchi Shōyō kenkyū*. Kyūshū Daigaku Shuppankai, 1988.
Isogai Hideo. *Mori Ōgai: Meiji nijūnendai o chūshin ni*. Meiji Shoin, 1979.
Itō Takashi, Sakeda Masatoshi, and Banno Junji, eds. *Tokutomi Sohō kankei monjo*. Kindai Nihon shiryō sensho, 7-1. Yamakawa Shuppansha, 1982.
Iwamoto Yoshiharu. "Ichikawa Danjūrō to Eisei shinshi." *Jogaku zasshi* 156 (April 6, 1889): 15–16.
Iwamoto Yoshiharu. "Kan'in no kūki, fujunketsu no kūki." *Jogaku zasshi* 150 (February 23, 1889): 1–7.
Iwamoto Yoshiharu. "Kenpō happu o shukushitaru uta." *Jogaku zasshi* 149 (February 16, 1889): 12–13.
Iwamoto Yoshiharu. "*Kokumin no tomo* dai gojū gō ni okeru 'Bungaku to shizen' o yomu, o kindokusu." *Jogaku zasshi* 162 (May 18, 1889): 15–17.
Iwamoto Yoshiharu. "*Kokumin no tomo* dai yonjūhachi gō: Bungaku to shizen." *Jogaku zasshi* 159 (April 27, 1889): 10–11.
Iwamoto Yoshiharu. "*Kokumin no tomo* shinnen furoku." *Jogaku zasshi* 195 (January 11, 1890): 7–8.
Iwamoto Yoshiharu. "Shiekusupia no risō." *Jogaku zasshi* 290 (November 7, 1891): 5–7.
Iwamoto Yoshiharu. "Shizen sūhaisha no kotae." *Jogaku zasshi* 165 (June 8, 1889): 30.
Jacobowitz, Seth. *Writing Technology in Meiji Japan: A Media History of Modern Japanese Literature and Visual Culture*. Harvard University Asia Center, 2015.
Jakobson, Roman. "Shifters, Verbal Categories, and the Russian Verb." In *Russian and Slavic Grammar: Studies 1931–1981*, edited by Linda R. Waugh and Morris Halle. De Gruyter, 1984. First published 1957.

Jakobson, Roman. "Two Aspects of Language and Two Types of Aphasic Disturbances." In *On Language*, edited by Linda Waugh and Monique Monville-Burston. Harvard University Press, 1990. First published 1956.
Jameson, Fredric. *The Political Unconscious: Narrative as a Socially Symbolic Act*. Cornell University Press, 1981.
"Jogakkō no akuhyō." *Yomiuri shinbun*, June 8, 1889.
"Jogakkō to joseito." *Yomiuri shinbun*, June 9, 1889.
"Jogaku no kyōkō." *Kokumin no tomo* 54 (June 22, 1889): 12-16.
"Jogakusei no hinkō." *Yomiuri shinbun*, February 18, 1890.
Kamei Hideo. *"Shōsetsu"-ron: Shōsetsu shinzui to kindai*. Iwanami Shoten, 1999.
Kamei Shino. "'Bibun Tennō' to 'Kannon': Tsubouchi Shōyō tai Mori Ōgai 'Botsurisō ronsō' ni tsuite." *Hokkaidō daigaku bungakubu kiyō* 47, no. 1 (October 1998): 29-111.
Kamuf, Peggy. *The Division of Literature: Or the University in Deconstruction*. University of Chicago Press, 1997.
Kanda Takao. "Mori Ōgai to E. V. Harutoman." In *Hikaku bungaku hikaku bunka*, edited by Shimada Kinji Kyōju Kanreki Kinenkai. Kōbundō, 1961.
Kant, Immanuel. *Critique of Pure Reason*, translated and edited by Paul Guyer and Allen Wood. Cambridge University Press, 1998. First published 1781.
Karatani, Kōjin. "Han-genpatsu demo ga Nihon o kaeru." *Shūkan dokushojin*, June 17, 2011.
Karatani, Kōjin. *Origins of Modern Japanese Literature*, edited by Brett de Bary. Duke University Press, 1993.
Karatani, Kōjin. "Henshū kōki." *Hihyō kūkan* no. 1 (1991): 258.
Karatani, Kōjin. "Henshū kōki." *Hihyō kūkan* 2, no. 12 (1997): 234.
"Kenpō." *Jogaku zasshi* 149 (February 16, 1889): 25-26.
Kim, Kyu Hyun. *The Age of Visions and Arguments: Parliamentarianism and the National Public Sphere in Early Meiji Japan*. Harvard University Press, 2007.
Kimura, Naoe. "'Hihyō' no tanjo." *Hikaku bungaku* 45 (2002): 7-22.
Kimura Naoe. *Seinen no tanjō: Meijiki ni okeru seijiteki jissen no tenkan*. Shin'yōsha, 1998.
"Kinkan zassho." *Kokumin no tomo* 17 (March 2, 1888): 33-34.
Kitamura Tōkoku. "Enseishika to josei." *Jogaku zasshi* 303 (February 6, 1892): 4-8.
Kitamura Tōkoku. "Enseishika to josei" [sequel]. *Jogaku zasshi* 305 (February 20, 1892): 6-8.
Kitamura Tōkoku. "Jinsei ni aiwataru to wa nan no ii zo." *Bungakukai* 2 (1893): 1-8.
Kitamura Tōkoku. "Jinsei no igi." *Bungakukai* 5 (1893): 3-6.
Kitamura Tōkoku. "Nihon bungakushi kotsu." *Hyōron* 1 (1893): 10-18.
Kobayashi Hideo. "Samazamanaru ishō." *Kaizō* (September 1929): 102-112.
Kobori Keiichirō. *Wakaki hi no Mori Ōgai*. Tokyo Daigaku Shuppansha, 1969.
Kōdokusha no hitori. "*Shuppan geppyō* e no jogen o kou." *Kokumin no tomo* 12 (November 18, 1887): 30.
Komori Yōichi. *Buntai toshite no monogatari*. Chikuma Shobō, 1988.
Komori Yōichi. "Kindai hihyō no shuppatsu." *Hihyō kūkan* 1 (April 1991): 69-84.

Komori Yōichi. *Kōzō toshite no katari*. Shin'yōsha, 1988.
Komori Yōichi. *Nihongo no kindai*. Iwanami Shoten, 2000.
Kōno Kensuke. *Shomotsu no kindai: Media no bungakushi*. Chikuma Shobō, 1992.
Kornicki, Peter. *The Book in Japan: A Cultural History from the Beginnings to the Nineteenth Century*. Brill, 1998.
Kuroda Shuntarō. "*Yomiuri shinbun* ni okeru 'shinbun shōsetsu' no hensei katei: Meiji nijūnen zengo, Shōyō no shikō to ishi no yukue." *Geibun kenkyū* 93 (December 2007): 1–28.
LaMarre, Thomas. "Bacterial Cultures and Linguistic Colonies: Mori Rintarō's Experiments with History, Science, and Language." *Positions: East Asia Cultures Critique* 6, no. 3 (1998): 597–635.
Latour, Bruno. "Why Has Critique Run out of Steam? From Matters of Fact to Matters of Concern." *Critical Inquiry* 30, no. 2 (Winter 2004): 225–48.
Le Feuvre, Lisa. *Failure*. Whitechapel Gallery and the MIT Press, 2010.
Levy, Indra. *Sirens of the Western Shore: The Westernesque Femme Fatale, Translation, and Vernacular Style in Modern Japanese Literature*. Columbia University Press, 2006.
Liu, Lydia. *Translingual Practice: Literature, National Cultures, and Translated Modernity—China, 1900–1937*. Stanford University Press, 1995.
Love, Heather. "Close Reading and Thin Description." *Public Culture* 25, no. 3 (2013): 401–434.
Love, Heather. "The Temptations: Donna Haraway, Feminist Objectivity, and the Problem of Critique." In *Critique and Postcritique*, edited by Elizabeth S. Anker and Rita Felski. Duke University Press, 2017.
Lozerand, Emmanuel. "The Rise of Criticism (1886–1889): Sohō, Hanpō, Ōnishi, Ōgai." *Cipango: French Journal of Japanese Studies* 2 (2013): 62–100.
Mack, Edward. *Manufacturing Modern Japanese Literature: Publishing, Prizes, and the Ascription of Literary Value*. Duke University Press, 2010.
Maeda Ai. "Kinsei kara kindai e." In *Nihon bungaku*. Vol. 9. Sanseidō, 1969.
Maeda Ai. "Ondoku kara mokudoku e." In *Kindai dokusha no seiritsu*. Yūseidō Shuppan, 1973.
Maeda Ai. "Tenpō kaikaku ni okeru sakusha to shoshi." In *Kindai dokusha no seiritsu*. Yūseidō Shuppan, 1973.
"Meiji nendai no bungaku o ronji awasete hihyō no hitsuyōnaru yuen o toku." *Meiji nippō*, August 4, 1883.
Mertz, John Pierre. *Novel Japan: Spaces of Nationhood in Early Meiji Narrative, 1870–88*. University of Michigan Center for Japanese Studies, 2003.
Miki Kiyoshi. "Hihyō no seiri to byōri." *Kaizō* (December 1932): 13–27.
Miyoshi, Masao. *Accomplices of Silence: The Modern Japanese Novel*. University of Michigan Center for Japanese Studies, 1996.
Moretti, Franco. *Distant Reading*. Verso, 2013.
Mori Ōgai. "Baishō no rigai." *Eisei shinshi* 1 (March 25, 1889): 15–18.
Mori Ōgai. "Futatabi, Kidori Han'nojō ni ataeru sho." *Kokumin shinbun*, April 28, 1890.
Mori Ōgai. "Gendai shoka no shōsetsuron o yomu." *Shigarami zōshi* 2 (November 25, 1889): 4–22.

Mori Ōgai. "Meiji nijūni-nen hihyōka no shigan." *Shigarami zōshi* 4 (January 25, 1890): 1–27.
Mori Ōgai. "Kidori Han'nojō ni atauru sho." *Shigarami zōshi* 7 (April 25, 1890): 20–27.
Mori Ōgai. "Maihime." *Kokumin no tomo* 69 (January 3, 1890): 1–17.
Mori Ōgai. "Sanbō ronbun: Sono ichi, Shōyōshi no 'Shinsaku jūnibanchū kihatsu shiban gappyō,' 'Baika shishū' hyō oyobi 'Azusamiko.'" *Shigarami zōshi* 24 (September 25, 1891): 1–28.
Mori Ōgai. "Sanbō ronbun: Sono jūichi, *Waseda bungaku* no bokkyaku-risō." *Shigarami zōshi* 30 (March 25, 1892): 1–9.
Mori Ōgai. "Sanbō ronbun: Sono jūni, Shōyōshi to Uyū sensei to." *Shigarami zōshi* 30 (March 25, 1892): 9–35.
Mori Ōgai. "Sanbō ronbun: Sono jūsan, *Waseda Bungaku* no kō-botsurisō." *Shigarami zōshi* 33 (June 25, 1892): 1–26.
Mori Ōgai. "Sanbō ronbun: Sono kyū, Emiru Zora ga botsurisō." *Shigarami zōshi* 28 (January 25, 1892): 21–24.
Mori Ōgai. "Sanbō ronbun: Sono shichi furoku, sono gen o torazu." *Shigarami zōshi* 27 (December 25, 1891): 9–10.
Mori Ōgai. "Sanbō ronbun: Sono shichi, *Waseda bungaku* no botsurisō." *Shigarami zōshi* 27 (December 25, 1891): 1–9.
Mori Ōgai. "*Shigarami zōshi* no honryō o ronzu." *Shigarami zōshi* 1 (October 25, 1889): 1–4.
Mori Ōgai. "Toyama Masakazu shi no garon o bakusu." *Shigarami zōshi* 8 (May 25, 1890): 14–50.
Mori Rintarō [Ōgai]. "'Bungaku to shizen' o yomu." *Kokumin no tomo* 50 (May 11, 1889): 18–22.
Mori Rintarō [Ōgai]. "Futatabi shizen sūhaisha ni tadasu." *Kokumin no tomo* 52 (June 1, 1889): 33.
Mori Rintarō [Ōgai]. "Shōsetsuron." *Yomiuri shinbun*, January 3, 1889.
Morris, Ivan. Introduction to Hayama Yoshiki's "Letter Found in a Cement-Barrel." In *Modern Japanese Stories: An Anthology*, edited by Ivan Morris. Tuttle Publishing, 1962.
Murphy, Joseph. *Metaphorical Circuit: Negotiations Between Literature and Science in 20th Century Japan*. Cornell University, 2003.
Nakamasa Masaki. *Shūchū kōgi! Nihon no gendai shisō: Posutomodan to wa nan datta no ka*. Nihon Hōsō Shuppan Kyōkai, 2006.
Nakano Shigeharu. "Akutagawa shi no koto nado." In *Nakano Shigeharu zenshū*. Vol. 9, edited by Matsushita Yutaka. Shobō, 1959. First published 1928 in *Bungei kōron*.
Nishi Amane. *Hyakugaku renkan*. In *Nishi Amane zenshū*. Vol. 1, edited by Ōkubo Toshiaki. Nihon Hyōronsha, 1945.
Noguchi Neisai [Takuten Jōsen]. "Maihime o yomite." *Shigarami zōshi* 4 (January 25, 1890): 50–52.
Noguchi Takehiko. "Kindai Nihon bungaku to 'hihyō' no hakken." *Hihyō kūkan* 1 (1991): 6–26.

North, Joseph. *Literary Criticism: A Concise Political History.* Harvard University Press, 2017.
Ochi Haruo. *Kindai bungaku seiritsuki no kenkyū.* Iwanami Shoten, 1984.
Odagiri Hideo. "Sannin no seinen sakka: Kitamura Tōkoku, Ishikawa Takuboku, Kobayashi Takiji." In *Kitamura Tōkoku ron.* Yagi Shoten, 1970.
Okada Akiko. *Jogaku zasshi to ōka: Kirisutokyō chishikijin to jogakusei no media kūkan.* Shinwasha, 2013.
Okada, Richard. "Areas, Disciplines, and Ethnicity." In *Learning Places: The Afterlives of Area Studies,* edited by Masao Miyoshi and Harry Harootunian. Duke University Press, 2002.
Ong, Walter. *Orality and Literacy: The Technologizing of the Word.* Methuen, 1982.
Ōnishi Hajime. "Hihyōron." *Kokumin no tomo* 21 (May 1888): 25–30.
Ōnishi Hajime. "Hōkon shisōkai no yōmu." *Rikugō zasshi* 100 (April 15, 1889): 15–23.
Ōsawa Satoshi. *Hihyō media ron: Senzenki Nihon no rondan to bundan.* Iwanami Shoten, 2015.
Ōsawa Satoshi. "Hihyō to media: 'Shi' ni setsuzokusuru tame no rejume." In *Gendai Nihon no hihyō 1975–2001,* edited by Azuma Hiroki, Ichikawa Makoto, Ōsawa Satoshi, and Fukushima Ryōta. Kōdansha, 2017.
Pavlov, Mikhail. "Gakujutsu to bijutsu no sabetsu," translated by Futabatei Shimei. *Kokumin no tomo* 19 (April 6, 1888): Appendix 7–11.
Poovey, Mary. "The Model System of Contemporary Literary Criticism." *Critical Inquiry* 27, no. 3 (Spring 2001): 408–38.
Popper, Karl. *Unended Quest: An Intellectual Autobiography.* Open Court Publishing, 1976.
Ri Takanori. *Hyōshō kūkan no kindai: Meiji "Nihon" no media hensei.* Shin'yōsha, 1996.
Ricoeur, Paul. *Freud and Philosophy: An Essay on Interpretation,* translated by Denis Savage. Yale University Press, 1970.
Ricoeur, Paul. *Oneself as Another,* translated by Kathleen Blamey. University of Chicago Press, 1992.
Rubin, Jay. *Injurious to Public Morals: Writers and the Meiji State.* University of Washington Press, 1984.
Saeki Junko. "'Bi' eno akogare." *Nihon no bigaku* 21 (July 1994): 178–90.
Saeki Junko. "'Shizen' to 'Shinjitsu.'" *Nihon no bigaku* 19 (December 1992): 142–59.
Saitō Mareshi. *Kanbunmyaku: The Literary Sinitic Context and the Birth of Modern Japanese Language and Literature,* edited by Ross King and Christina Laffin. Brill, 2021.
Saitō Mareshi. *Kanbunmyaku to kindai Nihon: Mō hitotsu no kotoba no sekai.* Nihon Hōsō Shuppan Kyōkai, 2007.
Sakai Takeshi. *Botsurisō ronsō to sono eikyō.* Bukkyō Daigaku Shibunkaku Shuppan, 2016.
Sakai Takeshi. "Ōgai ga Harutoman o eranda wake." *Bukkyō Daigaku bungakubu ronshū* 90 (March 2006): 1–10.
Sasaki Atsushi. *Nippon no shisō.* Kōdansha, 2009.

Satō Izumi. "Hachijū-nendai posuto modanizumu saidoku: Baburu to hihyō." In *Shiseiji no seishinshi: "Kikigaki" to teikō no bungaku*. Seidosha, 2023.
Satō Dōshin. *Meiji kokka to kindai bijutsu: Bi no seijigaku*. Yoshikawa Kōbunkan, 1999.
Satō Zen'ya. *Kitamura Tōkoku to jinsei sōshō ronsō*. NHK Bukkusu, 1998.
Satō Zen'ya. "Ōnishi Hajime no hihyōkan to sono gensen (chū)." *Rikkyō Daigaku Nihon bungaku* 42 (July 1979): 2–11.
Satō Zen'ya. "Ōnishi Hajime no hihyōkan to sono gensen (ge)." *Rikkyō Daigaku kenkyū hōkoku: Jinbun kagaku* 38 (1979): 23–58.
Satō Zen'ya. "Ōnishi Hajime no hihyōkan to sono gensen (jō)." *Rikkyō Daigaku Nihon bungaku* 41 (January 1979): 9–16.
Sedgwick, Eve Kosofsky. *Touching Feeling: Affect, Pedagogy, Performativity*. Duke University Press, 2003.
"Shakoku." *Kokumin no tomo* 9 (October 1887): n.p.
"Shakoku: 'Azusamiko,' Tsubouchi Shōyō saku." *Yomiuri shinbun*, May 15, 1891.
Shimazaki Tōson. *Haru*. In *Tōson zenshū*. Vol. 3. Chikuma Shobō, 1967. First published in 1908.
Shimazaki Tōson. *Sakura no mi no jukusuru toki*. In *Tōson zenshū*. Vol. 5. Chikuma Shobō, 1967. First published in 1919.
"*Shuppan geppyō* no hatsuda." *Shuppan geppyō* 1 (August 1887): 1–6.
"*Shuppan geppyō* no hyō." *Kokumin no tomo* 8 (September 15, 1887): 42.
"*Shuppan geppyō* no kōyō." *Kokumin no tomo* 11 (November 4, 1887): 31–32.
Sontag, Susan. *Against Interpretation and Other Essays*. Picador, 2001. First published 1964.
Suzuki Sadami. *Nihon no "bungaku" gainen*. Sakuhinsha, 1998.
Takahashi Gorō. "*Kokumin no tomo* naru Saidō-koji no 'Hihyōron' o yomu." *Rikugō zasshi* 90 (June 15, 1888): 223–32.
Takata Sanae. "Hihyō no hitsuyō." *Yomiuri shinbun*, May 4, 1887.
Takata Sanae. "*Tōsei shosei katagi* no hihyō." *Chūō gakujutsu zasshi* 21 (February 1, 1886): 28–40.
Tamura Mie, ed. *Gōtō: Dai Nihon kokumin sen'yō jitchi yūeki taizen*. Yūekidō, 1886.
Tanizawa Eiichi. *Bungōtachi no ōgenka: Ōgai, Shōyō, Chogyū*. Chikuma Shobō, 2012. First published 2003 by Shinchōsha.
Tanizawa Eiichi. *Meijiki no bungei hyōron*. Yagi Shoten, 1971.
Taylor, Mark. "The Lower Criticism." *Representations* 150, no. 1 (Spring 2020): 32–60.
Terayama Seisen. "Tsubouchi Shōyōshi no botsurisō ben o yomu." *Jōnan hyōron* 1 (March 21, 1892): 2–9.
Thomas, Julia. *Reconfiguring Modernity: Concepts of Nature in Japanese Political Ideology*. University of California Press, 2002.
Togawa Shinsuke. *"Dorama," "takai": Meiji nijūnendai no bungaku jōkyō*. Chikuma Shobō, 1987.
Tokutomi Sohō. "Genkon no Nihon wa tekiyō no jidai nari hihyō no jidai nari." *Kokumin no tomo* 20 (April 1888): 9–12.
Tokutomi Sohō. "Genron no fujiyū to bungaku no hattatsu." *Kokumin no tomo* 48 (April 22, 1889): 1–7.
Tokutomi Sohō. "Meiji nijūsan nen." *Kokumin no tomo* 69 (January 3, 1890): 1–5.
Tokutomi Sohō. "Seijijō no bungyō." *Kokumin no tomo* 21 (May 4, 1888): 1–6.

Tokutomi Sohō. "Shakai ni okeru shisō no sanchōryū." *Kokumin no tomo* 188 (1893): 1-8.
Tokutomi Sohō. *Shin Nihon no seinen*. Shūeisha, 1887.
Tokutomi Sohō. *Shōrai no Nihon*. Keizai Zasshi Sha, 1886.
Tokutomi Sohō. "Tekiyō no jidai, hihyō no jidai." *Rikugō zasshi* 89 (May 15, 1888): 167-74.
Tokutomi Sohō. "Tekiyō no jidai, hihyō no jidai" [sequel]. *Rikugō zasshi* 90 (June 15, 1888): 219-23.
Tomkins, Silvan. *Affect, Imagery, Consciousness*. Springer Publishing, 2008.
Toyama Masakazu. *Nihon kaiga no mirai*. Shūeisha, 1890.
Tsu, Jing. *Failure, Nationalism, and Literature: The Making of Modern Chinese Identity, 1895-1937*. Stanford University Press, 2005.
Tsubouchi Shōyō. "Azusamiko." *Yomiuri shinbun*, May 15-June 17, 1891.
Tsubouchi Shōyō. "Botsurisō no gogi o benzu." *Waseda bungaku* 8 (January 30, 1892): 1-5.
Tsubouchi Shōyō. "Botsurisō no yurai." *Waseda bungaku* 13 (April 15, 1892): 169-90.
Tsubouchi Shōyō. "Bunkai meisho sokoshirazu no mizuumi." In *Yomiuri shinbun 4866 gō furoku*. Nisshūsha, 1891.
Tsubouchi Shōyō. "Gazokusecchūnosuke ga gunbai." *Waseda bungaku* 14 (April 30, 1892): 1-22.
Tsubouchi Shōyō. "Hihyō no hyōjun." *Chūō gakujutsu zasshi* 58 (September 15, 1887): 1-8.
Tsubouchi Shōyō. "Jintō ni uma o tatete tekishōgun ni monomōsu." *Waseda bungaku* 13 (April 15, 1892): 1-7.
Tsubouchi Shōyō. "Jōnan Hyōron jōshu to Shōyōshi to no pārē." *Waseda bungaku* 13 (April 15, 1892): 7-16.
Tsubouchi Shōyō. "Monju Bosatsu no gōiken." *Waseda bungaku* 14 (April 30, 1892): 26-28.
Tsubouchi Shōyō. "Nyūdō Jōken ga gunhyōgi." *Waseda bungaku* 14 (April 30, 1892): 22-26.
Tsubouchi Shōyō. "Shēkusupiya kyakuhon hyōchū." *Waseda bungaku* 1 (October 20, 1891): 1-10.
Tsubouchi Shōyō. "Shinsaku jūniban no uchi kihatsu yonban gappyō." *Yomiuri shinbun*, December 7-15, 1890.
Tsubouchi Shōyō. "Shōyōshi ga hiru no yume." *Waseda bungaku* 9 (February 15, 1892): 12-22.
Tsubouchi Shōyō. "Shōyōshi ga yabumi." *Waseda bungaku* 14 (April 30, 1892): 28-29.
Tsubouchi Shōyō. "Sono i wa tagaeri." *Waseda bungaku* 10 (February 29, 1892): 17-20.
Tsubouchi Shōyō. *Tōsei shosei katagi*. Banseidō, 1886.
Tsubouchi Shōyō. "Uyū sensei ni kotau, sono ichi, sono ni." *Waseda bungaku* 9 (February 15, 1892): 1-12.
Tsubouchi Shōyō. "Uyū sensei ni kotau, sono san." *Waseda bungaku* 10 (February 29, 1892): 1-17.
Tsubouchi Shōyō. "Uyū sensei ni shasu." *Waseda bungaku* 7 (January 15, 1892): 16-17.

Tsubouchi Shōyō. "Ware ni arazu shite nanji ni ari." *Waseda bungaku* 3 (November 15, 1891): 1–3.
Tsubouchi Shōyō. "Waseda Bungaku-gayatsu Jibun Hyōron-mura no engi." *Waseda bungaku* 12 (March 30, 1892): 17–19.
Tsubouchi Shōyō. "Watashi no terakoya jidai." *Shōyō senshū*. Vol. 12. Daiichi Shobō, 1977.
Tsubouchi Shōyō. "Yosete higashi yori nishi yori semaru." *Waseda bungaku* 12 (March 30, 1892): 20–23.
Tsurumi Shunsuke. "Enchō ni okeru miburi to shōchō." *Bungaku* 26, no. 7 (1958): 1–12.
Ueda, Atsuko. *Concealment of Politics, Politics of Concealment: The Production of "Literature" in Meiji Japan*. Stanford University Press, 2007.
Ueda, Atsuko, Michael Bourdaghs, Richi Sakakibara, and Hirokazu Toeda, eds. *Literature Among the Ruins, 1945–1955: Postwar Japanese Literary Criticism*. Lexington Books, 2018.
Usui Yoshimi. *Kindai bungaku ronsō ge*. Chikuma Shobō, 1956.
Usui Yoshimi. *Kindai bungaku ronsō jō*. Chikuma Shobō, 1956.
"*Waseda bungaku* hakkō no shui." *Waseda bungaku* 1 (October 20, 1891): 1–2.
Watanabe, Kazuyasu. "Ōnishi Hajime: Criticism and Aesthetics." In *A History of Modern Japanese Aesthetics*, translated and edited by Michael Marra. University of Hawai'i Press, 2001.
Yagi Mizuho. "*Jogaku zasshi* o shiza to shita Meiji nijūninen no bungaku ronsō: Joshikyōikukai no moraru fuhai o meguru dōjidaigensetsu tono kōsaku." *Kindai bungaku shiron* 35 (December 1997): 1–12.
Yamaguchi Toratarō. "Maihime saihyō." *Shigarami zōshi* 4 (January 25, 1890): 46–50.
Yamaji Aizan. "Junbungaku." *Kokumin shinbun*. May 3, 1893.
Yamaji Aizan. "Meiji bungakushi." *Kokumin shinbun*, March 1–June 11, 1893.
Yamaji Aizan. "Rai Noboru o ronzu." *Kokumin no tomo* 178 (January 13, 1893): Appendix 39–52.
Yamaji Aizan. "Yuishinteki, hanshinteki keikō ni tsuite." *Kokumin shinbun*. April 19, 1893.
Yamamoto Takamitsu. *Hyakugaku renkan o yomu*. Sanseidō, 2016.
Yanabu Akira. *Hon'yakugo seiritsu jijō*. Iwanami Shoten, 1982.
Yanabu Akira. *Kindai Nihongo no shisō: Hon'yaku buntai seiritsu jijō*. Hōsei Daigaku Shuppankyoku, 2004.
Yanagida Izumi. *Meiji shoki no bungaku shisō*. In *Meiji bungaku kenkyū*. Vols. 4 and 6. Shunjūsha, 1965.
Yanagida Izumi. *Shōsetsu shinzui kenkyū*. Shunjūsha, 1966.
Yatabe Ryōkichi. "*Shuppan geppyō* hatsuda ni tsuki shokan o nobu." *Shuppan geppyō* 1 (August 1887): 35–37.
Yayoshi Mitsunaga. *Mikan shiryō ni yoru Nihon shuppan bunka*. Yumani Shobō, 1990.
Yeats, William Butler. "Among School Children." In *The Collected Poems of W. B. Yeats*. Macmillan, 1933.

Yoda, Tomiko. "First-Person Narration and Citizen-Subject: The Modernity of Ōgai's 'The Dancing Girl.'" *Journal of Asian Studies* 65, no. 2 (2006): 277–306.

Yoda, Tomiko. *Gender and National Literature: Heian Texts in the Constructions of Japanese Modernity*. Duke University Press, 2004.

Zhang, Dora. *Strange Likeness: Description and the Modernist Novel*. University of Chicago Press, 2020.

Zola, Émile. "Description." In *The Experimental Novel and Other Essays*, translated by Belle M. Sherman. Cassell Publishing, 1893.

Zola, Émile. "The Experimental Novel." In *The Experimental Novel and Other Essays*, translated by Belle M. Sherman. Cassell Publishing, 1893.

INDEX

Note: Page numbers in *italics* refer to illustrations.

academic disciplines, 102–3, 114, 180
aesthetic experience, 9, 200n50
aesthetic literature, 64, 87, 105, 106;
   boundaries of, 101, 104, 108–9,
   210n43; as pure literature, 163 (*see
   also* pure literature). *See also* creative
   production
Aizan, Yamaji, 28–29, 158–65, 168–69,
   172, 174, 220n12, 220n14, 221n15,
   222n35; "Rai Noboru o ronzu"
   (Discussing Rai Noboru [also known
   as Rai San'yō]), 161–62
Aizawa Kenkichi (fictional character).
   See "Dancing Girl" debate
Akutagawa Prize, 29, 160, 220n7
Akutagawa Ryūnosuke, 223n5
allegories, 135, 151–55, 219n77
Allibone, Samuel Austin, 151
annotations, 10, 45, 63, 136–38, 140, 143
Aono Suekichi, 180
Ara Masahito, 182
Aristotle, 214n45
Arnold, Matthew, 73, 75, 77–78, 207n35,
   207n49
Asada Akira, 183–86, 224n11; *Kōzō to
   chikara* (Structure and power), 183–86
Azuma Hiroki, 187, 224n20, 224n24

Bakhtin, Mikhail, 134, 154, 156, 188
Balzac, Honoré de, 99
Barthes, Roland, 169, 174, 222n40
Bashō, Matsuo, 166–69, 174
beauty, 86–88, 96–97, 101, 139–40; fine
   arts and, 106–7; poetry and, 116,
   213n16
Benveniste, Émile, 161, 173–74
Bernard, Claude, 83, 99
Best, Stephen, 18, 20
Blackmur, Richard P., 223n44

Bloom, Harold, 95
Boileau-Despréaux, Nicolas, 206n22
Boulous Walker, Michelle, 20
Bourdieu, Pierre, 90
Bowen-Struyk, Heather, 180, 223n4
Buddhism, 155, 219n77
bungaku (literature), 8, 62–63, 81, 204n52,
   220n14. *See also* literature
bungaku hyōron, 122
Bungakukai (The world of literature), 66,
   160, 162–63
bungei hihyō (literary criticism), 63
bunshō (writing), 202n17, 220n14
Byron, Lord, 71

caricatures, 139–40, 151, 215n14
carnivalistic laughter, 13, 134–35,
   154, 156
causality, 126–31, 214n45
chance (*gūzen*), 129, 143
Chian iji hō (Peace Preservation Law),
   181
Chiba Shinrō, 212n7
China: Western colonial expansion and,
   2, 34. *See also* classical Chinese studies
Chinese *hihyō*, 44–45, 49
Chinese writing system, 3, 10, 48,
   198n13, 203n22, 221n30
Christians, 50, 91, 93, 95, 163, 208n5
Chūō gakujutsu zasshi (Central academic
   journal), 48–49, 146
civilizational status, 34–35, 45–46, 62,
   71–74. *See also* Japan
class hierarchy, 4, 89–90
classical Chinese studies, 10, 63, 64,
   102–3
close reading, 22, 200n43
colonialism, 2–3, 34
commentaries, 45, 63, 135–38

237

INDEX

Craik, George Lillie, 151
creative production and *hihyō*, 2, 12–16, 27, 64–66, 74–78, 106–15, 117–18, 131, 156–57, 192, 207n49. *See also* fiction
critical language, 13, 25–28, 63; objective style of, 133; relationship between creative production and, 27, 77–78, 112–15, 117–18, 131, 156–57; spatialization of *hihyō* and, 102. *See also* language
critical reading, 1–12; alternative ways of "reading otherwise," 2, 6, 22, 29, 59, 188–92; creativity and, 192, 207n49; experimental forms, 2, 8, 27, 82–84, 98–100, 105, 108, 137, 176; and field of literature, 114; historicist/contextualist paradigm, 16–17, 20; institutionalization of, 147; methodologies of, 1, 21; self-reflective discussions about, 17–22; in twenty-first century, 14–22, 199n21; utopian vision of, 74; Western style of, 10–11 (*see also* criticism). *See also hihyō*
criticism (English term), 6, 9, 37–44, 197n6
cultural history, 16, 20

"Dancing Girl" debate, 25, 112–31, 214n45; alternative endings, 113, 124, 213n36; between fictional characters (Kidori/Ningetsu and Aizawa/Ōgai), 84, 112–13, 119–26, 128–30, 213n28, 213n36; luck and, 123–31; Ningetsu's *hihyō*, 112–13, 115–26, 128–31; Ōgai's response to Ningetsu, 116–26, 129–31; relationship between fiction and reality, 123–26
de Man, Paul, 60, 114, 185–86
defocalization, 144, 147–48, 150, 154–55
deictics, 29, 160, 169–70, 175
Deleuze, Gilles, 183
distant reading, 20, 200n43
division of intellectual labor, 27, 66–68, 75, 101–10, 117–18, 125

Edo period (1603–1868), 2, 38; *gesaku* (playful fiction), 150–52, 219n61; *gibun* (playful writing), 133, 150; literature of, 58
Eisei shinshi (New journal of hygiene), 94, 205n4
elites, 4, 9–10, 38, 47–48, 65, 67, 91, 95, 102–4, 112, 130

Emerson, Ralph Waldo, 96, 103; "Nature," 88
emptiness (*kū* or *kyo*), 168–69
Emre, Merve, 199n29
enpon (one-yen book) boom, 180
Episutēmē (Episteme), 183
Eubanks, Charlotte, 150, 218n60
Euro-Anglo-American cultures: colonial expansionism, 2–3, 34; encyclopedic knowledge, 38–42; literature and intellectualism, 2–3, 11, 71–73, 185. *See also* Western *hihyō*
evolution, 66–67
experimental forms of writing, 2, 8, 27, 82–84, 98–100, 105, 108, 137, 176

failure: creative possibilities of, 2, 12–16; negativity of, 12, 198n20. *See also* generative failures of *hihyō*
fairness, 12–13, 178
fault finding (*ana-sagashi*), 33, 218n51, 219n66
Felski, Rita, 20, 133, 200nn49–50
fiction: conflation of nonfiction with, 93; division of critical language from, 27, 112–15, 117–18, 131; *hihyō* becoming, 114–15, 118–26, 131; luck and, 131
Field, Norma, 180, 223n4
fields. *See* academic disciplines
fine arts: beauty and, 106–7; institutionalization of, 85–86
Fish, Stanley, 158, 161
free speech, 85, 187, 202n10, 209n27
Freedom and People's Rights Movement, 51, 90, 126, 209n26
Freud, Sigmund, 17
Fujiwara no Shunzei no Musume, 9
Fuss, Diana, 200n49
Futabatei Shimei, 102, 211n52; *Ukigumo* (*The Drifting Clouds*), 177

Garakuta bunko (Rubbish heap library), 64, 93
gendai shisō (contemporary thought), 7, 183–86
Gendai shisō (Contemporary thought [journal]), 183–84
gender, 34, 51, 56, 91–92, 126, 185. *See also* women's education and social status
gender-based inequality. *See* women's education and social status

generative failures of *hihyō*, 2, 12–16, 26, 67; *hihyō* becoming fiction in "Dancing Girl" debate, 114–15, 118–26, 131; Ōgai's misreading of "Literature and Nature," 101, 106–11; Ōgai's misreading of submerged-ideal, 133, 140–41; Ōnishi's theory and, 74; playful writing and, 133–34; postcritical reading and, 188–92
Genji monogatari tama no ogushi (The jeweled comb of *The Tale of Genji*), 9
Genron (Speech), 188
German philosophy, 34, 138–39
Germany, education in, 68, 95
gesaku (playful fiction), 150–52, 219n61
gibun (playful writing), 27–28, 133–35, 149–57, 215n6, 219n61
Goethe, Johann Wolfgang von, 71, 117
goodness, 88, 96–97, 103, 107
Gōtō: Dai Nihon kokumin sen'yō jitchi yūeki taizen (A collection of practical and useful matters for the people of great Japan), 3, 5
Gottschall, Rudolf von, 208n10
Guattari, Félix, 183
Guillory, John, 16, 197n6

Habermas, Jürgen, 36–37, 201n7, 201n9, 202n11
haiku, 166–69
Halberstam, Jack, 13, 16–17
Hartmann, Eduard von, 84, 138–42, 147, 215n11, 216n17, 216nn24–25. *See also* submerged-ideal debate
Hasegawa Izumi, 113
Hasegawa Tatsunosuke, 102
Hayama Yoshiki: "Letter Found in a Cement-Barrel," 189–90
Heian period (794–1185), 9
hierarchies: in East Asia, 2; social, 4, 89–90, 134–35. *See also* civilizational status; elites
higher education, 81, 102–3
hihyō: creativity and, 13–14, 27, 64–66, 74–78, 106–15, 117–18, 131, 156–57, 192, 207n49; debates, 25–29 (*see also* "Dancing Girl" debate; interrelation-with-life debate; "Literature and Nature" debate; submerged-ideal debate); elitism of, 48; emergence of, 24–25, 33–61, 180; failures of, 14, 19, 179 (*see also* generative failures of *hihyō*); historical context, 2–3, 8, 34–37; ideals of, 12–13, 25, 27, 29, 34–35, 69–74, 113, 122, 133, 137, 159, 178; information value created through, 47, 52–54, 62, 159; metadiscourses, 12, 55–61, 176; Ōnishi's theory of, 68–78; overview of, 22–29; peripherality in scholarship, 22–23; scope and meanings of, 6–8, 33–35, 47, 63, 67, 146–50, 185–87, 223n3; self-cancelation, 76, 176; self-referentiality of *hihyō*-on-*hihyō*, 55–61; self-reflection, 134, 156–57; Sohō on "age of *hihyō*," 33–37, 46, 64; translingual negotiations, 37–44, 96; in twentieth century, 179–88; uncertainty of, 82. *See also bungei hihyō*; Chinese *hihyō*; critical language; critical reading; interpretation-driven *hihyō*; personality *hihyō*; spatialization of *hihyō*; Western *hihyō*
Hihyō kūkan (Critical space), 185–87
Hill, Christopher, 113, 220n12
Hirabayashi Hatsunosuke, 180
Hirano Ken, 182, 185
Honda Shūgo, 182
Hongō Seinenkai, 34
Houghton, William A., 198n15
humanism, 7–8, 21, 63, 64, 182, 199n21

Ichikawa Danjūrō, 92
Iida Ō: *Mohō tetsugaku* (Philosophy of imitation), 57–58
immorality, 85–86, 89, 93, 96, 106–7, 210n34
impartiality, 12–13, 25, 137
Imperial Constitution, 91–92
Imperial Diet, 67, 91, 95, 127, 130, 209n26
Inakaya Bon'yari, 210n36
Inoue Tetsujirō, 47–48; *Tetsugaku jii*, 43–44, 44
intellectualism, 29, 67, 71–73; division of intellectual labor, 27, 66–68, 75, 101–10, 117–18, 125; twentieth-century trends, 183–86. *See also* knowledge; *specific intellectuals*
interpretation-driven *hihyō*, 1, 133–57; defined, 135
interrelation-with-life debate, 25, 28–29, 158–78; engaging with readers, 175–78; limits of linguistic representation, 164–69; purity of literature, 161–64 (*see also* pure literature); readerly community and, 169–75

Ishida Tadahiko, 215n6
Isogai Hideo, 215n6, 218n51
Iwamoto Yoshiharu: background, 89–90, 209n23; Chinese studies and, 103; on "The Dancing Girl," 212n11; "Literature and Nature" ("Bungaku to shizen"), 26–27, 81–98, 100–108, 110–11; on submerged-ideal, 136–37

Jacobowitz, Seth, 205n1
Jakobson, Roman, 144–45, 170–71
Jameson, Frederic, 17–18, 186
Japan: causal development, 126–31; civilizational status, 34–35, 45–46, 62, 64, 66, 71–74, 88, 118, 128, 130, 151; history of, 2–3, 8, 34–37, 220n12, 223n7; Imperial Constitution, 91–92; Imperial Diet, 67, 91, 95, 127, 130, 209n26; nation-building project, 4, 8, 22, 35, 91, 127–30; peripherality, 15; post-1945 occupation, 187. *See also* Edo period (1603–1868); Meiji period (1868–1912)
Japanese Communist Party, 223n5
Jiji shinpō (News on current events), 92
Jogaku zasshi (Women's magazine), 64, 85, 87, 90–92, 104, 203n36, 208n5, 209n25, 211n57
Jogaku Zasshi School (Society of *Jogaku zasshi*), 66, 88, 90–94
journalism, 7, 33, 51, 91–93, 180–81, 184, 188
journals, 7, 24, 36, 205n4; on *hihyō* of creative writing, 66; space for *hihyō*, 47 (*see also* spatialization of *hihyō*). *See also* periodicals; *specific journals*

kabuki, 92
Kagetsu shinshi (New journal of flowers and moon), 64
Kaihatsusha, 205n4
Kaizōsha, 223n5
Kamei Hideo, 150, 205n1, 216n20
Kamei Shino, 214n5, 215n6
Kamuf, Peggy, 81, 82
kanbun (Sinographic writing style), 48
kanbunmyaku (Literary Sinitic context), 198n13
Kanda Takao, 216n25
kansai-jutsu (art of reflection and judgment), 42, 44
Kant, Immanuel, 33, 34, 73
Kan'yu (Han Yu): "Gendō," 47

Karatani Kōjin, 16, 89, 143, 147, 185–88, 197n8, 199n26, 224n20, 224n24
Ken'yūsha School (Friends of inkstone society), 215n14
Ki no Tsurayuki, 9
Kidori Hannojō (fictional character). *See* "Dancing Girl" debate
Kikuchi Kan, 220n7
Kim, Kyu Hyun, 36
Kimura Naoe, 47, 126–28
knowledge: compartmentalization of, 110; division of intellectual labor, 27, 66–68, 75, 101–5; information value created through *hihyō*, 47, 52–54, 62, 159; organization of, 38–42, 67, 103–4
Kobayashi Hideo, 7, 181, 185, 223n5
Kobayashi Takiji, 180, 181
Kobori Keiichirō, 113, 208n10
Kōko shinbun (The public paper), 128
Kokumin no tomo (The nation's friend): Aizan in, 161; circulation, 115; creative writing in, 64; "The Dancing Girl" published in, 113; division of intellectual labor and, 66, 102; founding of, 90; *hihyō* section, 24, 36, 50–59, 69–70; "Literature and Nature" debate, 85–87; male readership, 56, 91–92, 204n47; metadiscourse on *hihyō*, 55–59; Min'yūsha School and, 213n25; Ōnishi's "Hihyōron," 68; politics and, 90–92, 126–30; "*Shakoku*" (announcement), 53; Sohō and, 34, 50, 90–91; Takahashi in, 206n20; on women's education, 93
Kokumin shinbun (The nation's paper), 213n25
Komori Yōichi, 52, 77, 113, 186, 201n6
Konakamura Kiyonori, 204n44
Kōno Kensuke, 4
Kornicki, Peter, 197n3
Kritik (German term), 6, 9, 37–44
Kurimoto Shin'ichirō, 184
Kuroda Shuntarō, 210
Kyōiku jiron (Education review), 205n4

Lacan, Jacques, 183
LaMarre, Thomas, 109, 208n4
language: limits of, 164–69; materiality of, 165; personal pronouns, 171–75, 222nn35–36, 222n40; physical gestures and, 177, 223n44; shifters, 170–74, 222n36; sign-referent

INDEX

relationship, 160–61; structural change in, 222n37; systematization of Japanese, 221n30. *See also* critical language; translingual practice
Latour, Bruno, 18–19
Le Feuvre, Lisa, 12
Levy, Indra, 151, 205n1
liberal arts, 8
literacy: of nonelites, 150; of samurai class, 4, 90
literary studies: linguistic turn, 183, 186, 224n10, 224n17; in twenty-first century, 14–22
literature: division of critical reading from, 112–15, 118–26, 131; field formation, 114; foreign elements in, 65–66; instrumentality of, 28–29, 158, 162–63; politics and, 181–83; schools of the novel, 139–40, 216n22; special relationship between *hihyō* and, 25, 62–67, 180, 183–86. *See also* aesthetic literature; fiction; proletarian literature; pure literature; *shōsetsu* (prose fiction)
"Literature and Nature" debate, 25–27, 81–111; beginning of, 85–89; context, 89–95; disconnect in, 82, 89, 94–95, 97; division between literature and science, 82, 88–89, 97; form of Ōgai's *hihyō*, 82; Ōgai's *hihyō*, 26–27, 81–84, 86–89, 94–111; Ōgai's misreading, 26–27, 83, 94–111
Liu, Lydia, 37, 42
Love, Heather, 199n29
Lozerand, Emmanuel, 10–11, 51, 55
luck (*gyōkō*), 123–31

Macaulay, Thomas, 71
Mack, Edward, 180, 197n3
Maeda Ai, 150, 159, 205n1
Marcus, Sharon, 18, 20
Marx, Karl, 17
Marxism, 180–81, 183, 199n26, 223n5
Masao Miyoshi, 113
meaning, 143–48, 214n4; singular locus of, 24, 132, 144–45, 148, 154–55, 171–73. *See also* sensemaking
Meiji Jogakkō (Meiji Women's School), 90, 208n5, 209n28
Meiji nippō (Meiji daily), 64
Meiji period (1868–1912): global dynamics during, 2–3, 8, 34–35; politics of, 67, 89–91

(*see also* political activism); systems of, 198n16
Merry Christmas Mr. Lawrence (1983), 190–91
Mertz, John, 152
metaphor, 145
metonymy, 144–46
Miki Kiyoshi, 178, 181, 197n9
mimesis, 165
Min'yūsha School (Society of people's friends), 34, 50–51, 89–92, 163, 213n25
misreading, 22; Ōgai on "Literature and Nature," 26–27, 83, 94–111; Ōgai on submerged-ideal, 133, 140–41
Miyako no hana (Flowers of the capital), 64, 93
Miyamoto Kenji, 223n5
modernization theory, 14–15, 19–20
Moretti, Franco, 20, 200n43
Mori Rintarō. *See* Ōgai
Morris, Ivan, 189
Motoori Norinaga, 9
Mumyōzōshi (The nameless book), 9
Murasaki Shikibu, 9
Murphy, Joseph, 102

Nakamasa Masaki, 183–84
Nakamura Masanao, 203n44
Nakano Shigeharu, 159, 182, 220n5, 221n25
Nakazawa Shin'ichi, 184
Naoki Prize, 220n7
national literatures, 200n43
Natsume Sōseki, 197n9
naturalism, 83, 97–98, 100, 108, 138, 217n35
nature: concept of, 87, 96–101. *See also* "Literature and Nature" debate
Nietzsche, Friedrich, 17
Ningetsu, Ishibashi: on beauty and poetry, 213n16; on division of intellectual labor, 104; *hihyō* on "The Dancing Girl," 27, 112–13, 115–26, 128–31, 212nn14–15; on importance of *hihyō*, 59–60; Min'yūsha School and, 213n25; pen names, 119, 213n27; scholarship on, 212n7; on separation of artistic expression from reality, 85–87, 89, 92–93; *Tsuyuko hime* (Lady Tsuyuko), 119–20; "Zaika ron" (Theory of causality), 128–29, 214n45

INDEX

Nishi Amane, *Hyakugaku renkan*, 38–42, 40, 44, 67, 96, 110, 202nn14–15, 202nn17–18
Noguchi Takehiko, 58, 169, 186
noninterpretation, 28, 133–35, 142–50
North, Joseph, 16, 19–20
novel, schools of, 139–40, 216n22
nyū akademizumu (new academism), 183–86, 224nn11–12

objective distance, 12–13, 27, 113, 122, 178
Odagiri Hideo, 159, 220n5, 221n25
Ōgai (Mori Ōgai Rintarō): "'Bungaku to shizen' o yomu" (Reading "Literature and Nature"), 86, 208n10; caricatures of, 215n14; on causality, 214n45; Chinese studies and, 103; on importance of *hihyō*, 59, 65–66; journals and, 205n4; "Maihime" ("The Dancing Girl"), 27, 112–31; pen names, 84, 119, 213n24; scholarship on, 22; *Shigarami zōshi* and, 65, 213n24; "Shōsetsuron" (The theory of the novel), 83, 100, 104, 108. *See also* "Dancing Girl" debate; "Literature and Nature" debate; submerged-ideal debate
Okada Akiko, 94, 209n25
Ōkuma Shigenobu, 48, 209n26
Ong, Walter, 54, 204n51
Ōnishi Hajime, 110, 192, 207n35; "Hihyōron" (A theory of *hihyō*), 25, 67–78, 206n22
oral performance, 177, 218n59
Ōsawa Satoshi, 23–24, 180–81, 184–85, 223n3
Ōshima Nagisa, 190–91
Ozaki Kōyō: *Fūryū kyōningyō* (Elegant Kyoto doll), 93

Paideia, 183, 224n9
paranoid reading, 18–22, 189
Pavlov, Mikhail G., 102, 211n52
pen names, 84, 119, 213n24, 213n27
periodicals, 36, 201n6; creative writing in, 64; in twentieth century, 183–87. *See also* journals
Perry, Matthew, 34
personality *hihyō* (*jinbutsu hihyō*), 180, 223n3
philology, 95–96
playful writing. *See gibun*
poetry, 9, 75, 166–69; beauty and, 116, 213n16

political activism, 51, 90, 126–30, 183–84, 188, 224n24
Poovey, Mary, 207n49
Pope, Alexander, 206n22
Popper, Karl, 192
popular literature, 220n7
postcolonialism, 16
postcritical reading, 16–22, 188–92, 200n49
print industry: availability of books, 2–3; commercial publishing, 35, 52; growth in nineteenth-century, 3, 35, 50, 62; "mixture of good and bad," 50, 52, 203n43; in twentieth century, 23, 180–81; woodblock printing and, 197n3. *See also* journals; periodicals
proletarian literature, 180–81, 189–90, 223n4
pronouns, 171–75, 222nn35–36, 222n40
prostitution, 85, 92, 94
pseudonyms. *See* pen names
public sphere, 36–37, 201n9, 201nn6–7, 202nn10–11, 204n47
pure literature (*junbungaku*), 28–29, 158–76, 220n7, 221n25; aesthetic literature as, 163; language and, 164–75; readerly communities, 161, 169–75

Rai San'yō, 158, 161–62; *Nihon gaishi* (Unofficial history of Japan), 162
readers: affective responses, 21; communities around pure literature, 161, 169–75; engagement with, 175–78; solitary reading, 177
reading aloud, 177, 218n59
reflective essays, 7, 26
Representations, 20
Ri Takanori, 205n1
Ricoeur, Paul, 17, 222n36
Rikugō zasshi (The universe), 34, 70
Rintarō. *See* Ōgai
riron (theory), 7, 183, 185–87
roundtable discussion (*zadankai*), 180, 223n3
Ryūtei Tanehiko, 150

Saeki Junko, 204nn53–54, 213n16
Saganoya Omuro: *Kusaretamago* (Rotten egg), 93, 210n34
Saitō Mareshi, 114, 170, 198n13, 221n30
Sakai Takeshi, 214n4, 216n25
samurai class, 4, 89–90
San'yūtei Enchō, 177
Sasabuchi Tomoichi, 113

INDEX

Sasaki Atsushi, 184
satire, 151–52, 219n77
Satō Dōshin, 208n7
Satō Izumi, 224n17
science: as distinct from literature, 26–27, 82–84, 97–101, 104–10; methodologies of, 98–100, 105
"season of politics" (*seiji no kisetsu*), 183–84
Sedgwick, Eve, 18, 21
semantics, 13, 26–27, 39–44, 82, 89, 94–97, 101, 136–38, 141, 187, 197n6, 217n32; of pure literature, 160–61, 164, 170–71, 175
semiotics, 113, 145, 183
sensemaking, 1, 146–49. *See also* meaning
Shakespeare, William, 71; *Hamlet*, 11, 116; *Macbeth*, 28, 132, 135–38, 140–41, 143–44
shifters, 170–74, 222n36
Shigarami zōshi (The weir), 59, 65–66, 118, 122, 212n11, 213n24
Shimazaki Tōson, 159, 220n4
Shinshōsetsu (New novels), 64
Shintoism, 219n77
shōsetsu (prose fiction), 152, 176–78
Shōwa period (1926–89), 185
Shōyō, Tsubouchi: "Azusamiko" (Shrine maiden), 151, 215n14, 219n62; education, 203n25; *gibun* (playful-writing style), 133–35, 141–42, 149–57, 215n6, 219n70; on *Hamlet*, 11; "Hihyō no hyōjun" (The criteria of *hihyō*), 6, 46, 65, 146; institutional affiliations, 48, 206n12; *Macbeth* annotation project, 28, 132, 135–38, 140–41, 143–44; scholarship on, 22; on schools of the novel, 139–40, 216n22; *Shōsetsu shinzui* (The essence of the novel), 138–39, 151–52; "Sokoshirazu no mizuuumi" (The bottomless lake), 151; submerged-ideal debate, 214n5, 215n9, 215n11; *Tōsei shosei katagi*, 44, 219n66; on Western-style *hihyō*, 6, 9, 44
Shuppan geppyō (Monthly reviews of publications), 24, 49–50, 52, 65, 203n44; metadiscourse on *hihyō*, 55–58
Sino-Japanese books, 3. *See also* Chinese writing system
Sino-Japanese war, 221n25
skepticism, 21
slow reading, 20
Sohō, Tokutomi, 8–9; on "age of *hihyō*," 33–37, 46, 64; Arnold and, 77, 207n35; background, 89–90, 209n23; Chinese studies and, 103; on division of intellectual labor, 102; first-person pronouns and, 173; on free speech, 209n27; "Literature and Nature" debate, 85–87, 89, 92–93, 104; on "new Japan," 206n13; New Year's address (1890), 127; "Seijijō no bungyō" (The division of labor in politics), 66–68, 75; *Shin Nihon no seinen* (The youth of new Japan), 128; *Shōrai no Nihon* (The future of Japan), 55, 222n38; on Tōkoku, 163
solitary reading, 177
Sontag, Susan, 17, 20, 132, 142
spatialization of *hihyō*, 24–26, 36–37, 47–55; information management and, 52–54; objective distance and, 122; and separation of critical language, 102
speech: academic field of, 180. *See also* free speech
storytelling, 177
strong theory, 18, 22
structuralism, 183
submerged-ideal debate, 25, 28, 132–57; arguments against interpretation, 133–35, 142–50; concept of "submerged-ideal" (*botsurisō*), 135–37, 140–41, 143; defocalization, 144, 147–48, 150, 154–55; failures of, 142, 147, 152–57; Ōgai's *hihyō* as Uyū-sensei/Hartmann, 138–42, 147, 152–57, 215n11, 216n17, 216nn24–25; Ōgai's misreading, 133, 140–41; Shōyō's *gibun* (playful-writing style), 133–35, 141–42, 149–57
surface reading, 20
suspicious reading, 17–22, 189
Suzuki Sadami, 204n52, 205n1
symptomatic reading, 18–22

Taiheiki (*A Chronicle of the Great Peace*), 219n70
Takahashi Gorō, 69–71, 73, 75, 206n20, 206n22
Takata Sanae, 44–46, 48–49, 65, 151, 203n25, 203n37; "*Tōsei shosei katagi* no hihyō" (A *hihyō* of *Tōsei shosei katagi* [The characters of modern students]), 49
Takizawa Bakin, 150
Takuten Jōsen (Noguchi Neisai), 212n11
The Tale of Genji, 9
Tamenaga Shunsui, 150
Tanizawa Eiichi, 214n5, 218n51

Taylor, Mark, 207n49
Terayama Seisen, 137, 215n11
Thomas, Julia, 105, 211n59
Togawa Shinsuke, 214n4
Tōkoku, Kitamura, 28–29, 211n57, 220n14; death of, 159, 221n25; "Enseishika to josei" (The pessimistic poet and a woman), 168; favoritism toward, 159, 175; friendship with Aizan, 221; Japanese language and, 221n30; "Jinsei ni aiwataru to wa nan no ii zo" (What does interrelation with life even mean?), 162; on pure literature, 158–78
Tokugawa shogunate, 2, 4, 36, 38, 89–91, 105, 151
Tokyo nichinichi shinbun (Tokyo daily newspaper), 201n6
Tokyo Senmon Gakkō, 44, 48–49, 140, 203n25, 206n12
Tolstoy, Leo, 145
Tomkins, Silvan, 18, 21
Toyama Masakazu, 216n24
Tōyō gakugei zasshi (Journal of Oriental arts and sciences), 47–49
transcendentalism, 69, 72–73, 181
translingual practice, 37–44, 96
truth, 16, 88, 96–97, 103, 106–7; *hihyō* and, 46, 50, 56, 76; shifters and, 175; submerged-ideal debate and, 142
Tsu, Jing, 198n20
Tsurumi Shunsuke, 176–77, 223n44

Uchida Fuchian, 215n14
Ueda, Atsuko, 182, 205n1, 216n20
University of Tokyo, 43, 47–49, 68, 102
Usui Yoshimi, 215n6
Uyū-sensei (fictional character). See submerged-ideal debate

warfare, 181–82
Waseda bungaku (Waseda literature), 66, 140, 152–53, 215n9, 217n27
Waseda University, 44, 140
weak theory, 21–22
Webster, Noah, 202n14
Western *hihyō*, 6–7, 9–11, 44–47, 49, 151, 203n37
Western knowledge. See Euro-Anglo-American cultures
women's education and social status, 85, 90–94, 97, 208n5, 209n25, 210n34, 210n36
wordplay, 28, 142, 150, 152. See also gibun (playful writing)

Yagi Mizuho, 210n34
Yamaguchi Toratarō, 212n11, 214n45
Yamamoto Takamitsu, 110, 202nn14–15
Yanabu Akira, 96, 173, 210n41, 222n37
Yanagida Izumi, 205n1
Yatabe Ryōkichi, 50, 203n44
Yeats, W. B., 112, 114
Yoda, Tomiko, 113, 205n1
Yomiuri shinbun (Reading by selling daily), 93, 210n36, 215n14, 219n62
Yoshimoto Takaaki, 197n8
youth: educated male intellectuals, 34, 51, 56, 65, 91–92, 95, 104, 130, 185; politics and, 126–30
Yūbin hōchi shinbun (Postal dispatch newspaper), 201n6

Zhang, Dora, 199n29, 220n8
Žižek, Slavoj, 186
Zola, Émile, 138, 141, 216n20; "The Experimental Novel," 27, 82–84, 97–101, 105, 108

www.ingramcontent.com/pod-product-compliance
Lightning Source LLC
Chambersburg PA
CBHW030537230426
43665CB00010B/926